UNITED STATES IMMIGRATION AND CITIZENSHIP

ALLAN WERNICK'S GUIDE TO THE LAW

PROFESSOR ALLAN WERNICK, Leader in U.S. Immigration Law

HIGHLINE

EDITIONS

High Line Editions
1441 Broadway, 5th Floor, Suite 5015
New York, NY
10018, USA

United States Immigration and Citizenship: Allan Wernick's Guide to the Law
Wernick, Allan © 2016

ISBN: Print 978-1-941286-17-3
ISBN: epub 978-1-941286-18-0
ISBN: epdf 978-1-941286-19-7
MOBI: 9781681200026
BISAC: LAW032000; LAW098000

Editor: Robert Astle
Interior Design and Layout: Kate Murphy
Cover Design: Ervin Serrano
Index: Jones Literary Services, Andrea M. Jones
Proof Reading: Jillian Ports, Brooke Kressel-Majin
Legal Advisors: Julie Dinnerstein, Andrew Fair, Phyliss Jewell
Contributors: Elinor Drucker-Rahmani, Tamara Bloom, Thomas Shea, Peter Rubie, Maria Violetta Szulc

Publisher's Disclaimers

Table of Contents

Addendum

Visa Bulletin Change

Expansion of F1 OPT STEM Program

Errata

Notes

How to Use This Guide

READ

My book has easy-to-read stories and has many examples of how people have succeeded in gaining their U.S. Immigration and Citizenship. Their stories are based on true events but the names have been changed. Others have had more difficulties, as the laws need to be strictly adhered to. All stories are indicated with this icon

LOOK

There are many possible mistakes to make. I've flagged these points with this icon.

FORMS

All the required forms are referred to in the book. Look for this icon. U.S. Government websites are also included so that you can easily reference the sites and the get the forms.

SEEK EXPERT ADVICE

This book offers many suggestions, tips and points out many exceptions; however, in all cases always seek the advice of a competent legal or para-legal advisor trained in U.S. Immigration law.

Preface

U.S. immigration law is incredibly complex and elastic. Moreover, new laws, regulations, court decisions, and agency interpretations change the law daily. That's why I regularly update my *Immigration Answers* web site, **www.allanwernick.com**. Through my web site, I keep you informed of the latest developments in immigration law and policy.

Throughout *United States Immigration and Citizenship: Allan Wernick's Guide to the Law,* I point out how important it is that you seek expert assistance if you have any doubts about your rights under U.S. immigration law. Heed that advice. Once you submit an application to the USCIS or to a U.S. consulate, it becomes part of your permanent record. This book will point you in the right direction, but you may need expert assistance to reach your goal.

Immigration law is constantly changing. In recent years, among the most important changes are the recognition by immigration laws of same-sex marriages, the efforts by President Barack Obama to grant legal status to undocumented immigrants through executive action, and the increased scrutiny of immigration and citizenship applicants. The later is the result of both the events of 9/11 and the economic crisis' having raised concern about immigrants taking jobs from U.S. workers.

When the U.S. Supreme Court found that Defense of Marriage Act unconstitutional, binational same-sex couples became eligible for the same benefits as different-sex couples. That includes the right of a U.S. citizen or permanent resident to petition for permanent residence for a same-sex spouse or a U.S. citizen to petition for a same-sex fiancé(e). The same is true for the right of the spouse of a U.S. citizen on the right to naturalize in three years instead of the usual five. No matter where the marriage takes place, in a U.S. state that allows for same-sex marriages or in a foreign country, U.S. immigration recognizes that a same-sex spouse qualifies as a "spouse" for all purposes. So, when you see the word "spouse," "husband," or "wife" in this book, the rules explained apply to both same-sex and different-sex couples.

As this book goes to press, the courts have enjoined, that is stopped, all but one of President Obama's deferred action programs for undocumented immigrants. I discuss the programs, known as DACA, expanded-DACA and DAPA in Chapter 20. The President sought to provide temporary protection from deportation and employment authorization to millions. Only his program announced on June 15, 2012 for children who came here before age sixteen is active. If and when the courts allow the program to proceed, you will be able to find information about the programs on my website.

The increased scrutiny of immigration and citizenship applications motivated by 9/11 and the economic downturn has led some to believe that our immigration laws have become more restrictive. That's not true. The most restrictive aspects of our current immigration laws come from the Illegal Immigration Reform and Immigrant Responsibility Act of 1996. That law put into place the "unlawful presence" bar to permanent residence discussed in Chapter 5, making it difficult for millions of undocumented immigrants to get green cards. Still, no question that immigration enforcement by U.S. Immigration and Customs Enforcement has increased and U.S. Citizenship and Immigration Services decision-making has become more restrictive. Immigrants, legal and undocumented need to be extra careful in preparing immigration and citizenship applications.

Hopefully, my book will help you with that task.

Allan Wernick, Esq.
Director, CUNY Citizenship Now!
Professor, Baruch College

About the Author

Photography: Andre Beckles

Professor Allan Wernick is a widely-noted authority and advocate on United States citizenship and immigration law. He serves as Director of CUNY Citizenship Now!, City University of New York-CUNY's free citizenship and immigration service project. He is professor at Baruch College, CUNY and has taught as a visiting professor in Chicana/o Studies at UCLA and California State University at Dominguez Hills. His informative columns on immigration law appear twice weekly in the *New York Daily News* and are syndicated by King Features Syndicate. He has served on the national Board of Directors of the American Immigration Lawyers Association (AILA), as Chair of the Immigration Committee of the Association of the Bar of the City of New York, and as President of the New York Chapter of AILA. He received his Bachelor's degree in Political Science from Stanford University and his J.D. from Loyola University in Los Angeles.

Prof. Wernick is renowned for his ability to clearly explain U.S. citizenship and immigration law to anyone interested in learning about this highly complex field. His more than twenty years of writing about immigration law issues in the *New York Daily News* and more recently for King Features Syndicate, have honed his ability to translate the complexity into easy-to-understand simple language. Over his career he has counseled thousands of immigrants, helping them down the path to permanent residence and citizenship. Immigrants, students, even lawyers have found his keen analysis and insights useful.

How to Contact the Author

www.allanwernick.com

or by mail:

Allan Wernick
CUNY Citizenship Now!
Suite 900, 101 W. 31st Street
New York, NY 10001

Introduction
United States Immigration and Citizenship:
Allan Wernick's Guide

Tom and Mary's Story

Tom was worried and upset—his wife, Mary, had just moved out. She had sponsored him for a green card, and his interview with the United States Citizenship and Immigration Services (USCIS) was just two weeks away. Tom was sure that because Mary left, his chances of staying in the United States had ended. Mary still loved Tom, and she hoped that he could get his immigration papers. But she felt their marriage wouldn't last, and she refused to live with him another day.

If Tom had read this book, he'd know that unless his wife withdraws his visa petition, he could still get his immigrant visa. He'd also know what documents to bring to his USCIS interview to help him win his case. Tom's story is typical of the thousands sent to me by readers of my weekly immigration law column published in the *New York Daily News* and my syndicated column for King Features Syndicate. Tom's story teaches you something about U.S. immigration law that you may not have known: Your husband or wife can help you get a green card even if you are separated.

Here are some other things you may not have known:

- Some permanent residents can become U.S. citizens without being able to speak, read, or write the English language.

- If you are married to a U.S. citizen, you can become a naturalized citizen after three years from the time you first became a lawful immigrant. If you have a college degree and an employer wants to sponsor you, you can get a temporary work status for up to six years—in certain circumstances, even longer. You can get this status even if you are less qualified than a U.S. worker who wants the job.

- If you are a U.S. citizen, you can bring your fiancé or fiancée to the United States by filing a K-1 Fiancé Petition.

- If you are a naturalized U.S. citizen, your children may have automatically become U.S. citizens when you did.

- Minor legal infractions such as traffic tickets and disorderly conduct usually won't keep you from becoming a naturalized citizen.

- Most applicants for asylum end up in removal proceedings (formerly called deportation proceedings).

- Sometimes you don't have to give up your native citizenship to become a U.S. citizen.

- An employer can sponsor you even if you are in the United States without papers.

- USCIS rules allow foreign students to work.

- Both men and women can petition to bring their out-of-wedlock children to the United States.

Who Needs This Book?

You need this book if:

- You are in the United States and want to stay.

- You are abroad and want to know how to come legally to the United States.

- You are lost in the complexity of U.S. immigration law or want to get legal status.

- You want to become a U.S. citizen.

- You are an employer, teacher, politician, or journalist who needs to know how our immigration system works.

Wernick's Guide to U.S. Immigration and Citizenship makes immigration law understandable. After answering hundreds of readers' questions, training hundreds of immigration law paralegals, and counseling immigrants for more than 30 years, I know what you need to know. If you want to make sense out of the U.S. immigration system, you need this book.

Getting Help with Your Immigration Problem

You have a lot at stake when you apply for legal immigration status or U.S. citizenship. Try to get some expert advice for your immigration problem before you submit papers to the INS. If you can't afford a lawyer, don't despair. Most people get visas without anyone's help. Others get advice from not-for-profit organizations, VOLAGS (voluntary agencies) or CBOs (Community Based Organizations that provide low-cost or free services to immigrants. The best tool for finding a VOLAG near you is **ImmigrationLawHelp.org**. There you can find an organization near you that handles your type of immigration case.

If I Read This Book, Do I Still Need a Lawyer?

If you can afford a lawyer to help you with your immigration problem, hire one. The USCIS is sometimes a difficult agency to deal with. Having an experienced immigration lawyer on your side may make a difference. Even if your case is easy, having a lawyer can help you relax as you go through the immigration process. If you decide to hire a lawyer, find one experienced in immigration and naturalization law. The best way to find a lawyer you'll be happy with is to follow the recommendation of a friend who is satisfied with his or her lawyer. Or, try the American Bar Association referral webpage, **http://apps.americanbar.org/legalservices/lris/directory/** or call your local bar association. Often they can refer you to an immigration lawyer who will charge you only a nominal amount for an initial consultation.

Getting Help from a Not-for-Profit Agency

Many not-for-profit agencies provide excellent immigration counseling services. Most agencies charge a nominal fee, but some provide free services. Some immigration counselors and paralegals employed by not-for-profit agencies are accredited by the Board of Immigration Appeals (BIA) to practice immigration law. You can find a list of agencies recognized to represent you in immigration court on the Internet at **justice.gov/eoir**. Search for "recognized agencies."

Representing Yourself

Most people represent themselves when they apply for legal immigration status. While it's best to have someone knowledgable about immigration and citizenship law, if you can't get help, at least make sure that you read the USCIS form instructions carefully. **USCIS.gov**, the USCIS website is constantly improving. I find it a useful resource.

The USCIS will send you forms for no charge if you call **800-870-3676**. You can also get the forms at the USCIS Web site, **uscis.gov**. Send completed forms and documents to the USCIS by certified mail with return receipt requested, and keep copies for your records.

Who's Who Under U.S. Immigration Law

Let's start our study of what immigration law can do for you by looking at how the law classifies people. I've included some stories to help you understand how the U.S. immigration system works. You'll find similar stories throughout the book.

U.S. immigration law divides all of us into two groups: U.S. citizens and aliens. The term "alien" includes permanent residents (green card holders), asylees, refugees, nonimmigrants, parolees, and undocumented immigrants. I try to avoid using the term "alien" in my writing and speaking, because it connotes strange beings from outer space. I prefer "foreign national." Our immigration laws however, still call foreign nationals "aliens."

U.S. Citizens

Whether natural born or naturalized, all U.S. citizens have the same rights except one: Only a natural born U.S. citizen can become president or vice president of the United States. Naturalized citizens may work in federal jobs, vote, and hold public office.

The government can't deport (remove) you for something you do after you become a U.S. citizen. However, the government can denaturalize a U.S. citizen who committed a fraud in becoming a citizen. Then the government can deport the denaturalized former citizen. You can also lose your U.S. citizenship by committing an act of expatriation. An example of an act of expatriation is joining a foreign government. You can renounce your U.S. citizenship. Renunciation takes place when you voluntarily, knowingly, and willfully give up your U.S. citizenship.

If you are a U.S. citizen, you may petition to bring to the United States as permanent residents your husband or wife; your children of any age, both married and single; and your parents. For more information on how to become a U.S. citizen, see section 2.

Permanent Residents (Green Card Holders)

Permanent residents are sometimes called green card holders, lawful permanent residents, and lawful immigrants. Permanent residents can travel freely into and out of the United States. However, if you are out of the United States for more than six continuous months, the government may question whether you have given up your residence. (See "Maintaining Your Permanent Residence," in chapter 1.)

Unlike U.S. citizens (including naturalized citizens), permanent residents can't vote in national, congressional, or state elections. In a few places permanent residents and undocumented immigrants can vote in community and school board elections.

Permanent residents qualify to work in most jobs. However, many federal and some state and local government jobs, such as police officer and firefighter, are reserved for U.S. citizens. Permanent residents may also be excluded from working for private employers, if the work is to be done under a U.S. government contract.

If you are a permanent resident, you can bring to the United States as permanent residents your husband or wife and unmarried sons and daughters. To learn how you can become a permanent resident, see section 1.

The USCIS gives a permanent resident a permanent resident card, formerly called an alien registration card. This card is also known as a green card. The permanent resident card is a plastic-covered card that shows that its legitimate holder is a permanent resident of the United States. The cards issued today are just like the first permanent resident card issued. The name stuck.

Nonimmigrants

Nonimmigrants are foreign nationals who come to the United States temporarily for a limited purpose (see section III). Pierre's and Ying's stories provide examples of how a person goes from being a nonimmigrant to a permanent resident and then a U.S. citizen.

Pierre's Story

Pierre came to visit the United States from France as a nonimmigrant visitor. He had only been in the United States for one month when he met Melanie, a U.S. citizen. They fell madly in love and decided to marry. Melanie then petitioned for Pierre to get an immigrant visa.

About three months after they filed his papers, the USCIS gave Pierre work authorization and he began working. A few months later, a USCIS officer interviewed him for his immigrant visa and Pierre became a permanent Resident.

Three years later, he was naturalized as a U.S. citizen. He qualified after only three years, instead of the normal five years, because he was still married to and living with his U.S. citizen wife.

Ying's Story

Ying came to the United States from China to study finance. She entered the United States using an F-1 nonimmigrant student visa. She successfully completed her master's program, so the USCIS gave her one-year of practical training work authorization. She immediately got a job with one of the largest financial institutions, Big Money, Inc., in Chicago. After six months on the job, the company offered Ying a permanent position. In order to keep her in legal working status while her permanent visa papers were processed, Big Money Inc. sponsored Ying for a temporary professional worker status called H-1B. Two months later, the USCIS approved a change of Ying's status from F-1 student to H-1B worker, valid for three years.

While Ying was in H-1B status, Big Money Inc. sponsored her for a permanent visa in the position of deputy director of their Asian Investment Department. Ying became a permanent resident and five years after that became a U.S. citizen. Once she became a citizen, Ying petitioned to bring her mother and father to the United States.

Asylees and Refugees

Asylees have a well-founded fear of being persecuted in their home country because of their race, religion, nationality, political opinions, or membership in a particular social group. They apply to the USCIS for asylum either after they enter the United States or while trying to enter the United States. Refugees are also people afraid of persecution if they return home, but who got refugee status before they came to the United States. For more on refugees and asylees, see section IV.

Lisa's story provides an example of a successful asylum applicant.

Lisa's Story

Lisa was running away from a country in turmoil. Her brother had been killed for his opposition to the government, and Lisa was sure that she was next on the government's list. She took what she could fit in a suitcase and using a phony passport, came to the United States. She left behind her husband and infant daughter. She was lucky to have gotten away.

Within a week after her arrival, she contacted an immigrants' rights organization, which advised her to apply for political asylum.

The USCIS granted Lisa asylum. She could then bring her husband and child to the United States, regardless of whether or not they had independent claims for asylum. One year after the USCIS granted Lisa asylum, she and her family applied for permanent residence. They qualified for permanent residence because Lisa had been an asylee for one year.

Undocumented Immigrants

We use the term "undocumented immigrants" for foreign nationals living in the United States who haven't yet established the legal right to be here. This includes people who entered the United States by evading inspection at the border as well as people who entered with fraudulent documents. It also includes people such as tourists who entered with a valid nonimmigrant visa but who have overstayed the time allowed them by the INS.

Parolees

Parolees are foreign nationals who the CBP lets into the United States, though at the time they apply to enter they don't qualify as either nonimmigrants or permanent residents. Parolee status is often used to let people into the United States for humanitarian reasons or in emergencies.

If you are in the United States with an application pending for permanent residence, you can sometimes get advanced parole. That's advance permission from the USCIS to be paroled back into the United States after travel abroad. (For more on advance parole, see chapter 6.) In rare situations, you can get parolee status if you have an urgent need to come to the United States. Most often this humanitarian parole is granted to people needing emergency medical care or to keep families united. **To apply for humanitarian parole, write to the USCIS Parole Branch at U.S. Immigration & Naturalization Service, Office of International Affairs, Attn: Parole Branch, 425 I Street, NW, Washington, DC 20536.**

The USCIS most often grants parolee status where it has some question as to a foreign national's admissibility as an immigrant, nonimmigrant, or asylee. An example is the thousands of Cubans who landed in Key West, Florida, in the early 1980s.

Section 1
Getting a Green Card

Maria and Andrew's Story

"Tomorrow is your green card interview, Maria. Don't forget to put our wedding pictures in your purse," said Andrew.

"Don't worry. I made sure to pack everything. Even this photo where you are dancing with my mother," Maria said laughingly.

Andrew is a permanent resident who received his green card when his employer, a U.S. corporation, sponsored him. Andrew and Maria were childhood sweethearts. When Andrew learned that Maria had come to the United States to study, he called her and they rekindled their romance. They married after just a few months. After their marriage, Maria continued her studies and maintained her student status.

Andrew petitioned for Maria based on his status as a permanent resident. Because of the long wait in the category for the spouse of a permanent resident, Maria couldn't get her green card right away. The USCIS approved the petition immediately, but because of the long waiting list for the spouses of permanent residents, Maria had to wait until she got to the front of the line in her visa category.

It took several years, but eventually Maria was able to become a permanent resident and then a U.S. citizen. Once she became a United States citizen, she then filed separate petitions for green cards for her mother and younger brother.

Getting an immigrant visa (a permanent resident card commonly called a green card) is the goal of millions of people in the United States and around the world. In this section, I explain the immigrant visa process.

In chapter 1, I give an overview of the ways that you might qualify for an immigrant visa. In chapters 2 and 3, I give you details on the two main green card categories: Family-Based permanent residence and Employment-Based permanent residence. In chapter 4, I explain who is eligible for the green card lottery and how you can enter. In chapter 5, I review the bars to permanent residence (problems that could prevent you from becoming a permanent resident).

Finally, in chapter 6, I explain the procedures for preparing your immigrant visa application, offering tips on how to prepare for the all-important interview where, in most cases, the final decision to grant or deny you permanent residence will be made.

Chapter 1 - Who Can Get a Green Card?

Most people get immigrant visas (green cards) because they are related to a U.S. citizen or permanent resident. The next largest group gets immigrant visas because they have a needed job skill or ability. Then there's a smaller group that gets immigrant visas in special ways, including a lottery, residence in the United States ten years or longer, through Congressional action, because they are crime or trafficking victims and children under twenty-one with a juvenile court protection order. I expand on the family-based, employment-based, and lottery categories in chapters 2, 3, and 4.

For now, let's begin our search to find out if you can become a permanent resident by summarizing the categories of immigrant visa eligibility.

Family-Based Visas

You may qualify for a Family-Based green card if you are the Immediate Relative of a U.S. citizen (a category for which there is no limit to the number of immigrant visas issued each year) or if you are in a Family-Based Preference group for which there is a limit, or quota, of 226,000 immigrants per year divided among four preferences.

Immigration laws define family relationships in a special way. An example is the term "child," which includes not only children born to a married couple but also certain adopted children, stepchildren, and children born out of wedlock. Details on these family relationships can be found in chapter 2.

The Immediate Relative of a U.S. citizen category includes the following:

- Spouse of a U.S. citizen.
- Unmarried child (under age 21) of a U.S. citizen.
- Parent of a U.S. citizen if the citizen is age 21 or older.
- Spouse of a deceased U.S. citizen.

As discussed in Chapter 2, some relatives, other than the spouse of a U.S. citizen, can get a visa despite the death of the petitioning relative. Note that the immigration law uses the term "child" for children under twenty-one years old and "sons and daughters" for children of any age.

The Family-Based Preferences

- **First Family-Based Preference**
  Adult unmarried sons and daughters (age twenty-one or older) of U.S. citizens.

- **Second Family-Based Preference A**
  Spouse and unmarried children (under age twenty-one) of permanent residents.

- **Second Family-Based Preference B**
  Unmarried sons and daughters (of any age) of permanent residents.

- **Third Family-Based Preference (formerly Fourth Preference)**
  Married children of U.S. citizens.

- **Fourth Relative Preference (formerly Fifth Preference)**
  Brothers and sisters of U.S. citizens if the U.S. citizen is age twenty-one or older.

Permanent Residence Based on Work, Talent, Investment

U.S. immigration laws recognize the value of immigrant labor to U.S. global competitiveness and job creation. Thus, you may be able to get a green card if you have unique education and skills, outstanding talent, or even willingness to work at a particularly unappealing job. You may also qualify for a green card by investing in a business. Permanent Resident visas in this category are referred to as Employment-Based visas.

There is a limit of 140,000 visas annually for all Employment-Based immigrants, but that doesn't always mean a long wait. How fast you can get an Employment-Based immigrant visa depends on your preference category as well as on how many people are applying for Employment-Based green cards from your native country. Following I list the Employment-Based Preferences. I also provide details for qualifying under these preferences in chapter 3.

The Employment-Based Preferences

- **First Employment-Based Preference**
  Priority Workers, Workers with extraordinary abilities, outstanding professors and researchers, and multinational executives and managers.

- **Second Employment-Based Preference**
  Members of professions holding advanced degrees or workers of exceptional ability.

- **Third Employment-Based Preference**
  Skilled workers, professionals, and other workers.

- **Fourth Employment-Based Preference**
  Special Immigrants, including certain religious workers, former U.S. government employees, Panama Canal employees, and certain foreign-language broadcasters working for Radio Free Europe or Radio Free Asia.

- **Fifth Employment-Based Preference**
  Employment creation (investor).

Other People Who Can Get Immigrant Visas

Even if you do not qualify in one of the relative or employment categories, you may still be able to get an immigrant visa through one of the following classifications:

1. Derivative Beneficiaries

A beneficiary is a person for whom a Family-Based or Employment-Based immigrant visa petition has been filed. A derivative beneficiary is the spouse or unmarried child under twenty-one of that person. The term "derivative" is used because your right to an immigrant visa derives, or comes from your spouse or parent, who is the primary beneficiary.

Under the derivative beneficiary rule, if you're coming to the United States under one of the Family - or Employment-Based Preferences, you can bring your spouse and unmarried children under age twenty-one with you. Your spouse and your children don't need to have separate petitions filed for them. Your spouse and children can even follow you to the United States after you've arrived, provided that you were married to your spouse and your children were born *before* you received your immigrant visa.

Immediate relatives of U.S. citizens cannot bring their family members with them as derivative beneficiaries. This means that if you're getting your immigrant visa as the spouse, parent, or unmarried child under age twenty-one of a U.S. citizen, you cannot automatically bring your spouse or children with you to the United States. This rule doesn't make much sense, but it's the law. Once you get your immigrant visa in the Immediate Relative category, you can then petition for your spouse and children.

Kim's and Jimmy's stories illustrate the law regarding derivative beneficiaries.

Kim's Story

Kim's mother, a U.S. citizen, petitioned for Kim to become a permanent resident. Kim is married to Harry. They have three children: Bertha, age eighteen and married; Aaron, age nineteen and single; and Cathy, age twenty-three and single. Kim will get her immigrant visa under the Family-Based Third Preference.

Let's see how the derivative beneficiary rules affect Harry, Bertha, Aaron and Cathy.

Harry is Kim's spouse, so he is automatically a derivative and can get his green card when Kim does. Aaron is still a "child" (under twenty-one) and single. Bertha, though under twenty-one, is married so she cannot get a derivative green card unless she becomes unmarried before Kim becomes a legal permanent resident. That would happen if her husband died or she and her husband divorced. Aaron qualifies as a derivative beneficiary because he is under twenty-one and unmarried. Cathy, being over twenty-one, is not a derivative beneficiary and cannot get a green card when Kim does.

Once Kim and Harry become permanent residents, either one can petition for Cathy under the Family-Based Preference 2B, provided she stays single. If Bertha stays married, she will need to wait until one of her parents becomes a U.S. citizen, and then the parent can petition for her under the Third Family Preference.

Jimmy's Story

Jimmy is a twenty-two-year-old U.S. citizen. His mother married his stepfather when Jimmy was just ten years old. Jimmy could petition for both his mother and stepfather for permanent residence. However, he doesn't like his stepfather, so Jimmy only petitions for his mother. Can Jimmy's mother bring the stepfather along as a derivative beneficiary?

No. Jimmy's mother qualifies for an immigrant visa under the Immediate Relative of a U.S. citizen category. Family members cannot derive in the Immediate Relative category. Once the mother gets her residence, she can petition for her husband under the Family-Based Preference 2A.

The Child Status Protection Act

Some children of Immediate Relatives and preference Permanent Residence applicants may benefit from a law enacted on August 2, 2002 called the Child Status Protection Act, CSPA. The purpose of the law is to protect certain children of U.S. citizens and permanent residents who may lose benefits because of long USCIS processing delays. For derivative beneficiaries, the law provides that the age of a child who is a derivative beneficiary of a preference green card applicant is fixed on the date a priority date becomes "current" for the primary beneficiary MINUS the time it takes the USCIS (or took the INS or BCIS - former designations for the agency) to approve the petition. The qualifying derivative child must begin processing for permanent residence within one year of qualifying.

Simone's story illustrates how the CSPA might benefit a derivative beneficiary.

Simone's Story

Simone's mother, a permanent resident, petitioned for her on January 2, 2003. Simone, as an unmarried daughter of a permanent resident at age fifteen, qualifies for residence in The Second Family Preference A category. One year later, on January 2, 2004, the BCIS approves the petition. Six years later, just after her twenty-first birthday, Simone's priority date becomes current. Despite turning twenty-one, she is able to get her immigrant visa under The Second Family Preference-A category. That's because her date was fixed on the date her priority date became current, MINUS the one year it took for the USCIS to decide the petition.

2. Visa Lottery Winners

Each year the U.S. Department of State holds a green card lottery through which they give out 55,000 permanent resident visas. The visas are for foreign nationals of countries with low levels of immigration during the previous five years. In some years the number of visas will be reduced to 50,000, with 5,000 visas going to NACARA (Nicaraguan Adjustment and Central American Relief Act) visa applicants. NACARA provides special opportunities for permanent residence for certain natives of Nicaragua, Cuba, El Salvador, Guatemala, and former Soviet Bloc countries. The filing dates for NACARA have passed. If you think you may have qualified for a NACARA green card, see an immigration law expert for advice. See chapter 4 for more on the visa lottery.

3. Asylees and Refugees

Asylees and refugees can apply for permanent residence after one year in that status. As I discuss in section 4, becoming an asylee or refugee is not always easy.

4. Registry

If you entered the United States before January 1, 1972, and you have resided in the United States continuously since you entered, you may qualify for permanent residence just because of your many years in the United States. Several of the usual requirements for a green card, like proving that you don't need welfare, do not apply to registry applicants.

5. Special Immigrants

The Special Immigrant category includes certain religious workers, juvenile dependents of a court who are eligible for foster care, some dependents of diplomats, certain long-term employees of the U.S. government working in foreign countries, holders of **S** (informers on terrorists, or criminals), **T** (victims of trafficking), and **U** (victims of other crimes) visas, and persons who have served in active duty in the U.S. armed services for twelve years or six years for those who reenlist for six additional years. This last category, for military personnel, is superceded by the rule that individuals in the military during wartime qualify immediately for U.S. citizenship.

Based on a declaration by President George W. Bush, for naturalization purposes we have been in a state of war since September 11, 2001.

6. Family Unity Visas

The spouse and unmarried children under twenty-one of "legalized" immigrants qualify for permanent residence under special rules. A legalized immigrant is one who got residence under one of the amnesty programs.

7. Unusual or Difficult Categories

The immigration laws provide a few unusual and especially difficult ways to become a permanent resident. You shouldn't try to get a green card in one of the following listed ways until you speak to an immigration law expert. These ways include:

- **Cancellation of Removal**

If you have resided continuously in the United States for ten years, you may be eligible for "cancellation of removal." For a battered spouse, child, or parent of a battered child, you need only continuously reside in the U.S. for three years.

The law provides different kinds of cancellation of removal. For the basic kind of cancellation of removal, you must prove "exceptional and extremely unusual hardship" to your U.S. citizen or permanent resident spouse, parent, or child. Hardship to yourself is not good enough. Cancellation of removal used to be called suspension of deportation and was far more generous than cancellation of removal is now.

Be warned: You can only apply for cancellation of removal in an immigration court.

Cancellation of removal can only be granted by an immigration judge in removal proceedings. If you apply for cancellation of removal and the judge grants your application, you become a permanent resident right then and there. If the judge denies your application, the judge may order you deported. If you think that you qualify for cancellation of removal, don't just walk into a USCIS office. They might detain you on the spot and deport you right away. If you want to apply for cancellation of removal, you should get advice from an immigration attorney or Board of Immigration Appeals accredited not-for-profit representative before trying anything.

The law also provides for specialized forms of cancellation of removal. If you are a battered spouse or child, or the parent of a battered child, you can apply for cancellation of removal if you have been in the United States for at least three years. To successfully apply for this kind of cancellation of removal, you should seek the help of an immigration attorney or BIA accredited not-for-profit representative.

- **Private Bills**

A Private Bill is an act of Congress granting permanent residence to an individual. Congress very rarely passes Private Bills. You need a member of Congress to sponsor the bill and push it through both the Senate and the House of Representatives. In order to get a green card based on a Private Bill, you would have to show an extraordinary humanitarian reason why you should get permanent residence.

- **Special Rules for Special Nationalities**

Over the years, Congress has seen fit to make green cards available to immigrants from certain countries, outside the normal immigrant visa system. In recent years, Nicaraguans, Cubans, Haitians, Salvadorans, Guatemalans, natives of former Soviet Bloc countries, and Syrian Jews have benefited from nationality-specific laws.

- **Amnesty and "Late Amnesty"**

In 1986 Congress passed a legalization or "amnesty" law. Under this law, people who had lived in the United States continuously, but unlawfully, since before 1982 could get permanent residence. Amnesty visas were given also to certain agricultural workers. The deadline to apply for amnesty was May 4, 1988.

After the deadline, many amnesty applicants complained that the USCIS unlawfully turned them away and did not let them apply. After some famous court cases, sometimes referred to as CSS/LULAC cases after the organizations that represented many of the late amnesty applicants, the USCIS was forced by the federal courts to accept some late amnesty applications. To qualify for late amnesty you must have been in the United States since before January 1, 1982, but failed to file for amnesty because the USCIS unlawfully discouraged you from filing. Some people think that the late amnesty was a new amnesty because applicants are allowed to file so long after the original deadline. Many of those who filed late got USCIS work permission. But if you came to the United States after January 1, 1982, and you filed for amnesty, your amnesty application is a fraud.

The CSS/LULAC cases did not end the amnesty controversies. In the year 2000, Congress passed the Legal Immigration Family Equity (LIFE) Act of 2000, which allows some late amnesty applicants who filed for amnesty before October 1, 2000, under any one of three of the late amnesty cases—*CSS v. Meese, LULAC v. INS*, or *Zambrano v. INS*—to qualify for permanent residence. Like all other legalization applicants, LIFE late amnesty applicants must have come to the United States before January 1, 1982, and lived here in an unlawful status until at least May 4, 1988. The applicants must also pass a U.S. citizenship language and civics knowledge test (or be taking a course in these subjects). The deadline for filing for permanent residence under the LIFE late amnesty provisions was June 4, 2003.

Special Juvenile Immigrant Status

An unmarried undocumented immigrant under age twenty-one can qualify for a green card if he or she is declared dependent in a juvenile court. Typically the child is placed with a family member or with foster parents. Once the family court issues its order, the child can immediately apply for permanent residence.

U and T Status Holders

Individuals with **U** status for crime victims and **T** status for sex and employment trafficking qualify to adjust status to permanent resident after three years in **U** or **T** status, sometimes sooner. More on this process in chapter 19 Lesser-Known Paths to Legal Status.

Maintaining Your Permanent Residence

Making the United States your primary home is a requirement for permanent residence. You can lose your permanent resident status if you spend too much time outside the United States.

If you plan to spend a great deal of time abroad, get a reentry permit before you leave the United States. A reentry permit is an USCIS travel document valid for entry into the United States after absences of up to two years. If you will be out of the country longer than two years, you must come back to the United States and apply for a new reentry permit. You file for a reentry permit using USCIS Form I-131, Application for Travel Document. When applying for the reentry permit, you must explain why you need to be abroad for so long. People get reentry permits for a variety of reasons, including to temporarily work abroad, to care for a relative who is sick, and to study.

Maintaining Your Residence

If an inspector at a port of entry believes that you have abandoned your U.S. residence, the government can try to take away your immigration status.

Usually, stays abroad of less than six months are not a problem. If you are abroad for more than six months, you should be prepared to explain to a border officer why you were out of the country for so long. Evidence that you have maintained your residence includes having a bank account, paying U.S. taxes, and having a place to live in the United States. If you get a reentry permit before you leave the United States, an inspector is more likely to admit you into the United States after a long absence.

If an inspector believes that the United States is not your primary country of residence, the inspector can deny you entry. If that happens, you have a right to a hearing before an immigration judge, who will decide whether you have really abandoned your residence.

Trips Abroad of More Than One Year

After one continuous year abroad, your permanent resident card is no longer valid for reentry. If you plan to be out of the United States for more than one year, apply to the USCIS for a reentry permit before you leave.

If you are outside the United States for more than one year without having first received a reentry permit, you can get a returning resident visa to ease your reentry into the United States. You can apply for the visa at a U.S. consulate abroad. You'll need to prove that you haven't abandoned your U.S. residence. If you return to the United States after three hundred and sixty-five days abroad without getting a returning resident visa, you may be detained at a port of entry or denied entry.

Proving that you are a returning resident after spending a year or more abroad can be difficult. Be very careful when planning long-term travel abroad.

The stories of Conrad, Danielle, Suresh, and Tony illustrate the issue of maintaining residency.

Conrad's and Mariel's Story

Mariel, a U.S. citizen, petitioned for Conrad, her husband, to become a permanent resident. Two years after Conrad became a resident, his wife's employer transferred her temporarily to the French branch of the company for a five-year assignment.

Conrad and Mariel decided to give up their New York apartment and rent an apartment in Paris. However, they still planned to spend the Christmas holidays in New York with their families.

Conrad is not abandoning his U.S. residence. He should submit USCIS Form I-131 with a letter from his wife's company explaining that they have sent her abroad to work. Conrad can then get a reentry permit, which is valid for only two years. He must return to the United States within two years to apply for a new reentry permit. He cannot apply for a new reentry permit from abroad.

Danielle's Story

Danielle, an actress, became a permanent resident in order to be ready to work when she got her big break as a Hollywood movie star. Meanwhile, she lived in Sweden until she got the call to stardom. Danielle traveled to the United States frequently for auditions but did most of her theatrical work in Europe. For several years, she made three trips per year to the United States, and was never in the country for more than a few weeks at a time.

Danielle's Story (Continued)

Five years after she became a permanent resident, an immigration inspector noticed the many entry stamps in Danielle's passport and asked her where her residence was. Danielle claimed that her residence was in the United States, but her only proof was a small bank account that she maintained in Los Angeles. The inspector at the airport referred her to what immigration officers call "deferred inspection." She was allowed to enter as a parolee (see the introduction for a definition of parolee status).

At the deferred inspection unit, Danielle claimed that she was residing in the United States, but she still had no proof. The inspector told her she had two choices: to leave the country or to try to convince a judge that she was residing in the United States.

Whether Danielle can keep her permanent residence will depend upon the evidence that she presents at her hearing. If she gives up and returns to Sweden, she can only become a permanent resident again if a relative or employer petitions for her.

Suresh's Story

Suresh works for a large American computer company, which sponsored him for his permanent residence. Suresh was promoted to International Sales Director, a job that required extensive trips outside the United States, and stays in hotels while abroad.

Though Suresh is spending most of his time outside the United States, he should have no problem convincing an inspector that he has not abandoned his residence. His job is in the United States, his home is in the United States, and he is only out of the country for lengthy periods because of his job.

Tony's Story

Tony learned that his father in the Dominican Republic was ill and went to visit him. When Tony arrived, he found out that things were worse than he'd thought. His father needed constant care, and Tony was the only one in the family that was available to help. Tony wrote to his employer, a small U.S. law firm, and quit his job. Sadly, a year-and-a-half after Tony had left the United States, his father died. Tony stayed another six months in the Dominican Republic to sell his father's business and then decided to return to the United States.

Since Tony did not get a reentry permit before he left for the Dominican Republic and had been abroad for more than one year, he must apply for a returning resident visa from the U.S. consulate. He will have to explain to a consular officer why he spent so much time out of the United States. He'll need evidence that he didn't intend to abandon his U.S. residence.

The fact that Tony maintained a bank account and a mailing address in the United States is helpful. Most important will be letters from his father's doctor and family business documents. This evidence proves that Tony didn't intend to abandon his U.S. residence; he was only in the Dominican Republic for an extended period of time to care for his father.

Green Card Expiration and Renewal

At one time, green cards, permanent resident cards, were issued without an expiration date. You only needed a new one if you lost your card, or you got your card as a child and an immigration inspector insisted that you to get a new card with an updated photo. Cards issued now are valid for ten years. When your card expires, you don't lose your permanent residence. That's a myth. It is just your card that expires, not your legal status as a permanent resident.

In 1994, the government required that certain permanent residents get new cards, even if their cards had not expired. Most of these cards were issued prior to 1979. If your card is one with a ten-year expiration date, you of course need to replace the card when it expires. If you have one of the older cards, you must replace the card unless it has the notation "I-551" on it.

Chapter 2 - Family-Based Immigration

Under what is called Family-Based immigration, you may qualify for an immigrant visa (or lawful permanent resident status, also known as "green card" status) if you are the spouse, parent, or child of a U.S. citizen or you are the spouse or unmarried son or daughter of a permanent resident. You can also obtain green card status if you are a married child of a U.S. citizen or a sibling of a U.S. citizen.

United States immigration law divides Family-Based immigration into two groups: the Immediate Relatives of U.S. citizens and the four Family-Based Preferences. Note one important difference between Immediate Relatives of U.S. citizens and preference applicants: A preference applicant can bring his or her spouse and/or unmarried child under twenty-one as accompanying family members. Immediate Relatives cannot. This illogical rule is called the "derivative beneficiary" rule. I discussed derivative beneficiaries in Chapter 1.

When discussing family-based immigration, the U.S. citizen or permanent resident filing for a relative (petitioning for the relative) is the petitioner. The relative trying to get lawful permanent resident status (who benefits from the petition), is the beneficiary. The form a petitioner files for a beneficiary is USCIS - Form I-130, Petition for Alien Relative. Before I explain how U.S. immigration laws define family relationships, let's review the family immigration categories.

The Immediate Relative Category

You are an Immediate Relative of a U.S. citizen if you are one of the following:

- Spouse of a U.S. citizen.

- Unmarried child (under 21) of a U.S. citizen.

- Parent of a U.S. citizen where the citizen is 21 or older.

- Spouse (and children of surviving spouse) of a deceased U.S. citizen, where at the time of your spouse's death, you were not legally separated, you self-petitioned within two years of your spouse's death, and you have not remarried, who lost citizenship status because of abuse within two years of the abusive U.S. citizen's death or loss of citizenship status.

- Former spouse (and children of former spouse) of an abusive U.S. citizen within two years of divorce if there is a connection between the divorce and the abuse.

- Unwitting victims of bigamy (and children of bigamy victims) of an abusive U.S. citizen.

- Children of former US citizen who lost citizenship status because of abuse within two years of the abusive U.S. citizen's loss of citizenship status.

If you qualify for the Immediate Relative category, you don't need to worry about a quota or waiting list. You can get a green card as soon as your papers are processed. That's because the number of people eligible to become lawful permanent residents in the Immediate Relative category is unlimited.

Some children of United States citizens may benefit from a law enacted on August 2, 2002 called the Child Status Protection Act, CSPA. The purpose of the law is to protect certain children of U.S. citizens and permanent residents who may lose benefits because of long USCIS processing delays.

Under the CSPA, when a U.S. citizen petitions for his or her unmarried child under twenty-one, the child's age is "fixed" on the date the USCIS receives the petition. Ida's story illustrates how an under twenty-one unmarried child of a U.S. citizen can benefit from the CSPA.

Ida's Story

Ida was twenty-years-old and unmarried when her mother, a U.S. citizen, petitioned for her. She remains qualified as the immediate relative of a U.S. citizen regardless of how long it takes the USCIS or U.S. consulate abroad to process her permanent residence application. That is true even if she turns twenty-one while waiting. Prior to the enactment of the CSPA, once she turned twenty-one, she would have moved to the first family preference category, with a long wait for permanent residence.

Family-Based Preference Categories

Under the four Family-Based Preference categories, you are subject to a yearly quota. For some preference categories the wait can be many years.

If you become a lawful permanent resident under a Family-Based Preference, your spouse and your unmarried children under age twenty-one can follow or accompany you to the United States as derivative beneficiary immigrants. (For more information on derivative beneficiaries, see chapter 1.) Note that immigration law uses the term "child" to refer to a child under twenty-one. A "son or daughter" includes all children, including those age twenty-one or over or is married.

The preference categories for the relatives of U.S. citizens and permanent residents are:

- **First Family-Based Preference**

Adult unmarried sons and daughters (age twenty-one or older) of U.S. citizens.

You qualify as an unmarried son or daughter if you have never married or your marriage has ended through annulment, divorce or death of your spouse. However, you cannot get a divorce for the sole purpose of getting a green card.

- **Second Family-Based Preference A**

Spouse and unmarried children under age twenty-one of permanent residents.

- **Second Family-Based Preference B**

Unmarried son or daughter of any age of permanent residents.

If you are applying in the Second Family-Based Preference category, you must remain unmarried until you become a permanent resident. Again, however, you cannot get a divorce for the sole purpose of getting a green card.

Mario's story illustrates that in order to get a green card under the Second Family-Based Preference, you must remain single until you become a permanent resident.

Mario's Story

Mario, a citizen of Ecuador, was single when his mother, a permanent U.S. resident, petitioned for him for a green card. Four years later, a U.S. consular officer called Mario in for his final immigrant visa interview at the U.S. consulate in Guayaquil.

All went well at Mario's interview; the consular officer approved his case and gave Mario his immigrant visa. Mario would have become a permanent resident upon his first entry into the United States. However, when Mario told his girlfriend, Maria, that the consular officer had given him an immigrant visa she was concerned that Mario would forget her once he got to the United States. Mario and Maria decided to get married right away, before Mario left for his new home in New York. When Mario arrived at JFK Airport, the USCIS inspector asked him if he was married and Mario answered yes.

Mario's Story (Continued)

The inspector, an employee of U.S. Customs and Border Protection (CBP), did not allow Mario to enter the United States, and he was forced to go back to Ecuador. This is because as a married man, Mario no longer qualified for a green card as the unmarried son of a permanent resident as required by the petition filed for him by his mother. When his mother becomes a U.S. citizen, she can file a new petition for him and eventually Mario will be eligible to get a green card under the Third Family-Based Preference as a married son of a U.S. citizen.

Had Mario waited until he had entered the United States before he got married, his entry would have made him a permanent resident. He could have flown home right away, married Maria, and then returned to the United States to petition for her.

- **Third Family-Based Preference**

Married sons and daughters of U.S. citizens.

- **Fourth Family-Based Preference**

Brothers and sisters of U.S. citizens.

Under the fourth preference, the U.S. citizen petitioner must be twenty-one years of age or older. This preference has long waiting lists.

The Special Problem of Deceased Petitioners

U.S. laws sometimes allows family members of U.S. citizens and permanent residents to get a green card despite the death of a petitioning relative. Different rules apply to these three groups: the Widow/Widowers of U.S. Citizens, family beneficiaries in the United States and family beneficiaries abroad.

Widow/Widowers of U.S. Citizens

A widow/widower of a U.S. citizen can self-petition for permanent residence if the couple was married at the time of the U.S. citizen's death and the beneficiary files USCIS form I-360, Petition for Amer-asian, Widow(er), or Special Immigrant within two years of the spouse's death. The U.S. citizen need not have filed a family petition for the widow/widower to self-petition. If the now-deceased petitioner had already filed USCIS form I-130, Petition for Alien Relative, the beneficiary can convert the I-130 petition to an I-360 petition. The unmarried children of the petitioner can benefit as well. This occurs when the child was not yet twenty-one at either the time the U.S. citizen filed the petition or, if the U.S. died before filing a petition, at the time the surviving spouse files form I-360.

Family Beneficiaries in the United States

Where a U.S. citizen or permanent resident who has petitioned for a family member dies and the beneficiary of the petition is in the United States, USCIS will allow the case to proceed. If the petition was filed in a preference case, and the primary beneficiary dies, a derivative beneficiary in the United States can continue processing his application for legal permanent residence.

Where the Beneficiary is Abroad

Where the beneficiary (other than a widow/widower of a U.S. citizen), is abroad and the petitioner dies, and USCIS approved the petition, USCIS can reinstate this petition for humanitarian reasons. In determining whether a beneficiary deserves reinstatement, USCIS will consider whether denying the beneficiary an immigrant visa will disrupt an established family unit; lead to hardship to U.S. citizens or lawful permanent residents. USCIS will also consider whether the beneficiary is elderly or in poor health; whether the beneficiary has spent a lengthy period of time in the United States, the conditions under which the beneficiary is living in his or her home country, whether undue government delay occurred in adjudicating the petition and the beneficiaries family ties in the United States.

Family Relationships

U.S. immigration laws are very specific in defining family relationships. In this section, we look at how the law defines husband and wife, child and parent, and brother and sister relationships.

Husband or Wife

In order to get a green card based on a petition filed by your spouse, you must prove that you didn't get married just to get a green card. If you or your spouse were previously married, you must prove that your and/or your spouse's prior marriages ended through divorce, annulment or death.

Real Marriages Versus Green Card Marriages

The USCIS will not recognize a marriage as bona fide or "real" if you married just to get a green card. If you try to get a green card using a phony marriage, you risk being permanently barred from becoming a permanent resident.

George's story illustrates what can happen if you try a "green card" marriage.

George's Story

George ran away from his home in London when he was 14. After several years of living on his own in Liverpool, he came to the United States, telling immigration officials when he entered that he was coming just for a visit. In reality he hoped to get work here as a welder. He went to live with a friend, Frank, in Los Angeles, California. Despite his skills, George found it almost impossible to find work because he didn't have work permission from the USCIS, and employers were afraid to hire him because of the employer sanctions law (see section V). Frank's girlfriend, Ginny, offered to marry George to help him get a green card. However, when the couple went to George's green card interview, Ginny was very nervous. When the officer questioned her about the marriage, Ginny broke down, admitting that she only married George to help him get legal papers. The USCIS officer denied George's green card application.

Some time later, George got a notice to appear for a removal hearing. This hearing used to be called a deportation hearing. By this time, he had divorced Ginny and married Sharon, a U.S. citizen, who was pregnant with George's child. George really loved Sharon, but because the USCIS had earlier caught George in a phony marriage scheme, he cannot get a green card by a petition filed by Sharon, another relative, or an employer. Ever.

To make sure that the USCIS approves your marriage petition, you and your spouse should present proof that your marriage is bona fide. Evidence of a real marriage includes:

- Photographs of your wedding, of your reception, and of you and your spouse together before or after you were married.
- Records of a joint bank account.
- A lease for an apartment or a mortgage agreement for a home with both your and your spouse's name.
- Letters from third parties addressed to you and/or your spouse at the same address.
- Affidavits from friends, relatives, or religious leaders about your marriage.
- Personal records showing your spouse as your emergency contact.
- Joint tax returns.
- Joint credit cards.
- Utilities and phone bills with both names.

You should attach any evidence to the I-130 petition when you submit the petition to the USCIS. By providing evidence that yours is a real marriage, you may avoid further inquiry from the USCIS about whether your marriage is bona fide. Plan to bring all supporting documents when you have your green card interview.

The Marriage Fraud Interview

If you and your spouse are both living in the United States, the USCIS may interview you about your life together. This may happen as part of your adjustment of status interview (see chapter 6) or in a separate marriage fraud interview. Actually, the USCIS approves many I-130 petitions filed by U.S. citizens and permanent residents without a marriage fraud interview.

You may bring an attorney or an accredited BIA representative to a marriage fraud interview. At the interview, the USCIS officer may separate you and your spouse and ask the two of you the same questions, such as whether you have ever met each other's relatives, the color of the walls in your apartment, when you met, what vacations you have taken together, if any, and whether you have a television. The purpose of the questions is to see if you and your spouse give the same answers. No matter how much you prepare, you'll find it difficult to pass the interview if yours is a phony marriage.

The story of Susan and Tom gives you a sense of what happens at a marriage fraud interview.

Tom and Susan's Story

Tom and Susan were truly a couple in love. Tom was a U.S. citizen. Susan, an Australian, had come to the United States on a visit and after meeting Tom, decided to stay. When Tom and Susan appeared for Susan's interview, they presented no evidence, other than their marriage certificate, to prove that their marriage was real. No photos, no letters, nothing. The USCIS officer decided to interview Tom and Susan separately to make sure that they didn't get married just so that Susan could get a green card.

Tom and Susan's Story (Continued)

The USCIS officer asked Susan what Tom had given her for her birthday. The truth was that Tom had forgotten all about Susan's birthday and had not given her a gift. Susan was afraid that if she told the interviewer the truth, the officer would think they weren't really a couple. So Susan answered, "A red sweater." Later when the officer asked Tom the same question, he told the truth, saying that he had not gotten Susan a present. Whoops!

Tom and Susan had forgotten the main goal of a USCIS marriage fraud interview: to see if the husband and wife say the same things.

Fortunately for Tom and Susan, their officer was especially nice. She asked Tom and Susan about the different answers to the question about the birthday gift and Susan explained the reason for her answer. Since Susan and Tom had given the same answer to so many questions, the USCIS officer gave them a day to bring in additional evidence that they were living together. Tom and Susan submitted the evidence that afternoon, and the USCIS interviewer approved the case.

If the USCIS officer believes that your marriage is real, the officer will approve the I-130 petition. If the officer believes that your marriage is not bona fide, the officer will deny the petition or ask the petitioner (your spouse) to withdraw it. This means that the USCIS is asking your spouse to stop the case. If your spouse withdraws the petition, you cannot get permanent residence from that petition. Often, whether the petition is denied or withdrawn, the USCIS will start proceedings to remove you from the United States.

Another possibility is that the officer will not decide right away but will instead send the case out for a field investigation. A USCIS officer may visit your home. USCIS field investigations of marriages are less common than people think, but they do happen. If the officer sends your case to the investigations unit, at some point in the future (sometimes several months after your initial interview), a USCIS investigator may appear at the residence you listed on the I-130 petition. The investigator is looking for evidence that you and your spouse are living together, such as men's and women's clothes, two toothbrushes, shaving cream, and perfume. The investigator may also talk to neighbors.

A USCIS investigator doesn't have the right to enter your house without either a warrant or your permission. Nevertheless, it is up to you and your spouse to prove that you are eligible for permanent residence. If you do not give the investigator access to your home, the USCIS may deny the marriage petition.

It's easy to see: You want to do all that you can to keep your case from being sent out for an investigation. Even if the investigator ultimately finds that your marriage is a valid one, the investigation itself can take weeks or months. If you want to avoid a long delay in your case, be sure to document your marriage well.

Self-Petitioning: Abused Spouse, Child or Parent - The Violence Against Women Act

If you or your child has been physically or mentally abused by your U.S. citizen or permanent resident spouse or your U.S. citizen child age twenty-one or over is abusing you, you may be able to "self-petition" for a green card. This means you don't need a sponsor. You can file for a green card without your spouse's help. An abused child may file a petition until age twenty-five if he or she can show that the "abuse was at least one central reason for the filing delay."

Men can also self-petition under The Violence Against Women Act.

In order to qualify to self-petition, you must have been battered or subjected to extreme cruelty by a U.S. citizen or legal permanent resident relative and you must be living in the United States. If you self-petition based on abuse to you or your child, at some time you must have lived with your spouse. If you are applying as an abused child, a period of visitation with an abusive citizen parent or step-parent qualifies. But you don't have to be living together at the time that you file the petition. The abuse must have happened sometime during your marriage. Abuse that takes place after you are legally divorced is not enough, although it might help prove that abuse took place during your marriage. You need not be married to your spouse at the time that you file your petition if there is a connection between the divorce and the battery or extreme mental cruelty. You can qualify even if your divorce was a "no fault" divorce. However, if you are divorced, the divorce must have occurred within two years of filing the petition.

To prove that you were abused, you must provide a statement about the abuse and any additional credible evidence of the abuse, such as a police record, a family court protection order, or a letter from a psychiatrist, psychologist, or social worker who has counseled you or your child. You can contact the National Domestic Violence hotline for a referral to legal assistance in your area. Call **1-800-799-SAFE (7233)**.

Once the USCIS approves your self-petition the USCIS will allow you to remain in the United States until you become a permanent resident.

If You and Your Spouse Are Living Apart

What if you and your spouse are not living together? Can your spouse's I-130 petition for you be approved?

- If the separation has nothing to do with your intentions to be together as husband and wife, the USCIS should approve the petition if you can satisfy any doubts about the validity of your marriage.

- If your marriage is in trouble and you and your spouse are living apart but you have not taken steps to legally separate or end the marriage, the USCIS can still approve the I-130 petition. However, if the two of you are living apart, it may be more difficult to establish that your marriage is bona fide.

- If you or your spouse ha filed a separation agreement or divorce action with a court, as far as the USCIS is concerned, the marriage is over. In some states, merely signing a separation agreement may be enough for a marriage to be considered ended.

The stories of Jim and Martha and of Jaime and Altagracia show that even if a husband and wife are living apart, the couple can still show that their marriage is bonafide or real.

Jim and Martha's Story

Jim, a U.S. citizen, and Martha, a citizen of Mexico, met when they were both students at the University of Chicago. Upon graduation, Jim got accepted to a law school in San Francisco and Martha was accepted to a medical school in Los Angeles. They decided that they would have to live apart. To express their commitment to each other, they got married.

By the time the USCIS interviewed Jim and Martha about Martha's permanent residence, they were already living in different cities. Jim and Martha brought evidence of their continuing relationship to the interview. This evidence included phone bills showing that they spoke every night, letters, and photographs of them together in Niagara Falls on their honeymoon. They also gave the USCIS photos taken on their visit to Martha's family in Mexico City. Based on this evidence, Martha had no problem becoming a permanent resident.

Jaime and Altagracia's Story

Jaime and Altagracia had known each other for many years before they got married. Jaime was a citizen of Costa Rica who was studying architecture at the University of California at Los Angeles (UCLA). Altagracia, a U.S. citizen of Mexican ancestry, was also a student at UCLA. They were college sweethearts since their freshman year, and after graduation they decided to marry. Altagracia then petitioned for Jaime to become a permanent resident.

Jaime and Altagracia found that there was a big difference between being married and being boyfriend and girlfriend. They didn't like being married so they decided to separate. While they were living apart, the USCIS called them to come in for the interview regarding Jaime's application for permanent residence.

Although they admitted that they were living apart and revealed that information immediately when they began their interview, Altagracia was able to prove that the marriage was bona fide. She explained that neither had begun divorce proceedings, and that they were truly a couple. They had several albums full of photographs taken together on trips and at parties. They also had photos from their lavish wedding, when twenty of Jaime's relatives had flown in from Costa Rica just for the ceremony. The USCIS officer was convinced that the marriage between Jaime and Altagracia was a real marriage and granted Jaime his permanent residence

Prior Marriages

If your former spouse, or your spouse's former spouse has died you must present a death certificate when submitting the I-130 petition. If your or your spouse's prior marriage ended in divorce, you must submit the divorce judgment (not just a certificate of divorce).

If the divorce took place in a foreign country, the USCIS verifies that the divorce was proper under the laws of that country. The USCIS also verifies that the divorce is valid under the laws of the state or country where the marriage ceremony between you and your spouse took place.

Evaluating whether a marriage has been properly terminated can be difficult. If you have questions about the validity of a foreign divorce, check with an immigration or family law expert.

Conditional Residence

If you get permanent residence based on a marriage that is less than two years old at the time you become an immigrant, you are a conditional permanent resident. Being a conditional permanent resident means that you have a temporary green card, which expires in two years, though your conditional resident status sometimes continues. You and your spouse must file a joint petition (USCIS Form I-751, Petition to Remove the Conditions on Residence) to make your permanent residence truly permanent.

You must file the joint petition in the 90 days prior to the second anniversary of your becoming a permanent resident. If you became a permanent resident more than two years after your marriage, the conditional residence rule does not apply. If you get divorced before the USCIS removes the condition, or your spouse refuses to sign the joint petition, you must apply for a waiver of the joint petition requirement as discussed below. Except for the need to remove the condition, a conditional permanent resident has the same rights as all other permanent residents. Time in conditional permanent resident status counts toward U.S. citizenship.

The stories of Carlos and Juanita and of Yoko and Yoshi illustrate the conditional residence rule.

Carlos and Juanita's Story

Carlos, a citizen and resident of Barcelona, met Juanita, a U.S. citizen, when Juanita was studying Spanish in Barcelona. Shortly after Juanita and Carlos met, they got married. Since Carlos had a good job as a language instructor, they decided to live in Barcelona, despite objections from Juanita's parents. Three years later, when they decided to move to the United States, Juanita filed a relative petition for Carlos. Several months later, Carlos became a permanent resident without condition. Because he had already been married to Juanita for more than two years when he became a permanent resident, there was no need for Carlos to apply for permanent residency.

Yoko and Yoshi's Story

Yoko, a U.S. citizen, met Yoshi, an exchange student from Japan, in Aspen, Colorado. Both were in Aspen on ski vacations. Yoko, although of Japanese descent, could speak very little Japanese, and Yoshi could speak very little English. Nevertheless, they fell head over heels for each other and flew to Las Vegas to get married. After their marriage they began living together in Los Angeles, and Yoko immediately filed papers for Yoshi. Yoshi became a conditional permanent resident about three months later. Because he became a permanent resident within two years of his marriage to Yoko, Yoshi's permanent residence was conditional.

When the time came for Yoshi to apply to have the condition removed from his permanent residence, he and Yoko had been living apart for well over a year. Since Yoko wanted Yoshi to get his green card, she agreed not to divorce him until the USCIS removed the condition from Yoshi's permanent residence. On the joint petition to remove the condition, Yoko and Yoshi gave separate addresses. The USCIS called them in for an interview. At the interview, they presented evidence, including photos from their many trips together, to show that they had not gotten married just so Yoshi could get a green card. The USCIS officer believed them and determined that the USCIS should remove the condition from Yoshi's permanent residence. He became a permanent resident without condition. After Yoshi became a permanent resident without condition, Yoko divorced him.

Removing the Condition Without Your Spouse's Signature

If your marriage has been terminated by the death of your spouse or by annulment or divorce, or if your spouse refuses to sign the joint petition, you may still apply to have your conditional status removed. This is a waiver of the joint petition requirement. The same form, USCIS Form I-751, is filed with the USCIS. For the USCIS to remove the condition from your residence without the signature and cooperation of your spouse, you must show one of the following:

- Removal will result in your suffering extreme hardship.
- You entered the marriage in good faith, and the marriage has been terminated by divorce or annulment.
- You were the victim of domestic violence.
- Your spouse is deceased.

If you are filing based on being the victim of domestic violence, you need not wait until the ninety day period prior to the expiration of your conditional permanent residence. If you entered the marriage in good faith, and the marriage has ended by divorce or annulment, your case will not be approved until you produce a divorce judgment. If you cannot provide USCIS with a divorce judgment once asked to do so, USCIS can deny your case.

If the USCIS denies your petition to remove the condition from your residence, you may be placed in removal proceedings. If you can convince the immigration judge that your marriage was valid, or that you would suffer extreme hardship upon removal, the immigration judge can reverse the USCIS's decision.

Jimmy and Karen's stories both illustrate the effect of divorce in a conditional residence case.

Jimmy's Story

Jimmy came to the United States from Ireland as a drummer in a rock-and-roll band. Partying after one of his concerts, he met Susan, a U.S. citizen. They were soon married, and Susan then petitioned for Jimmy. Three months later, he became a conditional permanent resident. Unfortunately for Jimmy, his new wife fell in love with the band's lead singer and filed for divorce. Jimmy agreed to the divorce. Twenty-one months after Jimmy became a permanent resident, he applied to have the condition removed from his permanent residence. Since his wife had divorced him, he had to file for a waiver of the joint petition requirement. He submitted the divorce papers and explained in an affidavit (a sworn statement) exactly what had happened during his marriage. He provided extensive evidence of their marriage, including a photo of them together at the MTV Video Music Awards ceremony published in Rolling Stone magazine. Jimmy convinced the USCIS officer that the marriage was bona fide. The officer granted the waiver, and the USCIS removed the condition from Jimmy's permanent residence.

Karen's Story

After a long courtship, Harry, a U.S. citizen, married Karen, a Canadian citizen. Unfortunately, Karen had become a conditional permanent resident. Harry lost his job and developed a drinking problem. He became very abusive and regularly screamed, yelled and threatened to hurt Karen. Although Harry never hit her, he often threatened to do so. When he came home drunk, he would throw furniture, dishes, and other items around the apartment, forcing Karen to call the police. Eventually, Karen obtained a protection order from the court banning her husband from their apartment and ultimately divorced him.

When Karen applied to remove the condition from her residence, she presented copies of the police reports (which, in addition to showing spousal abuse, proved that she and her husband were living together) as well as a copy of the protection order. She included a letter from her psychiatrist, who explained how Harry's abuse had inflicted psychological trauma upon Karen. Based on the evidence presented, the USCIS officer removed the condition from Karen's permanent residence.

> ### Getting Divorced and Filing for a New Spouse: The Five-Year Rule
>
> If you are a permanent resident based on marriage to a U.S. citizen or permanent resident, you cannot remarry and petition for your new spouse unless you can prove one of the following:
>
> - The death of your spouse ended the prior marriage.
> - You didn't enter the prior marriage only to become a permanent resident.
> - Five years have passed since you first became a permanent resident.

Some people think that a person cannot remarry and petition for a new spouse for five years after they become a permanent resident. That's not true. The law only makes it more difficult because you must show that not just one but two marriages were bona fide: the one where you received your original green card and the one for the spouse for whom you are petitioning.

Kitty's story illustrates the five-year rule.

Kitty's Story

Kitty, from England, became a permanent resident when her husband, Henry, sponsored her. Henry was born in California. Henry and Kitty had met at a friend's house, fallen in love, and decided to marry within two months. Three months later, Kitty became a permanent resident.

Shortly after the wedding, Kitty and Henry began having marital problems. They tried to make their marriage work, but after three years, they divorced. When Kitty went home to England for Christmas, she bumped into her high school sweetheart, Sam, and decided to give marriage another chance. Though she had become a permanent resident just three years before and the five-year rule applies, she can petition for Sam immediately after their marriage.

Kitty has a great deal of evidence to prove that her marriage to Henry was bona fide. They traveled together, and Kitty has photographs from trips with Henry before and after their wedding. Kitty and Henry had lived in the same apartment for more than two years, and both of their names were on their apartment lease. Henry had been the beneficiary on Kitty's pension plan, and their names were both on a family health insurance policy.

Kitty can prove that her relationship with Sam is bona fide as well. Kitty and Sam had been corresponding and she has Sam's letters and records of their phone calls. They had a big wedding, and invited both of their families, and they took lots of pictures. Because Kitty can prove that her marriages to both Henry and Sam were bona fide, the USCIS can approve her petition. Sam obtains his priority date and begins his wait for a green card.

Self-Petitioning for a Widow(er)

If you are the widow(er) of a U.S. citizen, you can petition for a green card for yourself and your children. The petition must be filed within two years of your spouse's death, and you must not have remarried at the time that you become a permanent resident. If you were legally separated or divorced from your spouse at the time of death, you don't qualify. To qualify for a green card as a widow(er), you may be able to convert a pending I-130 petition or, alternatively, must file a new USCIS Form I-360.

The Parent-Child Relationship

You must prove a parent-child relationship when you are filing for a parent or a parent is filing for you.

Mother-Child

You are considered the son or daughter (child) of your natural mother, regardless of whether your mother and father were married. The only exception is for adopted children who after adoption cannot sponsor their birth mother.

Father-Child

For immigration purposes, a person is considered the child of a natural father if one of the following conditions is met:

- The child was born to married parents.
- The child was legitimated before the age of eighteen.
- The country of nationality does not distinguish between legitimate and illegitimate children.
- The parent-child relationship was established prior to the child's twenty-first birthday.

To claim a father-child relationship, the father need not have legally recognized his relationship with the child as long as the father can establish an act of concern for the child's "support, instruction, and general welfare."

The story of Timothy and his son, Noah, illustrates the rule regarding father-child relationships where the child was not legitimate or legitimated.

Timothy and Noah's Story

Timothy was a permanent resident of the United States. On one of his visits to his home country, he spent time with his old high school girlfriend, and she became pregnant with his child whom she named Noah. Timothy did not know he was the father of Noah until fifteen years later when Noah's mother wrote to Timothy to ask if he would help his son with college expenses. Timothy was shocked to learn that he had a 15-year-old son, but decided that he wanted to help Noah.

On his next trip to his country, Timothy spent time with Noah and began a regular correspondence with him. Every month, he sent Noah $100 to help him pay for his expenses, and once or twice a year, he visited Noah.

Ten years later, when Noah was 25 years of age, he decided that he wanted to become a permanent resident of the United States. Timothy petitioned for Noah, and Noah came into the United States as the adult unmarried son of a permanent resident under the Second Family-Based Preference B. Although Timothy had never legally recognized Noah as his son, because Timothy had an established relationship with Noah that was typical of a father-son relationship, Noah qualified for a permanent resident as the unmarried son of Timothy.

Stepparent-Stepchild

U.S. immigration law recognizes a stepparent-stepchild relationship when the stepchild is less than 18 years old at the time of the marriage between the natural parent and the stepparent. This parent-child relationship is recognized by the USCIS regardless of the child's age when the petition is filed. Even if the natural parent and stepparent divorce, the USCIS will sometimes recognize the parent-stepchild relationship. Finally, the USCIS recognizes the relationship between a child and the child's natural parents, even after a stepchild-stepparent relationship is created. This means that a child can petition for his stepparents and his natural parents.

The stories of Michael, Martha, and their children and of Karen, Steve, Sally, and their children illustrate the stepparent-stepchild rule.

Michael, Martha and Their Children's Story

Michael is a U.S. citizen who married Martha, a citizen of Venezuela. At the time of her marriage to Michael, Martha had two children, Charlie (fourteen years of age) and Carmen (nineteen years of age). They all live in Venezuela, but Michael would like them to live in the United States as soon as possible.

However, only Martha and Charlie can become permanent residents as Immediate Relatives of a U.S. citizen. Since Charlie was younger than eighteen when Martha and Michael married, he is legally considered Michael's stepchild. Because of the unlimited number of green cards available for Immediate Relatives of U.S. citizens, both Martha and Charlie will become permanent residents as soon as their papers are processed.

Since Carmen was nineteen at the time of Martha and Michael's marriage, the USCIS does not consider her the stepchild of Michael. Carmen cannot become a permanent resident based on a petition filed by Michael. Carmen must wait until Martha becomes a permanent resident and then can petition for her. If Carmen remains unmarried, she must wait until her priority date (see chapter 6 for more on priority dates) is reached before she can get an immigrant visa under the Second Family-Based Preference B.

Karen, Steve, Sally and Their Children's Story

Karen and Steve, natives and residents of Australia, had both been married and divorced before they met, fell in love, and got married. Steve had a child, Chris, from a previous marriage. When Karen and Steve married, Chris was twelve years old. Under U.S. immigration laws, Chris is Karen's "child" under U.S. immigration laws.

When Chris was twenty-five years old, he became a U.S. citizen. He then petitioned to bring Karen and Steve from Australia. Though Chris is over eighteen, the stepchild-stepparent relationship created by the marriage of Karen and Steve lasts throughout both their lives. He could also petition for his natural mother since she is his natural mother.

Adopted Child

A child adopted before the age of 16 who has lived in the same household with and has been in the legal custody of his or her adopted parent for two years is considered by the USCIS to be a child of that parent.

Some countries still have informal or "customary" adoptions. In the case of customary adoptions, the USCIS will look to the laws of the country where the adoption took place. The USCIS will recognize the customary adoption if the adopted child has rights equal to a child formally adopted.

Orphan Child

A U.S. citizen can petition for an orphan child who is under the age of sixteen at the time the adoptive parent files the petition. An orphan petition can be filed after the child's sixteenth birthday, but before his/her eighteenth birthday if the child is the birth sibling of another child who has immigrated (or will immigrate) based on adoption by the same parent. The child must have become an orphan because of the death or disappearance of or abandonment by his or her parents. "Abandonment" may include a situation where a parent or parents are incapable of caring for the child. To petition for a specific orphan, a U.S. citizen must be married or at least twenty-five years old.

The adoptive parents must have adopted the child abroad, or the petitioner must prove that he or she will adopt the orphan child when the child comes to the United States. The adoptive parent(s) can do this by meeting the pre-adoption requirements in the state where the orphan will be residing.

Brother or Sister

To establish a sibling relationship, you must prove one parent in common under the rules for the parent-child relationship as discussed above. A U.S. citizen must be more than twenty-one years of age to petition for a brother or sister.

If siblings have the same parents and those parents were married, proving that they have a brother-sister relationship is easy. Birth certificates are usually enough to prove the sibling relationship. But suppose they have only one parent in common. What happens then is illustrated by the story of Miguel, Sonia and Reynaldo.

Miguel, Sonia and Reynaldo's Story

Sonia and Reynaldo have the same father, Miguel, but different mothers. Sonia, a twenty-five-year-old U.S. citizen, wants to petition for her half brother, Reynaldo.

Sonia is the legitimate child of Miguel, having been born to Miguel's wife, who passed away shortly after Sonia's birth. Reynaldo was born out of wedlock to Miguel and his girlfriend, Virginia. Under the laws of the country where Reynaldo was born, he is considered "illegitimate."

However, Miguel raised Reynaldo since his birth and has been Reynaldo's sole means of financial support and fatherly guidance. Miguel is also Reynaldo's father since he established a father-son relationship with Reynaldo before Reynaldo's twenty-first birthday. Thus, Reynaldo is Miguel's child under the law. Miguel is clearly Sonia's father because she is his legitimate daughter. Therefore, since Sonia and Reynaldo have one parent in common, Sonia and Reynaldo are sister and brother. Sonia can successfully petition for Reynaldo.

Chapter 3 - Employment-Based Immigration

Whether you're a housekeeper, gardener, designer, or scientist, you may be able to get an immigrant visa based on an offer of employment. Usually, your employer must prove that no qualified U.S. worker is immediately available to do the job. Sometimes you can get an immigrant visa simply because of the value of your skills, knowledge, or experience to U.S. society.

In this chapter, I give you an overview of how you can get an immigrant visa based on your work, talent, or investment. These categories are called Employment-Based Preferences.

If your employer must show that no qualified U.S. worker is available to do the job, the employer must get a labor certification from the U.S. Department of Labor (DOL). The labor certification will confirm the unavailability of U.S. workers for the position.

To get an immigrant visa based on employment, you must be the beneficiary of a USCIS-approved petition, USCIS Form I-140, Immigrant Petition for Alien Worker. Where the law requires a labor certification, it must be presented with the petition. Where the law doesn't require a labor certification, you file the petition with supporting documentation showing your qualifications under a particular Employment-Based visa category.

You sometimes can change jobs and continue with your Employment-Based case without filing a new labor certification and Form I-140 Immigrant Visa Petition. For more on this rule, see "Petition Portability for Employment-Based Cases," later in this chapter.

Your Employment-Based Priority Date

When a labor certification must support a petition, your priority date is the date when the U.S. Department of Labor first receives your labor certification application. Your priority date is your place in line under the preference system (for more on priority dates, see chapter 6). Where no labor certification is required, your priority date is the date that the USCIS receives your petition. In this case, proof of your education and/or experience must accompany the I-140 petition. Unless a well-known company is sponsoring you, your employer must submit proof of the company's ability to pay the offered salary.

Must You Stay at Your Job After You Get Your Immigrant Visa?

Just because your employer sponsored you doesn't mean you must stay with that job forever. However, if you quit soon after getting your immigrant visa, the USCIS may someday check whether the job offer was genuine. If the USCIS determines that the job offer was not genuine you run the risk of losing your green card.

Christine's and Joan's stories illustrate the rule about changing jobs for Employment-Based green card holders.

Christine's Story

Christine was working as a physical therapist in Holland when a hospital in Houston, Texas, offered her a job. She began work at the hospital in H-1B professional worker status (see chapter 14 for more on H-1B status). After Christine spent a year on the job, the hospital agreed to sponsor her for permanent residence. One year later, she became a permanent resident. Unfortunately for Christine, two weeks after becoming a permanent resident, the hospital replaced her supervisor. Christine started to have a miserable time at her job. She quit her position at the hospital and went to work teaching pottery to nursery school children, something she'd always wanted to do.

Christine's Story (Continued)

Five years after becoming a permanent resident, Christine applied for U.S. citizenship. At her USCIS naturalization interview, the examiner reviewed her work history. The examiner discovered that Christine had worked for her employer for only two weeks after she became a permanent resident. Christine had made very careful notes of all her experiences at the hospital. She convinced the USCIS naturalization examiner that the job offer was genuine and that she left her employment at the hospital because of circumstances beyond her control. The examiner approved her naturalization application.

Joan's Story

Joan was a skilled automobile repair worker living in Germany. Through a friend in the United States, she learned about a shortage of good German car repair specialists in Los Angeles. Joan always wanted to live in the city of the stars and decided to come to the United States on a visit. While in the U.S., she interviewed at a German auto repair shop. The owner of the repair shop agreed to sponsor her for a permanent visa. Joan would have liked to start work immediately, but she wasn't eligible for any temporary work-related visa. She also could not get H-1B status because she was not considered a professional. The job wasn't temporary, so she was not eligible for the H-2 temporary work visa for skilled workers (see chapter 11 for more on H-2 status).

She returned to Germany while her employer processed her green card application.

Two years later, the United States Department of Labor approved Joan's labor certification application. The employer petitioned for her, and six months after the USCIS approved the petition, the U.S. consulate called her in for her immigrant visa interview. A week before her interview, Joan received a letter from her employer stating that the job was still open. The letter said that they were interested in offering her a permanent position at the wage noted in the labor certification application. The U.S. consulate issued Joan a permanent visa. Before beginning her new life in the United States, she spent a month traveling in Europe. After her travels, she came to the United States and went right to Los Angeles to begin working at her new job.

Unfortunately, the night before Joan arrived in Los Angeles, the repair shop burned down. The employer did not have insurance, and Joan had no job. Though Joan had never worked for the employer who sponsored her, her permanent residence status is valid. If officers from the USCIS questioned Joan about how she received her green card, she would have to show that she intended to work for the company when she entered the United States. If asked for proof, she might submit to the USCIS a fire department report about what happened. She could also submit a letter from the employer who had originally sponsored her, explaining about the fire. She may also be asked for documentation that shows the company was financially healthy at the time of petitioning.

The Employment Preferences

If you get an Employment-Based immigrant visa, your spouse and unmarried children under 21 can accompany or follow you. They qualify for immigrant visas as your derivative beneficiaries (See Chapter 1 for more on derivative beneficiaries).

Let's review the Employment-Based immigrant visa preferences.

First Employment-Based Preference: Priority Workers

The term priority worker reflects the intent of the U.S. Congress to make green cards easily available for certain businesspeople, professors and researchers, and people with special talents. If you qualify in this category, you don't have to show that there are no U.S. workers available to do your job. A labor certification is not required from the Department of Labor.

The law divides priority workers into three subcategories: aliens with an extraordinary ability, outstanding professors and researchers, and multinational executives and managers.

Aliens with an Extraordinary Ability

To apply in this category, you must show extraordinary ability in the sciences, arts, education, business, or athletics. You must show sustained national or international acclaim with recognized achievements. To win an extraordinary ability case usually requires extensive documentation. You should be able to show at least three of the following:

- Receipt of a national or international award in your field.
- Membership in an association that requires outstanding achievement as a condition of membership.
- Published material about yourself in professional, trade, or major media publications.
- Reviews or discussions of your work in a major publication or other major media.
- Your participation as a judge of the work of others in the same or a related field.
- Original contributions, usually through publication, of major significance in your field.
- Authorship of scholarly articles.
- Display of your work at significant exhibitions.
- Performance in a significant role for organizations or establishments that have a distinguished reputation.
- Receipt of a higher salary than is usual in the field.
- Commercial success in the performing arts as shown by box office receipts or sales records.

While the law does not require a specific job offer in this category, you must present some evidence that you intend to continue work in your field. Examples are a contract with an agent or publisher. Suzie Shu's and Chudi's stories provide examples of workers of extraordinary ability.

Suzie Shu's Story

Suzie Shu is one of the world's leading Chinese zither players. Although little known in the United States, she is a household name in China and Chinese-speaking communities throughout the world. On her yearly visits to the United States, she plays to packed houses in New York and San Francisco. She has several bestselling albums, and has received many award. Shu is also is a member of the prestigious International Society of Musicians. Though most people in the United States do not know Shu, she is nonetheless an individual of extraordinary ability in her musical specialty.

Suzie Shu's Story (Continued)

To get a green card, Shu filed an I-140 petition with supporting documentation of her achievements. She included a letter from experts on Chinese music, many album covers, and articles about her in both American and Chinese newspapers. Her application included a letter from her agent showing that she had several performances scheduled for the next year. Once the USCIS approved her I-140 petition, she applied to become a permanent resident. She did not need an employer to sponsor her.

Chudi's Story

Chudi is a citizen of Nigeria. He came to the United States after several years of writing for Nigeria's leading national paper. He has been working for the last five years in H-1B temporary professional worker status at the Los Angeles Gazette, the city's leading daily paper. (For more on H-1B status, see chapter 14.) The Gazette is recognized as one of the outstanding daily newspapers in the United States. The managing editor promoted Chudi to chief international reporter. Chudi has won national and international awards, and his articles have been in many publications. He files an I-140 petition and includes letters from journalists, professors, and the editors of three leading newsmagazines in the United States. The letters state that he is recognized as a leading writer on the topic of international events. Chudi will have no problem becoming a permanent resident. He can petition for himself without the help of his employer.

Outstanding Professors and Researchers

To qualify in this category, you must show international recognition as being outstanding in a specific academic area. You must have at least three years of experience in teaching or research in the area. While this category doesn't require a labor certification showing the unavailability of U.S. workers, you must have a job offer from a college, university, research institute, or private company. For a college or university teacher, the job must be for a tenured or tenure-track position.

> To qualify as an outstanding professor or researcher, you must have at least three years of experience as a teacher or researcher and meet at least two of the following criteria:
>
> - Receipt of a major award for outstanding achievement in your field.
> - Membership in academic associations that require outstanding achievements as a condition of membership.
> - Published discussions of your work in professional journals.
> - Participation as a judge of the work of others in the same or a related field.
> - Original scientific or scholarly research.
> - Authorship of scholarly books or articles.

The stories of Suzanne and Julie help us understand the outstanding professors and researchers category.

Suzanne's Story

The Southern San Diego Research Institute in California offered Suzanne employment as a biomedical researcher. For the last four years, she has been working for the Institute in H-1B temporary professional worker status. Prior to that, she had worked for four years in a similar institute in her home country, France. Though she holds only a master of science in biology, she has co-authored several reports in the nationally recognized Journal of Biological Medicine. Her years of experience and her publications in a national journal qualify her as a priority worker under the outstanding professors and researchers category.

Julie's Story

Julie was not as fortunate as Suzanne. Julie was trying to get a green card as a professor of economics at Valley State University in California. She had been a professor at the college for three years working in H-1B status. However, other than her three years' experience, she was unable to qualify as an outstanding professor. She was in a tenure-track position and was considered the best teacher in the college, but she had not achieved much in other areas of professional activity. Julie always believed that her primary role as a professor was to teach and enlighten her students. However, her excellence as a teacher wasn't enough to qualify her for an immigrant visa as an outstanding professor and researcher. She had published many articles in popular newspapers and magazines but nothing in a professional journal. She had even written a book, Making Money in America, *which was published by a small press, but this still was not sufficient.*

Julie is able to apply for permanent residence as an employee of the college, but she will need to apply for a labor certification. Since she is professor, if the employer files a labor certification within eighteen months of the college having hired her, Julie can get a labor certification without her employer having to show that no U.S. workers are available to fill the position. The employer need only show that the search was fair and that they chose the person they believed was best for the position.

Multinational Executives and Managers

This category eases the transfer of international personnel. Prior to filing the I-140 petition, a branch, subsidiary, parent, or affiliate of the sponsoring company must have employed you abroad as a manager or executive for at least one of the previous three years. The U.S. company must have been doing business for at least one year. Most important, you must be coming to the United States to work as a manager or executive.

Katherine and Wei's stories provide examples of getting green cards as intracompany transferees.

Katherine's Story

Katherine works for a British bank with a branch office in New York. Her company transferred her to the United States to manage the international investment division of the company's New York branch. She entered the United States on an L-1 international transferee temporary visa. Katherine answers directly to the president of the bank's U.S. operations. She has several professional and nonprofessional employees working under her. These employees include investment advisors, financial analysts, and secretaries.

After two years of working in the United States, Katherine wanted to become a permanent resident. She emailed the main office and asked the company to sponsor her. The main office agreed to help Katherine become a permanent resident. The president of the New York branch of the bank filed an I-140 petition for her, and on the basis of this petition she became a permanent resident.

Wei's Story

Wei had been president of his own import-export company, Wei's Imports Ltd., based in Taiwan for more than twenty years. He did business around the world, but had not seen the need to establish a branch office in the United States.

Wei grew concerned about the long-range future of Taiwan and considered applying for a business investor visa. After speaking to several business and legal experts, he decided that the laws and regulations regarding permanent visas for international investors would interfere with his investment plans. Applying for a green card based on an investment was not worth the trouble.

Wei's Story (Continued)

Wei decided instead to expand his operations and open an office in New York. He hired two executives to help him run the business. His company, Wei International Ltd., which was incorporated under the laws of Taiwan, wanted to transfer him to New York to manage and run the new operations. After the New York office had been in operation for a year and was actively doing business, Wei had the company petition for him for permanent residence. That way he did not have to bother getting a nonimmigrant visa such as an L-1 for intracompany transferees.

After submitting detailed documentation regarding the development of the new office, he entered the United States as a permanent resident. His case took just over six months. He continued to manage the New York operations of the business and traveled to Taiwan one month out of every three to supervise the Taiwan business.

Second Employment-Based Preference: Members of Professions Holding Advanced Degrees or Aliens of Exceptional Ability

In this category you must be either **(a)** a member of the professions holding an advanced degree (or have the equivalent in education and experience) or **(b)** a person of exceptional ability. The term "member of the professions" means that to do your job a person would need at least a bachelor's degree or higher. Examples are teachers, engineers, architects, and college professors.

An "advanced degree" is the equivalent of a U.S. master's degree or higher. A bachelor's degree followed by five years of progressive experience may be considered to be the equivalent of a master's degree.

The fact that you hold an advanced degree is not enough. Your job must also require the degree you hold. Rachel's and Paul's stories illustrate the relationship between the position and the degree for professional workers.

Rachel's Story

Rachel studied mathematics in her home country of Poland. Her English was excellent and Rachel also had her transcripts evaluated by a professional credential evaluation company in the United States. The evaluation showed that she had the U.S. equivalent of a master's degree in mathematics. A cousin in the United States told her about a job as a math teacher at a local private school, and Rachel applied for the job from Poland. The school got her a labor certification from the Department of Labor and then filed a petition for her in the Second Employment-Based category. The school explained that a master's degree or higher in the subject to be taught was a normal requirement for an instructor at the school. The USCIS approved the petition, and about one year later Rachel came to the United States with a permanent resident visa.

Paul's Story

Paul received his Ph.D. in art history from the University of Moscow. His father had been the manager of a large factory. While Paul had no formal business training or work experience, because of his father's job, he was very well connected in the growing Russian business community.

When Paul came to the United States to present a paper at a conference on twentieth-century Russian art, a friend introduced him to an executive of the Bulls and Bears stock brokerage firm. The firm was based in San Francisco, California. The executive offered Paul a job at two-hundred-thousand dollars a year, plus bonuses, if Paul could help the company with business development. His chief responsibility would be to introduce the company to Russian investors and to entertain Russian business executives when they came to the United States.

Paul can't qualify under the Second Employment-Based Preference. He has an advanced degree, but his job doesn't require a degree in art history.

The Second Employment-Based Preference category also includes individuals who can show "exceptional ability" in the sciences, arts, or business. To qualify as a person of exceptional ability, you must show at least three of the following:

- An official academic record showing that you have a degree related to the area of exceptional ability.
- Evidence that you have at least 10 years of full-time experience in the job you are being petitioned for.
- A license to practice your profession.
- Evidence that your salary reflects your exceptional ability.
- Membership in professional associations.
- Evidence of recognition for achievements and significant contributions in your field.

In the Second Employment-Based Preference category, your employer must obtain a labor certification certified by the Department of Labor unless the USCIS grants you a national interest waiver (discussed later this chapter).

Third Employment-Based Preference: Professionals, Skilled Workers, and Other Workers

Professionals are individuals who hold United States bachelor's degrees or the academic equivalent. The degree must be a normal requirement for the job. Skilled workers perform labor requiring at least two years of education, training, or experience. Other workers perform un-skilled labor requiring less than two years of training or experience. No more than ten-thousand visas annually are available for the category of "other workers."

In the category of Third Employment-Based Preference, your employer must get you a labor certification. Billy's story helps us to understand the difference between "skilled" workers and workers in the "other worker" category.

Billy's Story

Billy came to the United States from Trinidad as a student in F-1 status. He soon tired of school and decided to go to work. He convinced an employer to hire him as a chef's assistant in a twenty-four-hour restaurant. The job required one year of experience, which Billy had gained before coming to the United States. Billy worked the midnight to 8AM. shift in the same position for two years. His employer agreed to sponsor him for permanent residence. Because of the late hours, no U.S. workers with the necessary experience were ready, willing, and able to take his position.

The Department of Labor approved Billy's labor certification. Billy realized, however, that because of the backlog in the quota for less-skilled workers, it could be many years before he would qualify for permanent residence.

Meanwhile, in the two years that had passed since Billy's employer first filed the labor certification application, the head chef in the restaurant trained Billy to cook the homemade pastries that had made the restaurant famous. A different restaurant offered Billy a pastry chef position, based on his four years of experience as a chef's assistant and his two years of training as a pastry chef. Now Billy was doing a job that required at least two years of experience.

Billy's new employer filed a labor certification for him, and two years later the Department of Labor approved his labor certification. In contrast to the long waiting list for less-skilled workers, there was no waiting list for skilled workers from Billy's country.

Fourth Employment-Based Preference: Religious Workers and Certain Special Immigrants

Religious workers with two years of experience, ministers, religious professionals, some religious nonprofessionals, and certain foreign-language broadcasters working for Radio Free Europe or Radio Free Asia can get green cards as special immigrants.

The Fourth Employment-Based Preference special immigrant category also includes Afghanistan or Iraq nationals who supported the U.S. as translators, some dependents of diplomats, employees of the American Taiwan Institute for at least fifteen years, and persons who have served in active duty in the U.S. armed services for twelve years or after six if they have reenlisted for six additional years.

Fifth Employment-Based Preference—Employment Creation (Investor)

To get an employment creation visa, the investor must establish a NEW commercial enterprise or invest in one of the regional job creation centers recognized by USCIS. The person must invest, or be in the process of investing, a minimum of one million dollars. The minimum is five-hundred-thousand dollars if the investment is an area that has an unemployment rate at least 150 percent of the national average or a rural area with a population of less than twenty thousand. The enterprise must create full-time employment for at least ten U.S. citizens, permanent residents, asylees or refugees. Under the regional center program, rather than starting a new business yourself, you can invest in a USCIS-approved enterprise. Under this program, the investor can show indirect job creation. That means the applicant invests with the regional job creation center and it, rather than the investor, runs the enterprise that qualifies you for permanent residence (and creates the needed ten jobs). You can find a list of regional centers at the USCIS website, **www.uscis.gov**. Search for "Immigrant Investor Regional Centers."

If you get your green card under the investor provisions, you become a conditional permanent resident. You must apply to the USCIS to have the condition removed within the ninety-day period preceding the second anniversary of your having become a permanent resident.

To get the USCIS to remove the condition, you must prove that a commercial enterprise was established, that you actually made the investment, and that you are sustaining the investment as a commercial enterprise.

The Labor Certification Requirement

As noted above, some Employment-Based green card categories require certification from the Department of Labor. The Department of Labor certifies that no lawful U.S. worker is ready, willing, and able to fill the job offered. "Lawful U.S. workers" include U.S. citizens, permanent residents, asylees, and refugees. The labor certification is, in most cases, a requirement for applying for permanent residence.

Many people have the mistaken impression that in order to get a labor certification, you must be must speak several languages, have advanced technical skills or unique talents. True, unique ability is important in some cases. However, you will find that you might establish unavailability of lawful U.S. workers in jobs that require a substantial amount of experience. You can prove unavailability even in some selected job categories requiring little experience, such as live-in domestic household workers.

Melissa and Johnny's stories provide examples of workers who qualified for labor certifications.

Melissa's Story

Melissa came to the United States from Ireland on a visitor's visa and overstayed. Though she had no children of her own, Melissa loved children and began working as a childcare attendant for a young couple. The children's parents both worked as lawyers, and they needed a live-in housekeeper. Melissa had her own room with a separate bathroom in the house. After a year working for the family, Melissa and her employer decided that they would begin the process of getting Melissa a green card. Though Melissa's job does not require a large amount of experience and training, finding housekeepers and child care workers willing to live in is hard. Melissa's employers applied for a labor certification for her and it was approved.

The problem for Melissa is that under current law the waiting list for a lesser-skilled worker is long and because of the unlawful presence bar to permanent residence, she may never get her green card. Melissa's has her labor certification, but that does not give her the right to work. Melissa may never get a green card based on this labor certification. By the time her number comes up under the quota system and her priority date becomes current, the family may not even need a childcare attendant. Additionally, unless Melissa can interview in the United States for permanent residence, she will be barred from returning for three or ten years. It is unlikely her employer would wait so long for her to return. For more about the unlawful presence bar, see chapter 5.

Johnny's Story

Johnny also came to the United States on a visitor's visa and overstayed. He is the assistant manager in a supermarket in a largely Chinese community. He speaks Cantonese and Mandarin, two of the most common Chinese dialects. He learned the business of supermarket management in Hong Kong, where he lived until he was 25 years of age. Johnny is responsible for maintaining inventory, hiring and firing, and managing the supermarket when the senior manager is not available. Because of his skills and language ability, Johnny can do a job that few Americans are ready, willing, and able to perform. His employer can most likely get a labor certification for him. If the employer can convince the Department of Labor and the USCIS that his job requires at least two years of experience, he will be eligible under the skilled worker category and he will not have as long a wait for his immigrant visa. His big problem will be overcoming the bar to residence for people out of status (see chapter 5).

You Can't Tailor the Job

The Department of Labor will be careful to ensure that your employer doesn't tailor job requirements to your particular experience. Your employer must justify any unusual job requirement based on a business necessity, not just a personal preference.

Jim's story shows how the Department of Labor may deny a labor certification application if they believe that the employer is tailoring the job requirements to a particular employee

Jim's Story

Jim came to the United States from England on a visit. Jim asked his employer to sponsor him for permanent residence. Jim's boss decided to help him and filed a labor certification for a receptionist. Jim had studied languages in school in England and was fluent in French, Italian, and Spanish. To keep other qualified workers from applying, Jim's employer included in his recruitment ad the requirement that the receptionist speak French, Italian, and Spanish. Nobody else applied for the position.

Jim's Story (Continued)

When Jim's employer submitted the labor certification application, the U.S. Department of Labor challenged whether the employer had a genuine business necessity for a worker who could speak the listed foreign languages. Unfortunately for Jim, no such need existed. None of the other employees or the firm's clients or business associates spoke foreign languages. Since Jim's employer could not prove the need for the foreign language requirement, he had to re-advertise the position using the genuine job requirements: "word processing skills, secretarial/receptionist skills, two years' experience."

Whether the Department of Labor will approve the labor certification will depend on whether qualified people apply for the position. That, in turn, will depend on the job market in existence at the time the ad appears. If many qualified people in the area have the skills required, Jim cannot get a labor certification. If no qualified applicants are ready, willing, and able to take the position, Jim can get the labor certification. There may be many receptionists in New York City with the skills that are required for the position. However, if they are all working and not looking to change jobs, and thus no qualified people apply, then Jim can get the labor certification.

The Labor Certification Process

Under current procedures, known as the Program Electronic Review Management — or PERM— process, the employer starts the process by determining the prevailing wage for the position. The employer then tests the market to determine whether any U.S. workers are ready, willing, and able to perform the job duties. Under PERM, the employer typically finds the prevailing wage by requesting a prevailing wage determination from the Department of Labor based on the job description. The employer can challenge the wage determination, but success is rare. Where a wage is set by a collective bargaining agreement, known also as a union contract, the prevailing wage is the union wage for the position.

Usually the employer will wait until the prevailing wage is agreed to before testing the labor market through advertising. The employer may reject any worker who does not meet the minimum job requirements or who fails to meet typical job-related standards such as appearing at interviews on time and dressing appropriately.

If no qualified worker applies for the position, the employer files the PERM application and reports an unsuccessful search. The DOL will then either certify that no qualified workers are available, deny the application or audit the search. Where the DOL denies an application, the employer can seek reconsideration or appeal the denial.

Where the Employee Is Already Employed by the Employer

Often an employee whom the employer wants to sponsor is already working for the employer when the advertising begins. If the employer makes a good faith effort to find a qualified worker, the employer may sponsor an employee already on-the-job. We say that the employer is "testing the market" to determine whether the employee qualifies for a labor certification. If a qualified U.S worker applies, the employer need not hire that worker. However, whether the market test reveals that a qualified worker is ready, willing, and able to accept the position, the employer cannot file a labor certification application for the foreign national worker.

National Interest Waivers

If you are coming to the United States to do work that will benefit the national interest of the United States, you might qualify for an immigrant visa without a labor certification. You don't even need an employer to sponsor you; you can sponsor yourself. You will need to prove that you will work in the United States in your field.

To get a national interest waiver, the USCIS usually (but not always) requires you to have at least the equivalent of a U.S. master's degree. It's become more difficult to get a national interest waiver since the program began, but it remains available particularly for well-published scientists and biomedical researchers and others making significant societal contributions.

Petition Portability for Employment-Based Cases

If you change jobs while your application for adjustment of status (application for permanent residence filed in the United States) is pending, your Employment-Based petition may continue to be valid. That means that the USCIS will continue to process your permanent residence application based on sponsorship from your new employer. You'll keep the priority date, place in line, that you were assigned based on your old job. Your new employer need not file a new I-140 petition. To qualify for this portability, the following must be true:

1. You applied for adjustment of status based on an approved Employment-Based petition.

2. You filed for adjustment of status (see chapter 6), and your application has been pending for 180 days when you change jobs.

3. The new job is in the same or a similar occupation to the job for which your original petition was filed.

4. You are applying for permanent residence in the First, Second or Third Employment-Based Preference category.

Chapter 4 - Lottery Green Cards

One of the more unusual (some say bizarre) ways that the United States hands out immigrant visas is the Diversity Visa, or, as people commonly call it, "the green card lottery." Each year, the U.S. government gives up to fifty-five thousand visas to applicants who are natives of low-admission countries. Low-admission countries are countries where fewer than fifty thousand people have immigrated during the preceding five years. For the next few years, the government will give only fifty thousand visas. Of the usual fifty-five thousand, up to five thousand will go to NACARA applicants. For more on NACARA, see chapter 1.

No matter where you are currently residing, if you are a native of a qualifying country, as the law defines "native" under the lottery rules, you may win the lottery. You may be living in the United States, your native country, or any other country in the world. If after reading this chapter you are still not sure whether you qualify, go ahead and enter.

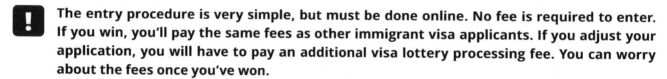

The entry procedure is very simple, but must be done online. No fee is required to enter. If you win, you'll pay the same fees as other immigrant visa applicants. If you adjust your application, you will have to pay an additional visa lottery processing fee. You can worry about the fees once you've won.

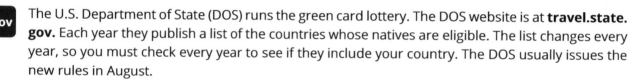

The U.S. Department of State (DOS) runs the green card lottery. The DOS website is at **travel.state. gov.** Each year they publish a list of the countries whose natives are eligible. The list changes every year, so you must check every year to see if they include your country. The DOS usually issues the new rules in August.

If You Don't Win, Will Immigration Deport You?

Some people living in the United States are afraid to apply for the lottery. They think that if they don't win, Immigration Customs and Enforcement will arrest them and they'll end up deported. You need not be afraid to apply for the lottery. First, you don't have give your own address when applying, you just need to give the DOS a mailing address so that they can notify you if you are a winner. Second, even if you were to put your home address, it is unlikely that immigration will come looking for you.

The Families of Lottery Winners

If you win the lottery, your spouse and any of your children who are under age twenty-one and unmarried when you become a permanent resident can get lottery green cards when you do.

The USCIS and U.S. consuls will sometimes deny lottery green card applications if you don't list your spouse and/or children on your lottery entry. That rule does not apply if you do not list your children U.S. citizens or over twenty-one. If you did not list children over age eighteen but under twenty-one, the government will excuse your omission only if you can successfully argue that you thought children over eighteen were excluded from getting a lottery green card as your dependent.

Some unmarried minor children of Diversity Visa lottery winners will benefit from the Child Status Protection Act (CSPA) enacted on August 2, 2003. For diversity lottery CSPA purposes, you must determine the period for which the case is pending. This is first day of the DV mail-in period and the date on the applicant's "congratulatory" letter. The congratulatory letter is the letter applicants receive notifying them that they are lottery winners. The days the petition is pending are subtracted from the DV lottery derivative beneficiary's age on the date the visa became available. Once you make this calculation you know the DV Lottery derivative beneficiary's CSPA age.

Rosemary's story illustrates how The CSPA might benefit a child of a DV lottery winner.

Rosemary's story

Rosemary's mother entered the DV lottery for 2005 on November 1, 2003. On that date, Rosemary was twenty years and five months old. Her mother was a lucky winner. The congratulatory notice was dated August 1, 2004. Though her real age was over twenty-one, Rosemary's age was counted by the law as being nine months earlier, April 1, 2004 (the period between the lottery entry date November 1, 2003 and the notice date August 1, 2004).

Rosemary's mother's application was approved January 1, 2005. Though Rosemary had already turned twenty-one, she qualified for a derivative DV lottery visa because using the date the law allows under the CSPA, she was not yet twenty-one on her mother's eligibility date.

Who Is Eligible to Win the Green Card Lottery?

To qualify to win the green card lottery, you must be a native of a country with low immigrant admission over the past five years. You must also have at least a high school education or its equivalent or have worked in an occupation requiring at least two years of training or experience.

Who Is a Native?

You are a native if you meet one of the following requirements:

- You were born in the qualifying country.
- Your husband or wife was born in the qualifying country.
- You are under twenty-one and unmarried, and one of your parents was born in a qualifying country.
- One of your parents is a native of a qualifying country, and your parents didn't reside in your country of birth.

If you are not sure whether or not you are a "native" of a qualifying country, go ahead and enter the lottery anyway.

The stories of Claudette, Jason, and William illustrate how the law defines the term "native" for the purposes of the lottery.

Claudette's Story

Claudette was born in Canada. The year she entered the lottery, Canada was not considered to be a low-admission country. So she was not a qualifying country native. However, Claudette was married to George, who was born in Sweden, which was a qualifying country. Claudette and George lived together in Canada, where George was a landed immigrant, the Canadian equivalent of a permanent resident. Because George is a native of a qualifying country, Claudette and George can each make separate entries in the visa lottery. If either George or Claudette wins the lottery, the other can get an immigrant visa at the same time as the winner.

Jason's Story

Jason is seventeen years old and single. He was born in the People's Republic of China (not a qualifying country the year that he wished to enter the lottery). However, Jason's mother was born in Laos, which was a qualifying country that year. Thus Jason qualifies as a "native" because his mother is a native of a qualifying country. Of course, his mother can also apply separately and if she wins, Jason can then get an immigrant visa when she does. However, if Jason wins, he cannot get an immigrant visa for his mother at that time.

William's Story

William was born in Canada to Egyptian parents. His parents were in Canada working on a short-term assignment from a Canadian bank. Though Canadian natives were not eligible to win the lottery the year William entered, he nonetheless qualified. He benefited from the rule which states that a person who is born in a country where his parents weren't residing qualifies as a native of his or her country of birth.

The Education/Work Experience Requirement

Once you win the lottery, you must prove that you meet the education/work requirements. You can meet the requirements in one of two ways. One way is by having at least a high school degree (or higher) or its foreign equivalent. The second way is by proving that you have worked for two of the past five years at a job that requires at least two years of training or experience. You don't have to prove that you meet the education requirement until you win the lottery and apply for your immigrant visa.

If you have completed high school in the United States, your diploma provides enough evidence. A "foreign equivalent" of a high school diploma is proof that you have completed a twelve-year course of elementary and secondary education that is the same as a high school degree in the United States. The USCIS view is that a high school equivalency diploma (GED or TASC), which is valid to enter college in some states, does not meet the education requirement for the lottery.

If you don't have a U.S. high school diploma or the foreign equivalent, you must have worked two out of the past five years in a job that requires two years of experience. It is not just the number of years work experience you have that counts. Even if you have more than two years of work experience during the last five years, the two years' experience must have been in a job that required two years' experience. The Department of State uses the U.S. Department of Labor's O*NET OnLine database, **www.onetcenter.org**, to determine which jobs require two years' experience.

The stories of Karen, Constantine, and Susan illustrate the lottery work experience requirement.

Karen's Story

Karen came to the United States from the former Soviet Union ten years ago on a visitor's visa to visit her sister, who was attending school in the United States. Karen was 16 years old when she came to the United States. She had not yet finished high school and had no work experience. She ended up staying in the United States, working for various employers as a housekeeper or child care worker. She wanted to become an artist, so she took various painting and drawing classes, but never made much money in that field. Natives of the former Soviet Union qualify for the lottery, but Karen is not eligible for a lottery visa. Though she has more than five years' work experience, she has never worked in a job that requires at least two years of experience.

Constantine's Story

Constantine's situation is much more complicated than Karen's. Constantine is a native of Greece and has never been in the United States. He dropped out of school when he was fifteen, and for the last twenty-eight years he has worked at many different jobs. Most of his work has been in restaurants and cafés. During the last five years, he has worked in a variety of cooking jobs. For instance, he worked as a cook in a fast-food restaurant preparing sandwiches and salads—a job that the U.S. Department of Labor says requires no more than one year of experience. He has also been the chef in an upscale French restaurant, a job that the U.S. Department of Labor says needs from two to four years of experience.

Constantine's Story (Continued)

In order for Constantine to get a lottery immigrant visa, he must show that over the last five years he has worked more than two years in the chef position. Even if he's worked a few days at a time in each restaurant, if he can prove that he has worked a total of two years in the chef position, he meets the requirements for a lottery green card. He should be prepared to show letters from his employers, pay stubs, or other documentation. Constantine should enter the lottery. He can worry about whether he meets the lottery requirements if he is chosen as a winner.

Susan's Story

Susan worked as an electrician in Israel before she came to the United States to study electrical engineering at the University of California at Berkeley. While studying, she also worked on campus twenty hours a week as an electrician, a job that the U.S. Department of Labor says requires four years or more of training and experience. Therefore, Susan qualifies for a lottery immigrant visa.

Entering the Green Card Lottery

The U.S. Department of State now accepts lottery green card lottery entries only online. The application form is simple. You must submit a digital photo. That means that you must either have your photo taken with a digital camera, or scan a photo into your computer. When you complete the form, you receive an electronically generated filing receipt.

The law allows you only one entry per year. The Department of State claims that they have disqualified up to five hundred thousand entries in the past because people send in more than one entry. Of course, each qualifying applicant can send in an entry. That means that if you, your spouse, and your children all are natives of qualifying countries and meet the education or work requirements, you may each submit a separate entry.

Do I Need a Lawyer to Help Me Enter the Lottery?

A lawyer can't increase your chances of winning the green card lottery. A lawyer can help you prepare your entry, but the application is very simple and the Department Of State provides clear instructions. A lawyer can help you figure out if you are a native of a qualifying country or if you meet the education or work requirement, but you can worry about this once you're a winner. If you win the lottery, you must apply for an immigrant visa by adjustment of status or consular processing (see chapter 6 for more on applying for your immigrant visa). At that point, you must prove that you are not inadmissible (ineligible) for an immigrant visa. That's the time when it's worthwhile to speak to an immigration lawyer or other immigration law expert.

What if I am in the United States Unlawfully?

If you can interview in the United States, the adjustment of status process discussed in chapter 6, you may be able to adjust status despite your being here unlawfully. If you must travel home for your visa, you may not be able to get your green card because traveling abroad may make you inadmissible as discussed in chapter 5. If you win the DV lottery and you are here unlawfully, get advice from an immigration law expert.

Where Do I Get Information on the Next Green Card Lottery?

The U.S. Department of State, Bureau of Consular Affairs, provides green card lottery information at the DOS website **travel.state.gov.**

Chapter 5 - Overcoming the Bars to Permanent Residence: Exclusions and Waivers

To get an immigrant visa, you must prove that you are not "inadmissible" (before April 1, 1997, the USCIS used the term "excludable" rather than "inadmissible"). Being inadmissible means that you cannot get a visa even though you qualify for one under one of the immigrant or nonimmigrant visa categories. You may be inadmissible and thus barred from permanent residence, for instance, because you have engaged in criminal activity or you have insufficient financial resources. Sometimes the USCIS will forgive, or waive, your inadmissibility, although getting a waiver is often very difficult. If the USCIS grants you a waiver, you can get your immigrant visa despite the inadmissibility.

In this chapter, I discuss the most common grounds of inadmissibility and how to overcome them. A complete list of the bars to permanent residence (grounds of inadmissibility) can be found in Appendix A, "Grounds of Inadmissibility/Exclusion."

The Six Most Common Grounds of Inadmissibility

- Having been unlawfully present in the United States.
- Likelihood of becoming a public charge (needing welfare or other public assistance).
- Criminal activity.
- Misrepresentations to the USCIS or U.S. consul.
- Political activity.
- Medical conditions.

Unlawful Presence Bar

The government may bar (forbid) you from obtaining permanent residence for three years if you have been in the United States unlawfully for more than one-hundred and eighty continuous days, and then you leave the country. The bar is ten years if you leave after having been in the United States unlawfully for three hundred and sixty-five or more continuous days. If these unlawful days occurred prior to April 1, 1997, they will not be counted against you

The USCIS may waive these bars (and thus you can become a permanent resident despite the bar) if you are the spouse, son, or daughter of a U.S. citizen or permanent resident.

The unlawful presence bar doesn't apply to applicants for permanent residence under the special rules for battered women and children and the parents of battered children if you can show that your unlawful status was related to the battering you or your child received. Nor does the bar apply if you are a family member of an amnesty permanent resident (a "Family Unity" case).

The USCIS won't count time spent in the United States unlawfully while you were under eighteen years of age. Nor will the USCIS count the time your asylum application is pending, including while you are making an asylum claim to an immigration judge or appealing a denial of an asylum claim, unless you work without USCIS authorization during that time. If you file for adjustment of status (see chapter 6), the time while your application is pending before the USCIS does not count. The clock is stopped.

Finally, if you make a "timely" (before your lawful stay expires) application for a change of status or extension of stay, you don't start counting your unlawful presence unless and until the USCIS denies your application. If the USCIS approves your application, you were never unlawfully present. If the USCIS denies the application, you start counting unlawful presence from the date of the denial. To benefit from this "tolling-until-denial" policy, you must apply for the extension or change of status before your current status expires, and you must not engage in unauthorized employment.

The "tolling-until-denial" policy is a generous interpretation of the law by the USCIS based on their inability to quickly decide cases. Actually, the law provides only a one hundred and twenty-day tolling (stopping) based on a pending application for change of status or extension of stay. This tolling applies only to the count of one hundred and eighty days under the three-year bar, not for the three hundred and sixty-five days for the ten-year bar.

If you are a Canadian or Commonwealth citizen residing in Canada, a special rule applies. If you entered the United States after inspection by an USCIS officer, you are considered lawfully present for the purpose of this bar, regardless of whether you violate your status. You will only be considered to have violated the unlawful presence rule if an immigration judge or immigration officer finds that you violated your status. This is similar to the rule that applies to nonimmigrants granted "duration of status," discussed in the following section.

Perhaps the most important rule regarding the unlawful presence bar is that it only applies to those who leave the United States after unlawful employment. That means that if you can get permanent residence without leaving the United States, the process we call adjustment of status, the bars don't apply.

More on this later in the chapter.

What is Unlawful Presence?

The USCIS will consider you unlawfully present if you do one of the following:

- Remain here longer than permitted on a temporary stay.
- Enter the United States without USCIS authorization.
- Enter with phony papers.
- The immigration judge finds that you violated your status.

If you are here in lawful nonimmigrant status, which I discuss in Section 3, violating the conditions of your stay will not make you subject to the unlawful presence bars unless the USCIS or an immigration judge decides that you are out-of-status. So, if you work without permission, or otherwise violate your status but you don't get caught, you don't automatically become unlawfully here for the purpose of these bars.

If the USCIS catches you, you could be deported for violating your status, but you can't be barred under the three- and ten-year bars. If the USCIS allowed you to remain in the United States for duration of status (as is commonly done in the cases of most F-1 International Students, J-1 Exchange Visitors, and I Journalists), you'll never become subject to the three- and ten-year bars unless the USCIS or an immigration judge finds you out of status. If this approach sounds strange to you, you're not alone. However, that's how the USCIS has interpreted this rule.

The cases of Dan, Tim, Liz, and Gary help us understand what the USCIS means by unlawful presence.

Dan's Story

Dan entered the United States on an F-1 visa to study engineering at San Diego State University in California. When he arrived at San Diego International Airport, the USCIS inspector at the border admitted him for "D/S". Prior to April 23, 2013 the USCIS inspector would have wrote on his USCIS Form I-94, Arrival/Departure Document. "D/S" stands for "duration of status," meaning that Dan can stay in the United States as long as he maintains lawful student status. To maintain status, Dan must remain a full-time student and not work in violation of U.S. immigration laws. Dan decides to drop out of school and become a professional surfer. He begins working part-time in a sporting goods store.

Dan isn't subject to the unlawful presence bars, despite having violated his status. Ten years later, an employer sponsors him for permanent residence as a senior instructor in a surfing school. Because he's violated his status by dropping out of school and working, he may have to leave the United States to get an immigrant visa. (See chapter 6 for more on who must leave the United States to get an immigrant visa.) However, because the USCIS granted him duration of status, he won't be inadmissible for having been unlawfully present in the United States.

Tim's Story

Tim entered the United States as an F-1 student to study at Iowa State University. After two years, he dropped out of school for one year to write a novel. When the year was up, he applied to New York University and was admitted. He applied to the USCIS for reinstatement of his student status, and the USCIS denied his application on August 1, 2010. Because the USCIS denied his application for reinstatement, he is now considered out-of-status for the purpose of the three and ten-year bars to permanent residence. If he remains in the United States beyond one hundred and eighty days from the day the USCIS denies his reinstatement and then leaves the United States, he'll face the bars. Had he not applied for reinstatement, the USCIS would never have decided that he was out-of-status, and he would not be subject to the bars. However, though not subject to the bars, he would have been removable.

Liz's Story

Liz came to the United States in H-1B temporary professional worker status on January 1, 2010. She worked as an engineer. The USCIS admitted her for three years, until January 1, 2013, the maximum for an H-1B worker (unless she extends her H-1B status). After just one year working as an engineer, she quit her job to try a career as a lounge singer. Liz is out of status and if the USCIS catches her, they could remove her from the United States. To make sure she can stay in the United States, should her singing career fail, Liz asks a company to sponsor her for permanent residence. Her green card case goes smoothly, and on December 1, 2012, Liz left the United States to apply for an immigrant visa at a consul abroad. Since Liz left the United States before her stay expired, she wasn't subject to the unlawful status bars. This is because violating status doesn't make a person subject to the bars.

Gary's Story

Gary came to the United States to attend his sister's wedding. The USCIS inspector at the airport gave him six months to stay in the United States. He decided to stay longer, and two years later he still hasn't left. Gary is subject to the new bars for people out of status since he has overstayed the time given him by the United States by more than one year. If he leaves the United States, he'll be barred for reentry for ten years unless the USCIS grants him a waiver of the bar.

The Three-Year Bar for One Hundred and Eighty Days in Unlawful Status

The three-year bar applies to applicants for permanent residence who were in the United States unlawfully for more than one hundred and eighty continuous days and then left the country. As I discuss in detail later in this chapter, if you qualify to get permanent residence without leaving the United States, this bar won't be a problem.

Under the three-year bar rule, the law says that the USCIS can excuse up to one hundred and twenty days of your being out of status. The USCIS calls this a "tolling" of the unlawful status period. This law has little relevance now that the USCIS has ruled that any time you spend in the United States waiting for an extension of stay or change of status won't count as unlawful presence. However, you must have been in lawful status when you applied and not have worked without authorization.

The Ten-Year Penalty for One Year in Unlawful Status

The law bars you from permanent residence for ten years if you have been here unlawfully for one year or more. Unlike the one hundred and eighty-day bar, the USCIS won't excuse or toll any time if you are subject to the ten-year bar.

What the Unlawful Status Bars Mean to You

The three- and ten-year bars apply only if you leave the United States. So if you're in the United States and can get your permanent residence status without leaving, the new bars don't apply. Not everyone can become a permanent resident without leaving the United States, the process called "adjustment of status." In chapter 6, I detail who can adjust status.

The stories of John, Steve, Regina, and Nilda help us understand the unlawful presence exclusion.

John's Story

John came to the United States from Ghana to visit his brother Paul, a U.S. citizen. He arrived on February 10, 2000, and entered on a B-2 visitor's visa. The USCIS gave him permission to visit with his family for six months. He liked life here so much that he decided he wanted to stay. In December, 2001, Paul filed a family-based immigrant petition for John. Six weeks later, the USCIS approved the petition. Unfortunately, because of the long quota backlog for brothers and sisters of U.S. citizens, it will be many years before John can apply for adjustment of status. To apply he must be in the front of the line for an immigrant visa (he must have a priority date that is "current").

John can avoid the ten-year bar to permanent residence for having been in the United States unlawfully, provided he doesn't leave the country until he gets USCIS travel permission or becomes a permanent resident. It may take many years before he can apply for adjustment of status. He has to remain here unlawfully without employment authorization until his number is current under the visa quota system. Still, under the rules for adjustment of status, he has the right to get his permanent residence without leaving the United States and thus can avoid the ten-year unlawful presence bar.

Steve's Story

Steve, from Moscow, entered the United States by sneaking across the Canadian-U.S. border in November 2007. He had tried to get a visitor's visa at the U.S. consul, but the consular officer denied his visa application. Steve's son, a twenty-one-year-old U.S. citizen, filed a family-based petition for him on June 1, 2011. Though Steve is an Immediate Relative of a U.S. citizen, he must return home for his immigrant visa interview. However, if he leaves the United States to go to his immigrant visa interview, after having been here unlawfully for more than one hundred and eighty days, the consul will deny him an immigrant visa because of unlawful status bars to permanent residence.

Steve's Story (Continued)

Since the law does not provide a waiver for the parent of a U.S. citizen, Steve has two choices. He can remain in the United States unlawfully, unable to ever get a permanent visa (unless he marries a U.S. citizen and applies for a waiver or Congress changes the law). Or he can leave and wait three years (if he's overstayed more than one hundred and eighty days) or ten years (if he's overstayed three hundred and sixty-five days or more) before applying for an immigrant visa.

Regina's Story

Regina is a French cook. She came to the United States in 1998 on a visitor's visa and then overstayed the six months the USCIS gave her to visit. Her employer sponsored her for permanent residence. The employer filed a labor certification application for her on December 30, 1999. The U.S. Department of Labor certified that no U.S. workers were ready, willing, and able to do her job. On July 1, 2002, when her priority date became current under the visa quota system, she became eligible for permanent residence (see chapter 6 for more on the quota system).

Under the rules for adjustment of status discussed in chapter 6, she received her permanent residence without leaving the United States. She didn't have to worry about the unlawful presence bar. She became a permanent resident, and she didn't need a waiver of inadmissibility. The USCIS will interview her in the United States.

Nilda's Story

Nilda came to the United States as an H-1B temporary professional worker in March 2010. (See chapter 14 for more on H-1B status.) She grew tired of her job and quit in March 2011 to pursue a career as an artist and fell out-of-status. In June 2014, she met John, a U.S. citizen, and they married four months later. Nilda immediately filed for permanent residence.

Although she has been in the United States unlawfully for more than one year, Nilda didn't have a problem with the unlawful presence bar—it didn't apply to her. Because she entered the United States legally (with a visa) and she is an Immediate Relative of a U.S. citizen, she won't have to leave the United States to become a permanent resident.

Waivers of the Unlawful Presence Bars

The USCIS may waive the three- or ten-year bars to permanent residence. To qualify for a waiver, you must be the spouse, son, or daughter of a U.S. citizen or permanent resident. In addition, you must prove that your U.S. citizen or permanent resident relative will suffer extreme hardship if the USCIS or a consular officer doesn't grant you permanent residence.

One problem for waiver applicants is that in many cases, the USCIS will not consider a waiver application until the individual applies for permanent residence. So, if you must leave the United States to apply for your immigrant visa at a U.S. consulate (see chapter 6 for who must can and cannot interview here for permanent residence) and by leaving, you face an unlawful presence bar, you can't apply for a waiver until you are already abroad. If the USCIS denies your waiver application, you can't return for three or ten years.

In some cases, however, USCIS will consider an unlawful presence waiver request while the applicant is still in the United States. If USCIS approves the waiver, the applicant can travel to the immigrant visa interview abroad confident that his or her unlawful presence won't be a problem. These are called "provisional unlawful presence waivers".

To be eligible for these waivers you must be an immediate relative of a U.S. citizen, a son or daughter of United States citizens or the spouse and unmarried children of permanent residents. USCIS calls the waivers "provisional" because the agency wants to emphasize that getting the waiver doesn't guarantee getting the immigrant visa. Still, if USCIS grants the waiver, an immigration law expert can usually tell you whether you will have a problem getting your visa. If you have an otherwise clean record, you shouldn't have a problem passing your interview.

The cases of Marco, Leticia, and Carrie illustrate what happens when a person in the United States unlawfully faces the unlawful presence bar.

Marcos' Story

Marco entered the United States without a visa from Mexico in 2004, by evading the U.S. border patrol. He got a job working "off the books," meaning that his boss didn't report his earning to U.S. tax authorities. In 2013, he met Patrice, a U.S. citizen. They married and Patrice petitioned for Marco to become a permanent resident. USCIS approved the petition, but because Marcos entered the United States without inspection, he must return home to Mexico to apply for his immigrant visa.

However, since he is the spouse of a U.S. citizen, he is applying in the immediate relative category and he qualifies for provisional stateside waiver processing. He applied to USCIS for a waiver and proved to the USCIS that Patrice would suffer extreme hardship if the couple were to be separated for many years. USCIS granted the waiver, so when the U.S. consul in Mexico City called Marcos for his immigrant visa interview, unlawful presence was not an issue for him. He met all requirements to become a permanent resident and the U.S. consul issued him an immigrant visa.

Leticia's Story

Leticia qualifies for a green card based on a petition filed by her U.S. citizen mother. She is thirty years old and married, so she can get her green card in the third family preference category. However, Leticia, a native of Nigeria, entered the United States from Canada in 2009 by hiding in a truck. Because she was not inspected at entry, she must return home to Nigeria to apply for her immigrant visa. She needs a waiver of the unlawful presence bar to permanent residence, but as the daughter of a U.S. citizen, she can apply for the waiver before traveling to her immigrant visa interview. Her mother is disabled and Leticia is the only family member in the United States who can care for her mother. USCIS grants her the wavier based on the hardship her U.S. citizen mother would face if the two were separated for ten years. She travels to Nigeria for her immigrant visa interview. With the waiver, the interviewing U.S. consular officer does not consider her having been in the United States unlawfully a negative factor and she gets her immigrant visa.

Carrie's story

Carrie qualifies for permanent residence because her sister is a U.S. citizen. She came to the U.S. from France in 2010 for a visit and decided to stay. Once Carrie gets to the front of the line for an immigrant visa, after a wait of many years, she will be eligible to apply for her immigrant visa. However, she would need to travel home for her interview and apply for a waiver of the unlawful presence bar.

USCIS may approve the waiver or may not. But since Carrie cannot apply for the waiver until she travels home to France for her interview, she decides not to take the risk and stays in the United States. If she travels home and USCIS approves the waiver application, she would get her immigrant visa. If USCIS denies the waiver request, she will be stuck in France for ten years. She decides to stay in the United States and hope that the law changes.

Likelihood That You'll Become a Public Charge

To get an immigrant visa, you must prove to the United States government that once you become a permanent resident, you won't need public assistance—in the words of the immigration law, you won't become a "public charge." Needing food stamps, Medicaid, and other "means-tested" benefits for poor or disabled people would make you a public charge. Needing public assistance is not a problem if you are applying for permanent residence based on your status as an asylee, a refugee, a Cuban Adjustment Act beneficiary, a NACARA beneficiary, a registry applicant, or a self-petitioning abused spouse, abused child, or parent of an abused child.

An affidavit of support is one way to prove that you won't become a public charge. An affidavit of support is a form signed by a person promising to support you, if you need support, once you become a permanent resident. Under the 1996 Immigration Act, an affidavit of support is required in Family-Based cases (except for those based on spousal or child abuse). The law also requires an affidavit of support if you are coming to the United States to work for a relative or for a business where relatives own five percent of the company. In other cases, the affidavit is just one of many ways to prove you won't become a public charge.

We begin by discussing the rules that apply in cases where an affidavit of support is required. Then we will discuss proving that you'll not be a public charge in other cases.

When an Affidavit Is Required

The 1996 immigration law made an affidavit of support a required document in most Family-Based cases. Where the law requires an affidavit, the person who signs for you must prove the ability to support you at 125 percent of the federal poverty guidelines. If you are an active member of the armed forces petitioning for a spouse or child, you need only show support at one hundred percent of the poverty level.

If your petitioner doesn't have enough income, he or she can find a joint sponsor to submit an affidavit. You or your sponsor can also use liquid assets (money in bank accounts, stocks, or mutual funds—more on the use of assets to follow) to prove you won't become a public charge.

A sponsor can use income from some family members who have been living in their household to support the affidavit. The USCIS issued a form, USCIS Form I-864, Affidavit of Support Under 213A of the Act, which you must use where the law requires an affidavit. Perhaps the most significant change in the law is that which makes affidavits of support binding contracts.

 Note: A sponsor under the new rule must submit notice to the USCIS of a change of address until the sponsorship requirement expires.

Is an Affidavit of Support Absolutely Required in Your Case?

If you're getting your immigrant visa based on a petition from a family member, the law now requires you to submit an affidavit of support from that person. The USCIS calls the relative the "sponsor." The only exceptions are when the beneficiary of the petition has worked forty quarters (ten years) in the United States, the petitioner has died, or the beneficiary is self-petitioning under the special rules for a battered spouse, a battered child, or a parent of a battered child or as the widow or widower of a U.S. citizen. Even if you're wealthy, you need someone to sign for you. There's one other situation where the law insists that you get an affidavit of support. That's the unusual situation where you're getting your immigrant visa based on an offer of employment and your employer is a relative or a company in which relatives own five percent.

Josie's story illustrates the requirement that a family-based sponsor submit an affidavit of support.

Josie's Story

Josie, twenty-five years of age, wishes to become a permanent resident of the United States. So, her mother, Marsha, is a U.S. citizen and petitions for her. Though Josie has a good job, the law requires an affidavit of support from Marsha. Marsha must prove that she can support herself, her household, and Josie at one hundred and twenty-five percent of the federal poverty level. If Marsha doesn't have sufficient income and/or assets, she may ask a person with more resources to be a joint sponsor. If a relative of Marsha's has been living with her for at least six months, Marsha can include that relative's income if she becomes a "contract sponsor."

Finally, if Marsha, Josie or a joint sponsor, have liquid assets (i.e. money in the bank), Josie can use those assets to prove she won't become a public charge. However, even if Josie's individual assets are enough to prove that she won't become a public charge, Marsha must still submit an affidavit of support.

Who Can Be a Sponsor?

Sponsors must be U.S. citizens, nationals, or lawful permanent residents, must be age eighteen or older, and must have their primary residence in one of the fifty states, Washington, D.C., or a U.S. territory or possession. If you are a sponsor, you'll need to submit your tax returns for the past three years or prove that you weren't required to file returns.

Proving You Can Support a Relative: The One Hundred and Twenty-Five Percent Rule, Household Size, Income, and the Income of Household Members

Where the law requires an affidavit of support, your petitioning sponsor (or your sponsor and a cosigner) must prove that he or she can support you at one hundred and twenty-five percent of the federal poverty guidelines. The poverty guidelines specify the minimum amount you can earn andstill qualify for public assistance. You can find current poverty guideline information at **uscis.gov**. See form I-864P. If you are an active member of the U.S. armed forces, your unmarried children under age twenty-one and your spouse need only prove that you can support them at one hundred percent of the guidelines.

Mark's story illustrates the one hundred and twenty-five percent of income rule.

Mark's Story

Mark is single and twenty-five years old. His mother, a permanent resident of the United States, petitioned for him to become a permanent resident. Though he has a good job, immigration law requires that he get an affidavit of support from his mother. His mother is unmarried and has two other children, so when Mark begins to live with them, they will be a family of four. In 2009 the poverty line for a family of four in New York, where his mother is living, was $22,050. Mark's mother (and/or a cosigner) must show income of at least one hundred and twenty-five percent of that amount ($27,562) or use their assets to supplement the income. The amount typically increases every year.

Under the one hundred and twenty-five percent rule, the amount you need to show depends on the size of your household including the sponsor and the newly arriving immigrants. Household size also includes anyone living with the sponsor for at least six months who is related to the sponsor by birth, marriage, or adoption. Also included are dependents listed on the sponsor's federal income tax return for the most recent tax year and some immigrants previously sponsored using form I-864.

Household Sponsor Rule

If any of the sponsor's household members are working, sometimes you can include the household members' income with the sponsor's income to meet the "One hundred and twenty-five percent of the poverty level" standard. The household member must submit USCIS Form I-864A, Contract Between Sponsor and Household Member. This contract makes the household members jointly responsible with the sponsor to reimburse the costs of any means-tested public benefits used by the sponsored immigrants.

A "household" member must be related to the petitioning sponsor by birth, marriage, or adoption. Also, the contract sponsor must have lived in the sponsor's household for at least six months and must be living there when the sponsor submits the affidavit, or the primary sponsor must have listed the household member on his or her income tax.

The Joint Sponsorship Rule

If your petitioning relative doesn't earn enough to provide for you, then you can get another person to act as a cosponsor. Both your sponsor and cosponsor must submit affidavits of support. While relatives are often the best cosponsors, the law doesn't require that the cosponsor be a relative—of either the applicant or the primary sponsor. Joint sponsors (unlike persons living in the same household) cannot add their income to that of another sponsor to reach one hundred and twenty-five percent of the poverty guideline. A joint sponsor, by himself or herself, must meet the full one hundred and twenty-five percent income requirement.

Sally's story illustrates the joint sponsorship rule.

Sally's Story

Sally, a U.S. citizen, wants to bring her mother to the U.S. from Italy. She and her husband both work, but they barely make enough money to support themselves and their three children. Sally petitions for her mother as an Immediate Relative of a U.S. citizen (see chapter 2). When her mother goes to her immigrant visa interview, she must submit an affidavit of support from Sally. However, Sally doesn't have the income and assets to support her mother at one hundred and twenty-five percent of the federal poverty level. So she must have another person, preferably a close relative, be a joint sponsor. Sally and the joint sponsor must both sign affidavits that Sally's mother submits with her immigrant visa application. Sally asks her cousin Cathy to be a joint sponsor and sign a separate USCIS Form I-864, Affidavit of Support, for Sally's mother to submit with her application. Cathy is an executive in a bank and makes enough to support her family, and her aunt as well. By submitting both Sally's and Cathy's affidavits, Sally's mother can prove that she is unlikely to become a public charge.

The Affidavit of Support As a Contract Rule

Under the 1996 Immigration Act, the affidavit of support is now a contract between you, the government, and the person(s) who signed for you. If your sponsor won't provide you financial assistance, you can sue them. If you receive certain public benefits (benefits where your income is an eligibility factor) from a federal, state, or local government agency, the agency could collect the cost of that benefit from your sponsor. For instance, if you get food stamps, the government could try to collect the cash value of those food stamps from your sponsor.

Your sponsor's obligations continue until you become a United States citizen or you have worked forty quarters (the equivalent of ten years).

The rule that makes your relative responsible for the public benefits you receive does not apply to emergency Medicaid; immunization; some testing for communicable diseases; short-term, noncash emergency relief (like shelter during a hurricane); child nutrition, including the WIC (Women, Infant & Children) program and school meals; foster care and adoption assistance; higher education loans and grants; elementary and secondary education; Head Start; the Job Training Partnership Act (JTPA); and some noncash programs such as soup kitchens.

The legal responsibility of the person who signs an affidavit of support for you applies only to public benefits, not to private debts. So if you go into debt by buying a car or an appliance, the relative signing the affidavit is not responsible for that debt.

Using Assets to Prove You Won't Become a Public Charge

If your sponsor, your cosponsor, or a household contract sponsor doesn't have sufficient income to prove that you won't become a public charge, your assets or a sponsor's assets can make up any difference between required income and the poverty guidelines. The assets must equal five times the difference between the sponsor's income and the minimum income requirement under the poverty guidelines. You and/or your sponsor must be able to convert the assets to cash within one year. Examples of assets are money in bank savings or checking accounts, stocks or mutual funds, certificates of deposit, and real estate. The real estate may not be the affiant's (the person signing the affidavit) primary residence.

Scott and Margaret's story illustrates how you can use assets to prove you won't become a public charge.

Scott and Margaret's Story

Margaret a U.S. citizen, petitioned for her son Scott. He and his wife, Winona, are graduate students and have no income. Margaret inherited $100,000 when her husband died, and is supporting herself as well as Scott's three brothers and sisters. She doesn't work, but she receives an income of $20,000 per year from her husband's pension.

Scott's mother must submit an affidavit of support and show income for a family of six. The poverty level in 2009 for a family of six when Scott and his family applied for permanent residence was $29,530.00—one hundred and twenty-five percent of the guideline was $36,912. Margaret's yearly income was only the $20,000 from her deceased husband's pension. The difference between the one hundred and twenty-five percent guideline and Margaret's income was $16,912. To support an affidavit for Scott and his wife, she must have at least $84,560 in savings (five times the difference between her income and the poverty guidelines). Since she still has the $100,000 she inherited from her husband, she has sufficient assets to prove that Scott and his wife will not become a public charge.

Using Employment to Prove You Won't Become a Public Charge

If you are the beneficiary of an affidavit of support and you have lived six months with the affiant, you can use your income to make up any difference between the sponsor's income and the amount of one hundred and twenty-five percent of the poverty level. You'll need to prove that your income is likely to continue.

The Change of Address Rule

If you are a primary sponsor, joint sponsor, or household contract sponsor and you move, you must report a change of address to the USCIS within 30 days. You report the change using USCIS Form I-865, Sponsor's Notice of Change of Address. You must also report the change to the state government where you resided when you submitted the affidavit to the USCIS and to the state government where you now reside.

Proving That You Won't Become a Public Charge in Lottery Cases and Other Cases Where the Law Doesn't Require an Affidavit of Support

As mentioned above, not every case requires that you follow these rules and use the I-864 affidavit of support form. You may use the affidavit of support, USCIS Form I-134 (and your own income and/or assets without a sponsor's affidavit), in the following cases:

- You and your family members are applying in an employment-based case except the I-864. The affidavit is required if a close relative owns five percent or more of the business, unless the relative is a U.S. citizen or permanent resident not living in the United States.
- You are a self-petitioning widow or widower.
- You are a self-petitioning battered spouse or child.
- You are applying under the diversity visa lottery program (see chapter 4).
- You are applying under the Cuban Adjustment Act.
- You are a returning resident.
- You are a registry applicant.
- You are an applicant under the Nicaraguan Adjustment and Central American Relief Act (NACARA) of 1997.
- You are required to present evidence that you won't become a public charge as part of a nonimmigrant visa application.
- You are applying for permanent residence based on cancellation of removal.
- You are applying for a nonimmigrant visa, including a B-2 visitor's visa or a K visa for a spouse or fiancé(e) of a U.S. citizen.

Among the ways to prove that you are not likely to become a public charge in these cases is by:

- Showing that you are ready, willing, and able to work and have an offer of employment, or if you are in the United States, that you are already working.
- Presenting affidavits, supported by tax returns from close family members, to the effect that the family members will provide you financial support if necessary.
- Showing sufficient personal assets to prove that you don't need to work.
- Showing a combination of employment, support, and assets.
- Presenting, if you are in the United States and working, a current job letter explaining the type of work you are doing, whether the job is full-time and permanent, your salary, and income tax forms filed with the IRS.

Even if you're working "off the books" and your boss is paying you "under the table" (meaning that your employer doesn't keep records of your wages), you can still use your work history to prove that you can support yourself. One way to do this is by filing tax returns. If you do not have a social security card, you can still file your tax return using an Individual Tax Identification Number (ITIN).

An ITIN is a nine-digit number used for tax purposes by people not eligible for a social security number. You apply for an ITIN using IRS form W-7, Application for IRS Individual Taxpayer Identification Number. For information about the ITIN on the Web, go to **www.irs.gov/ind_info/itin.html**. If you don't have an ITIN, and you want to file a tax return, include your ITIN application with your return.

Criminal Activity

The most difficult ground of inadmissibility to overcome involves criminal activity. Not all crimes will make you ineligible for a green card. If you have been convicted of a crime, speak to an immigration law expert before making any application to the USCIS.

Two major areas of criminal activity that may make you ineligible to become a permanent resident of the U.S. are crimes involving moral turpitude and crimes involving drugs.

The USCIS may waive some of these grounds of inadmissibility. Other criminal activities may make you inadmissible as well. You can find a complete list of the grounds of inadmissibility in appendix A, "Grounds of Inadmissibility/Exclusion."

Crimes Involving Moral Turpitude

Moral turpitude is hard to define, but generally it means a crime involving acts committed by people who are mean or evil-spirited or who cheat the government. Most crimes involving theft and violence involve moral turpitude. Simple assault often doesn't involve moral turpitude. If you have committed or admit to a crime involving moral turpitude, you may be ineligible to become a permanent resident unless you first get a waiver of inadmissibility.

Drug-Related Crimes

The immigration laws are especially harsh toward the sale or use of illegal drugs. If you are convicted of any crime involving a controlled substance, you are probably barred from immigrating. A waiver is available in only one situation: a single offense of possession of 30 grams or less of marijuana. No waiver of exclusion is available for immigrant visa applicants for other crimes involving drugs. The "no waiver" rule applies to even minor drug-related activity such as more than one marijuana possession conviction, selling marijuana (even a small quantity), and possession of any amount of cocaine.

Forgiveness of Criminal Activity—Exceptions and Waivers

Under an exception for youthful offenders, you aren't barred from residence and do not need a waiver if (1) you were convicted of only one crime involving moral turpitude, (2) you were under 18 at the time, and (3) more than five years have passed since the time that the crime was committed or since you were released from jail. Under a petty offense exception, you are also not inadmissible for a conviction of a single crime involving moral turpitude where the maximum possible sentence is one year and you were sentenced to no more than six months in jail. This exception is available no matter your age.

Other Options

Options other than a waiver may be available to you if you are inadmissible for criminal activity. If you received a full and complete pardon (forgiveness granted by a governor or president), your conviction may not count against you. If a U.S. conviction was totally expunged from your record, the conviction may not count against you. The expungement must result in your record showing that it is as if you had never been convicted. Whether an expungement eliminates a conviction for immigration purposes is an area of law that is constantly changing. Check with a legal expert for updated information about the rules applying to pardons and expungements.

Regardless of the rule applied to expungements, some drug-trafficking crimes will make you inadmissible, expunged or not.

If you're inadmissible because you committed a crime involving moral turpitude or you were convicted of only a single count of simple possession of thirty grams or less of marijuana, you may be eligible for a waiver of inadmissibility. To get the waiver, you must prove that either **(1)** you are the spouse, parent, son or daughter of a U.S. citizen or permanent resident and that your relative would suffer extreme hardship if you were not admitted as a permanent resident or **(2)** the offense happened more than fifteen years before your application, you have rehabilitated, and your admission to the United States would not be contrary to the welfare, safety, or security of the country.

To apply for a waiver of a criminal ground of exclusions, you must file USCIS Form I-601, Application for Waiver of Grounds of Excludability.

Fraudulent Misrepresentations

If you have ever made a "fraudulent misrepresentation" (a lie or falsehood) when applying to enter the United States, for a visa or for any other immigration benefit, you may be inadmissible (ineligible for a visa or entry) because of that act. The misrepresentation must have been "knowing" (on purpose), "willful" (also, on purpose), and "material" (significant). That is, the USCIS shouldn't punish you for meaningless lies.

If you have made a fraudulent misrepresentation, you may be able to get an inadmissibility waiver. To get the waiver, you must be the spouse or son or daughter of a permanent resident or U.S. citizen, and you must be able to prove that extreme hardship would result to your spouse or parent if you don't get a permanent visa.

John's story provides an example of a fraudulent misrepresentation.

John's Story

John applied for a visitor's visa at the U.S. consulate in his home country of Costa Rica. He told the consular officer that he was attending college and presented a student identification card (ID) with his picture on it as proof. However, the picture ID was a phony. John had substituted his picture for another student's. In fact, John was unemployed and had been living on the streets for five years. He had never attended college.

This lie would most likely be considered a knowing, willful, and material misrepresentation. It is material because if the consular officer had known that John was not in school, he would not have granted John a visitor's visa. In order to obtain a visitor's visa, John had to prove that he had not abandoned his residence in Costa Rica. He also had to prove that he intended only to visit the United States and that he would leave the United States after his visit (for more on visitor's visas, see chapter 12).

John's Story (Continued)

Whether or not John is in school is important to the question of whether he will return to his country once his visit to the United States is over.

The consular officer didn't discover that John was lying and issued John a visitor's visa. Upon John's arrival in the United States, the CBP (Customs and Border Protection) admitted him for a six-month visit. Shortly after his arrival, he met and fell in love with Susan, a U.S. citizen. If John applies for an immigrant visa based on Susan's petition, the USCIS may discover that he lied when he got his visitor's visa. He may still get his immigrant visa, but he probably will need a waiver of inadmissibility.

Marriage Fraud

The immigration laws are particularly harsh on people who marry just to get an immigrant visa. A person who enters into a phony marriage can never get a green card through a Family-Based or Employment-Based Petition. No waiver is available—ever—for marriage fraud. If you are found guilty of marriage fraud, your only hope for getting an immigrant visa is through asylum, through cancellation of removal, as a derivative beneficiary, or through a private bill. (See chapter 1 for an explanation of cancellation of removal and private bills.)

Political Activity

If you were a member of a totalitarian or communist party, either in the United States or abroad, you are inadmissible (with a few exceptions). Sometimes a Communist Party member can get an immigrant visa, but usually with some difficulty. If the U.S. government believes that you would be a foreign policy risk or that you participated in genocide or persecution, U.S. immigration law bars you from permanent residence without exception. Exclusions based on political activity are far less common than in the past.

Even if you were a member of a communist organization, you can still immigrate if you were age sixteen or under at the time you joined the organization or if you joined the organization because you had to.

You are also admissible if you have terminated your affiliation connection with the communist organization at least two years before applying for permanent residence. If your membership was in a communist party that controlled the government of your country, you must have ended your membership at least five years before making your application. These exceptions apply only if you are not a threat to the security of the United States.

Even if you're inadmissible because of membership in a communist or totalitarian organization, a waiver is available if you are the spouse, parent, son, daughter or sibling of a U.S. citizen, or the spouse or son, daughter of a permanent resident. In order to get the waiver, your admission to the United States must serve a humanitarian purpose, assure family unity, or otherwise be in the public interest. Again, you must not be considered a threat to the security of the United States.

If your membership in a communist or totalitarian organization wasn't meaningful, willful, or voluntary, it cannot be a basis for denying you permanent residence.

You may be barred from the United States if you have engaged in terrorist activity. The law defines "terrorist" to mean either committing an act of terrorism or "affording material support" to any individual, organization, or government in conducting a terrorist activity. The law defines "material support" as, among other things, the soliciting of funds or other items of value for terrorist activities or for any terrorist organization.

Health Issues

Unless you submitted a medical exam as part of an earlier application to come to the United States, for instance as a K-1 (finacee) or refugee status, you must take a medical examination prior to becoming a permanent resident. The examination includes a chest X ray and a blood test. If you are pregnant, you may be excused from being X-rayed. You don't have to take the blood test if you can prove a legitimate religious objection to taking the test. You must also be vaccinated against communicable diseases.

The most common medical conditions that make you ineligible for residence are, having a sexually transmitted disease (STD) like syphilis and gonorrhea, or being mentally retarded or ill.

If you are inadmissible because you test positive for tuberculosis or other treatable diseases, you will be given time to obtain treatment, take a new medical examination, and be admitted as a permanent resident.

If you are mentally ill or retarded, you can only become a permanent resident if you first obtain a waiver of inadmissibility. If you have a communicable disease of public health significance the waiver is available if you are the spouse or unmarried son or daughter of a permanent resident or U.S. citizen, or if you have a son or daughter who is a U.S. citizen, who is a lawful permanent resident, or who has been issued an immigrant visa. Unlike some other waiver applications, you need not show that your relative will suffer hardship if you don't get your immigrant visa. Apply for the waiver using USCIS Form I-60 Application for Waiver of Grounds of Inadmissibility.

In the United States, only an USCIS-authorized physician can do the medical exam. Abroad, the physician must have been authorized by the U.S. Department of State. You can obtain a list of doctors from your local USCIS district office or a U.S. consulate. Under the 1996 immigration laws, you must present proof that you have been vaccinated against vaccine-preventable diseases, which include mumps, measles, rubella, polio, tetanus and diphtheria toxoids, pertussis, influenza type B, and hepatitis B. You can be exempt from the vaccine requirement if getting the vaccine would not be medically appropriate or because you have religious or moral objections to vaccinations.

Other Grounds of Exclusion

On the application for permanent residence, whether it is USCIS Form I-485, Application for Adjustment of Status, or DS-260 from the Department of State, many questions relate to inadmissibility.

 Read the list carefully, and if you must answer "Yes" to any of these questions, contact an immigration law expert before submitting the application form.

Chapter 6 - Applying for an Immigrant Visa

When You File, Where You File, Preparing for Your Immigrant Visa Interview, Your Right to Appeal

In this chapter, I review the filing procedures for an immigrant visa. Once you know that you qualify for an immigrant visa based on your family ties or work, you need to know when and where you can get your visa. I explain how to know if you qualify for a visa immediately or if you must wait for a visa under the quota system. I then explain your options as to where you can be interviewed for the visa followed by tips on preparing for that interview. Finally, I explain your right to appeal or seek review of a denied application.

When You Qualify to Get Your Immigrant Visa: The Preference, or "Quota" System

As I explained in chapters 2 and 3, in order to get a Family-Based or Employment-Based immigrant visa, USCIS must approve a petition filed by you or on your behalf. But that doesn't mean that you can always get an immigrant visa immediately. Under the preference, or "quota," system, an immigrant visa may not be available right away.

If you are an Immediate Relative of a U.S. citizen (see Chapter 2 for a discussion of who qualifies under this category), you don't come under the quota system. With no limit on the number of immigrant visas available, you can get your immigrant visa as soon as your petition is processed.

However, in many preference categories, more people want visas than are available in a given year for a given country. If that's true in your case, even if the USCIS has already approved a petition for you, you can't get your immigrant visa immediately. You'll have to wait your turn. Your place in line to get a preference immigrant visa is called your priority date. Some preferences have a long waiting list. Some categories have no wait. Whether you must wait and for how long depends on your native country and your preference category.

In a **Family-Based Preference** case, the date your relative files the petition establishes your priority date. It doesn't matter how long USCIS takes to process the petition—the priority date is set when USCIS receives the petition. Sometimes, when there is no waiting list, you can file your petition and application for permanent residence at the same time.

In most **Employment-Based Preference** cases, you establish your priority date when your employer files a labor certification application with the U.S. Department of Labor. Where the law does not require a labor certification, your priority date is the date USCIS received the employment-based petition. The time it takes to process the application has no effect on your priority date. (For more on the question of labor certifications, see chapter 3.)

If you are a preference applicant, you must look to the current USCIS Visa Bulletin to learn if a visa is immediately available for you. If a visa is available, we say that your priority date is current. How do you know if your priority date is current? Each month, the Department of State issues a Visa Bulletin with the cutoff dates for the following month.

You can find out the cutoff dates for each category yourself at **travel.state.gov** or by calling **(202) 485-7699.** You get the visa bulletin by E-mail by sending an E-mail to **listserv@calist.state.gov.** In the message body, type: Subscribe Visa-Bulletin.

Reading the Visa Bulletin:

Let's look at the immigrant visa cutoff dates in the Visa Bulletin for July 1996 and see how to read the Visa Bulletin. Though long out-of-date, I use the July 1996 bulletin below for illustration because it shows the full range of possibilities regarding the preference cutoff dates. I wanted to use this chart because we can see that some categories are unavailable. Though this bulletin is many years old, the rules for reading the bulletin are the same as they are today. Preference applicants whose priority date was before the date listed in the Visa Bulletin qualified for immigrant visas in July 1996. The Department of State issued this bulletin in June 1996.

FAMILY-BASED PREFERENCES
(Refer to page 233 for 2015 update)

	ALL CHARGEABILITY AREAS EXCEPT THOSE LISTED	INDIA	MEXICO	PHILIPPINES
1st	C	C	U	01 May 86
2A	22 Dec 92	22 Dec 92	15 May 92	22 Dec 92
2B	01 Mar 91	01 Mar 91	01 Mar 91	01 Mar 91
3rd	01 Aug 93	01 Aug 93	15 Oct 87	01 Apr 85
4th	15 Feb 86	08 Oct 84	01 Jul 85	08 Oct 77

EMPLOYMENT-BASED PREFERENCES

	ALL CHARGEABILITY AREAS EXCEPT THOSE LISTED	INDIA	MEXICO	PHILIPPINES
1st	C	C	C	C
2nd	C	U	C	C
3rd	C	U	C	01 Feb 95
Other Workers	08 May 87	U	08 May 87	08 May 87
4th	C	C	C	08 Mar 95
Certain Religious Workers	C	C	C	08 Mar 95
5th	C	C	C	C
Targeted Employment Areas/ Regional Centers Targeted	C	C	C	C

To use the Visa Bulletin to figure out if you could qualify for an immigrant visa in July 1996, you must know what preference category you are in. Suppose you are in the First Family-Based Preference. That means that you are over twenty-one and your mother or father, a U.S. citizen, haspetitioned for you. Except for Mexico and the Philippines, you find a "**C**" under the countries listed for the First Family-Based Preference for July 1996.

The "**C**" means "current," a way of saying that in July 1996 a visa was immediately available for First Family-Based Preference applicants born in all countries except Mexico and the Philippines. Only applicants born in Mexico and the Philippines have to wait. For Mexico, you find a "**U**." The "**U**" means that until October 1, 1996, when the new USCIS fiscal year begins, no visas at all will be available for First Family-Based Preference applicants born in Mexico. For the Philippines, an unmarried child of a U.S. citizen who had a parent file for them before May 1, 1986, received immigrant visas in July 1996.

If the Visa Bulletin doesn't mention your country by name, you come under the all chargeability category. Notice that in July 1996 in the Fourth Family-Based Preference (the brothers and sisters of U.S. citizens) for the Philippines, the U.S. citizen would have to have filed the petition prior to October 8, 1977. At the time the Visa Bulletin came out, these applicants had already been waiting more than seventeen years.

The stories of Aida, Tomas, Marcia, and Pilaf illustrate how the Visa Bulletin works.

Aida's Story

Aida, a citizen of Mexico, came to the United States on an F-1 student visa. While studying at the University of California, Los Angeles, she met Ruben, a U.S. citizen of Mexican ancestry. Ruben and Aida married and he petitioned for her permanent residence. As the spouse of a U.S. citizen, Aida doesn't have to check the Visa Bulletin since she has an immigrant visa immediately available to her. Since the law places no limit on the number of Immediate Relatives of U.S. citizens who can come to the United States every year, they are not part of a preference category. The Visa Bulletin is irrelevant.

Tomas' Story

Tomas is a 22-year-old married man from Dominican Republic. His mother came to the United States many years ago and is now a U.S. citizen. Tomas wanted to come to live in the United States, so on July 31, 1993 his mother filed a relative petition for him. By reading the Visa Bulletin for July 1996, we can see that in that month he had a current priority date and could get an immigrant visa immediately.

Any Third Family-Based Preference applicant whose petition in the all chargeability category was filed before August 1, 1993, was eligible for permanent residence in July 1996.

Marcia's Story

Marcia, a native of Venezuela, worked in New York as a live-in domestic household worker. Her job required only one month's experience. Marcia's employers wanted to petition for her for a green card. They filed a labor certification for her on January 15, 1992. Because finding live-in help is hard, the employer could prove that no qualified U.S. workers wanted the job. The Department of Labor approved the labor certification application. On February 1, 1994, the employer filed a petition for her with the USCIS. The USCIS approved the petition on October 1, 1994. Marcia didn't yet qualify for an immigrant visa in July 1996. Her priority date was January 15, 1992.

Marcia's Story (Continued)

When an Employment-Based Preference case requires a labor certification, the priority date is the date the Department of Labor receives the petition. Applicants born in Venezuela whose labor certifications the Department of Labor received before May 8, 1987, were at the front of the line to get immigrant visas in July 1996. Marcia still has a long wait before she qualifies for an immigrant visa. At the time her priority date becomes current, her employer will need to prove that he or she still needs a live-in housekeeper. Otherwise, Marcia won't qualify for an immigrant visa.

Pilaf's Story

Pilaf is a citizen and a native of France. She has a sister in the United States who is a U.S. citizen. In the hope that Pilaf would join her in the United States, the sister petitioned for Pilaf USCIS received the petition on January 15, 1989. Pilaf's priority date is January 15, 1989, and she is eligible for a permanent residence under the Fourth Family-Based Preference. By July of 1996, Pilaf had been waiting to become a permanent resident for almost seven years, and she may still have a long wait before she'll get an immigrant visa. She can get her immigrant visa when French natives whose cutoff petitions were received by the USCIS before February 15, 1986, are current. Since the Visa Bulletin cutoff dates move are unpredictable, it is hard to tell how long Pilaf must wait, but it could be many more years.

Cross-Chargeability: Qualifying Under the Country of Your Spouse or Parent

Sometimes you can claim an immigrant visa under the country of birth of your spouse or parent. If you are a Preference immigrant visa applicant, your unmarried children and your spouse can get an immigrant visa when you do. We call your children or spouse derivative beneficiaries. If your derivative beneficiary spouse is a native of a different country, you can claim eligibility from that country. If you are accompanying your parent, your visa may be changed to either parent.

! Note that a parent cannot charge his or her visa to the country of a child.

If you were a U.S. citizen but lost your citizenship, your visa may be charged to country of current citizenship or, if citizenship is nonexistent, to country of last residence. Finally, if you were born in a country where neither of your parents was born or had residence (for instance, your parents were studying in that country), you may be charged to the country of either parent.

Migdalia's story provides an example of how cross-chargeability works.

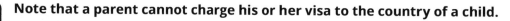

Migdalia's Story

Migdalia was born in Mexico. When she was twenty, she married David, a native of the Dominican Republic. Migdalia's father immigrated to the United States, and when he became a U.S. citizen on July 31, 1993, he petitioned for her under the Third Family-Based Preference. If we look at the July 1996 Visa Bulletin, we see a long wait under the Third Family-Based Preference for citizens of Mexico. However, since David will be immigrating to the United States with Migdalia, she can claim her immigrant visa under the quota for the Dominican Republic, which is current under the Third Family-Based Preference for applicants whose petitions were filed for them before August 1, 1993. The Dominican Republic is in the all chargeability areas category for July 1996. Migdalia and David can get their green cards as soon as the U.S. government can process the papers.

Can You Wait in the United States Until Your Priority Date Becomes Current?

If you don't have a visa immediately available, can you wait here until your priority date is reached? If you're in lawful nonimmigrant status, you can stay in that status until your status expires. The same is true if USCIS has granted you temporary status such as Temporary Protected Status and Deferred Action for Childhood Arrivals. Even if you are not here legally, U.S. Immigration and Customs Enforcement (ICE) the immigration enforcement agency, won't come looking for you just because you are waiting for your priority date to become current.

The government may try to deport you if you come to the attention of ICE in a factory raid, you commit a serious crime or you get caught up in an "anti-terrorist" investigation. The government will almost certainly try to remove you if you apply for asylum and USCIS doesn't approve your application. Of course, the policy described here could quickly change if public sentiment or public policy turns against all, or a specific group of immigrants.

Where to Apply for Your Immigrant Visa

If you are in the United States, sometimes you can get immigrant status without leaving the United States. This process is called adjustment of status. If the law doesn't allow you to adjust status, you must apply at a U.S. consulate abroad, a procedure called consular processing. If you are in the United States and qualify for adjustment of status, you may still choose to apply at a U.S. consulate abroad, but I advise most people to apply in the United States if they can.

Getting Your Green Card Here Is Usually Best

If you are in the United States, adjustment of status is almost always the best way to become a permanent resident. Adjustment of status is more convenient than consular processing. It is also safer. If you are applying for adjustment of status and a problem arises in your case, or the USCIS denies your application, you can often remain in the U.S. while you try to resolve the problem. And if the USCIS tries to remove you, you can renew your application with the immigration judge. If you are trying to get a visa at a U.S. consulate, you have a limited right to review if a consular officer denies your application. Any problems you face are harder to solve. Also, certain grounds of inadmissibility apply only if you leave the United States (see chapter 5).

If you go home for an interview at a U.S. consulate and a problem arises with your case, you may have to remain outside the United States until you can resolve the problem.

When you apply for adjustment of status, you can get permission from the USCIS to work while your application is pending. And in most cases, you can travel abroad and return to the United States while your application is pending. We call this permission to travel advance parole.

The stories of Barbara and Arthur show why it is usually best to apply for your green card here in the United States through the adjustment of status process.

Barbara's Story

Barbara applied for adjustment of status based on her marriage to Roberto, a United States citizen. Roberto had been married once before in his native country, the Dominican Republic, but he was divorced. When Roberto and Barbara went to Barbara's adjustment of status interview, they brought Roberto's certificate of divorce, but they did not have the complete divorce judgment. The USCIS examiner who interviewed them insisted that she could not approve the case until she saw the actual divorce judgment with a translation.

Barbara's Story (Continued)

When Roberto took too long to get it, the examiner denied Barbara's adjustment of status application. USCIS usually does not try to enforce an applicant's departure in a situation like that faced by Barbara and Roberto. Roberto got the divorce judgment and Barbara applied again for adjustment of status. The USCIS approved the new application.

If Barbara had applied for her immigrant visa at the U.S. consulate abroad, she would have had to wait outside of the United States until Roberto obtained the documents. Because she applied for adjustment of status, she could wait in the United States and stay with her husband.

Arthur's Story

Arthur applied for adjustment of status based on sponsorship by his employer. Arthur had been arrested when he was seventeen years old for demonstrating against the Italian government. He had been a member of a socialist student group, and the police had charged and convicted him of disorderly conduct and for assaulting a police officer. Arthur answered the questions on the application honestly, admitting that he had been arrested. He believed that he would have no problem becoming a permanent resident. His lawyer told him that since simple assault is not a crime involving moral turpitude and he was under eighteen at the time of his conviction, he could become a permanent resident, despite the conviction. He was a socialist and was never a member of a communist party. He told his story to the USCIS examiner at his adjustment of status interview, but still the examiner denied his application, claiming that Arthur was barred from permanent residence under the law that makes Communist Party members inadmissible. When the examiner denied the application, Arthur was placed in removal proceedings. For more on inadmissibility for political activity, see chapter 5.

Arthur has the right to present evidence at his removal hearing about the student organization he belonged to in Italy. He can bring witnesses to testify, such as university professors who are knowledgeable about the political system in Italy. He can testify himself about his beliefs and the beliefs of the organization as he understood them.

If the immigration judge does not agree with Arthur's analysis and upholds the decision of the USCIS, Arthur can appeal to the Board of Immigration Appeals and remain in the United States while the appeal is pending. On the other hand, if Arthur had applied at a U.S. consulate abroad and they denied his application, his only right to review would be a nonbinding advisory opinion by the U.S. Department of State in Washington, D.C., a slow and unreliable process. He would not have the right to appeal the denial nor could he come and live in the United States pending a favorable decision on his case.

Who Can Get an Immigrant Visa Without Leaving the United States?

Not everyone in the United States who qualifies for permanent residence can get their immigrant visa without leaving the country. Some people who qualify to have the USCIS interview them in the United States have to pay an additional $1,000 for the privilege. You qualify to become a permanent resident without leaving the United States if you meet one of the following criteria:

- You were inspected upon entry by an USCIS officer, you were never out of status, and you never worked without permission.

- You were inspected and admitted upon entry by an USCIS officer and you are applying for permanent residence as an Immediate Relative of a U.S. citizen. If you are in the Immediate Relative category and USCIS inspected you at entry, you can adjust status even if you are in the United States unlawfully. The immediate relative category includes the spouse of a U.S. citizen, unmarried children under age twenty-one of U.S. citizens, and the parents of U.S. citizens, who are twenty-one or older, and the spouse of a deceased U.S. citizen where, at the time of your spouse's death, you had been legally married and were not legally separated.

- You are applying based on your status as a refugee or asylee.

- You are an employment-based immigrant visa applicant or a special immigrant religious worker, you entered the United States lawfully, and you were not out of status or worked without authorization for more than one hundred and eighty days in the aggregate (total) since your last lawful nonimmigrant entry.

- You are applying based on an approved self-petition under the Violence Against Women Act (VAWA).

 Or, under what many refer to as the "245(i) grandfather clause," you can adjust status if you pay a $1,000 filing penalty over and above the regular filing fee and meet one of the following criteria. These categories are discussed in Section 5, Special Rules for Special People.

- You're applying as a family-based immigrant and your relative petitioned for you by January 14, 1998.

- You are an employment-based visa applicant and your employer filed a labor certification for you with the State Department of Labor, or you or your employer filed a petition with the USCIS by January 14, 1998.

- A relative petitions for you or an employer files a labor certification or employment-based petition for you on or before April 30, 2001, and you were in the United States on December 21, 2000.

- You are a derivative beneficiary of a "245(i) grandfathered" individual. See chapter 1 for the definition of derivative beneficiary.

- You benefit from a special law that gives a selected group of individuals, I.E. Cuban entrants, the right to adjust status.

Note that the "physical presence in the United States on December 21, 2000," rule applies only if the petition or labor certification was filed for you after January 14, 1998, but on or before April 30, 2001. If your family- or employment-based papers were filed by January 14, 1998, the physical presence rule doesn't apply. Note also that once you get grandfathered under 245(i), you can adjust status regardless of whether you qualify for your immigrant visa through your original petition or in another category.

On January 26, 2001, USCIS issued a memorandum explaining how to prove physical presence in the United States on December 21, 2000. USCIS prefers that you submit a federal, state, or city-issued document. However, the memorandum instructs USCIS officers to accept other documentation as well, including letters and affidavits. USCIS recognizes that sometimes several documents taken together may prove physical presence on December 21, 2000. The memorandum gives the example of a person who makes a mortgage payment on December 1, 2000, and another on January 1, 2001.

The USCIS memorandum clarifies also that dependent (derivative) spouses and children need not prove physical presence on December 21, 2001, to qualify for 245(i). The derivative beneficiary however, must prove that the principal beneficiary (the person for whom a petition or labor certification was filed) was in the United States on that date. Suppose that you qualify for permanent residence as the married daughter of a U.S. citizen.

You were here on December 21, 2001, having entered as a visitor in 1999. Your U.S. citizen mother files for you on April 30, 2001. It may take five or more years for you to qualify for permanent residence under the preference quota system. When you do qualify, USCIS will interview you in the United Staes. USCIS will also interview your spouse and your unmarried and under-twenty-one children, regardless of whether they, too, were in the United States on December 21, 2001.

EXCEPTIONS: If you entered in **C** or **D** crew member status, or with permission to enter in Transit Without Visa status, you can only adjust status if you are 245(i) grandfathered. If you came here with a **K** visa, you cannot adjust status unless you marry the U.S. citizen who petitioned for you to get **K** status. Generally, if you qualify for an immigrant visa and you did not marry the K-1 petitioner, you must return home for the immigrant visa interview. The 245(i) grandfather clause won't help you.

The stories of Timothy, Sharon, Katy, Ruth, Manuel, and Samson illustrate who can get an immigrant visa without leaving the United States.

Timothy's Story

Timothy came to the United States in August 1995 on an F-1 student visa to study at a community college. He did well and continued his studies through college and law school. He worked part-time on campus with the permission of his international student advisor. After law school, he got permission from USCIS to work for one year under the practical training program for F-1 students. His employer liked him and sponsored him for an H-1B temporary professional work visa. Three years later, his employer sponsored him for an immigrant visa. Timothy can become a permanent resident without leaving the United States. He can adjust status since he never worked without permission, and he was never unlawfully in the U.S.

Sharon's Story

Sharon entered the United States on a visitor's visa using a phony foreign passport with her picture. She married Jim, a U.S. citizen, on February 1, 1998. Jim immediately petitioned for her to become a permanent resident. Unfortunately, Sharon may have to go home for her permanent resident interview. Though she qualifies for an immigrant visa as an immediate relative of a U.S. citizen, the fact that she entered unlawfully may result in the USCIS finding that she's ineligible for adjustment of status.

Still, some applicants in Sharon's situation have successfully adjusted status, though they need USCIS to grant them a fraud waiver. For more on fraud waivers, see chapter 5.

Katy's Story

Katy and her husband came to the United States from the Philippines with tourist visas and decided to stay. Katy's mother is a U.S. citizen, and on January 5, 1997, Katy's mother petitioned for Katy. Katy qualifies for permanent residence under the Third Family-Based Preference for the married sons and daughters of U.S. citizens. Her husband will get his immigrant visa as a derivative beneficiary of Katy. Because of the long wait in the third preference for nationals of the Philippines, it may be ten years before Katy and her husband get to the front of the immigrant visa line. Still, USCIS will interview them here if they each pay a $1,000 penalty. Though they overstayed the time, USCIS granted them, Katy's mother petitioned for Katy before the January 14, 1998, cutoff.

Ruth's Story

Ruth entered the United States on December 1, 2000, on a visitor's visa. USCIS gave her permission to visit for six months, but she decided to stay. She was an experienced engineer and was offered a good job working in the U.S. The company filed a labor certification application for her on April 30, 2001. Since Ruth was physically present in the United States on December 21, 2000, and her employer petitioned for her on or before April 30, 2001, she is able to adjust status once the U.S. Department of Labor approves her labor certification and USCIS approves an employment-based petition for her. To adjust status, she'll need to pay the $1,000 filing penalty.

Manuel's Story

Manuel entered the United States from Mexico on December 22, 2000 and was not inspected by a CBP officer. In January 2001, he married a U.S. citizen. His wife petitioned for him a month later. Though Manuel is married to a U.S. citizen, he must return to Mexico to process for permanent residence. He cannot adjust status because he entered without inspection. He cannot benefit from the 245(i) law because he was not physically present in the United States on December 21, 2000. If he remains in the United States 180 days after his initial entry and then leaves to process at a U.S. consulate in Mexico, he'll face the three-year bar to admission. He'll only get his permanent residence if USCIS grants him a waiver. For more on these waivers, see chapter 5.

Samson's Story

Samson's uncle Alfred, a U.S. citizen, petitioned for Samson's mother. Samson's mother was Alfred's sister. Samson was fifteen years old when his uncle Alfred filed the petition on January 14, 1998, and thus was 245(i) grandfathered as a derivative beneficiary of his mother. Samson and his mother had come to the United States in visitor's status and then overstayed. The wait is so long under the category for the brothers and sisters of U.S. citizens, the Fourth Family-Based Preference, that when Samson turned twenty-one, his mother's priority date was not yet current. Under USCIS law, he had lost his right to immigrate as a derivative beneficiary at the age of twenty-one.

Samson was unable to qualify under the Child Protection Act. However, he did not lose the right to interview in the U.S. under the 245(i) rule. Suppose that five years later, an employer gets a labor certification approved for Samson. Once his II-140 petition is approved and his priority date is current, he can adjust status under the 245(i) rule. His rights that he earned as a derivative beneficiary under 245(i) remain with him for the rest of his life.

Who Must Pay an Extra Fee for Adjustment of Status?

Some people qualify for adjustment of status only because relatives or employers began cases for them by January 14, 1998, or because the papers were filed by April 30, 2001, and they were in the United States on December 21, 2000. These applicants must pay a $1,000 penalty in addition to the regular filing fee for the right to have the USCIS interview them in the United States.

If you're applying for permanent residence as the immediate relative of a U.S. citizen and you entered legally, you don't have to pay the penalty. That's true even if you're not now in legal status. You can also adjust status and avoid the penalty if you entered lawfully, you are applying in an employment-based category, and you weren't in the United States unlawfully or worked without authorization for more than 180 days since your last entry. If you are applying in a family preference category, you can avoid the penalty if you entered the United States lawfully, you never worked without permission, and you were never out of status.

If you're a crew member of a ship and USCIS gave you a pass to come ashore while your ship docked here, or you were admitted to the United States on a **C** or **D** visa to join a ship, you must pay the $1,000 penalty to adjust status. The same is true if you were admitted to the United States on the way to another country and you entered with Transit Without Visa (TWOV) permission.

Refugees, asylees, and some, Cuban and others applying under special adjustment acts don't have to pay the extra fee. Some older special adjustment programs were based on nationality and are now closed for the most part, such as the Chinese Student Protection Act and the Haitian Refugee Immigration Fairness Act (HRIFA). You are also exempt from paying the extra fee if you are under seventeen years of age at the time the USCIS decides your application for adjustment of status.

The stories of Javier, Lloyd, Marla, Wanda, and Priscilla show how the adjustment of status penalty rule works.

Javier's Story

Javier, a native of Haiti, entered the United States from Canada. He had lost his passport and U.S. visa, so he entered by evading U.S. border officers. On January 1, 1998, he married a U.S. citizen. She petitioned for him on January 13, 1998. Javier can adjust status, but because he entered the United States without inspection, he must pay a $1,000 penalty for the right to have his interview here.

Lloyd's Story

Lloyd came to the United States on an F-1 student visa in 1995. He finished four years of college and worked for one year as an F-1 practical trainee. After he finished his F-1 trainee status, he decided to spend a year traveling around the United States. He was out of status, but he guessed that USCIS wouldn't catch him. He did not have to work because he had a rich uncle who sent him a check every month. After his one year of fun,, Lloyd wanted to start his career as an industrial designer. Lloyd found an employer who successfully sponsored him for a permanent visa based on a labor certification (see chapter 3). The employer filed the labor certification application on April 30, 2001. No matter how long it takes to process his labor certification application, Lloyd can apply to become a permanent resident without leaving the United States. That's because he filed his case before the April 30, 2001 cutoff. However, he still must pay the $1,000 penalty because he had been out of status in the United States.

Wanda's Story

Wanda came to the United States from Poland on a B-2 visitor's visa. She told the consular officer who issued her visa that she wanted to visit colleges in the United States, and intended to continue her studies in economics. The University of Texas accepted her in their graduate economics program, she changed status to F-1 student, and she began her studies. She graduated and began work in H-1B status. In December 1997, Wanda's employer filed a labor certification application for her to begin the process of making her a permanent resident. While she was still in lawful status, the U.S. Department of Labor approved the labor certification application, and she applied for adjustment of status. Wanda was never out of status and never worked without permission. The USCIS will interview her in the United States, and she need not pay the $1,000 penalty.

Priscilla's Story

Priscilla came to the United States on an "I" visa for international journalists. Le Monde sent her here to write about the 1992 presidential elections. In the excitement of the campaign, she met and fell in love with Jay, a U.S. journalist who is a United States citizen. They married, but they were too busy covering the campaign to file papers with the USCIS so that Priscilla could become a permanent resident. Priscilla quit her job with Le Monde and began doing freelance work for several U.S. newspapers. Eventually, her husband petitioned for her and she applied for adjustment of status.

Because Priscilla qualifies for permanent residence as an Immediate Relative of a U.S. citizen and she entered the United States legally, she doesn't have to pay the $1,000 penalty. The fact that she violated her status by working for U.S. newspapers doesn't disqualify her from adjusting status.

Consular Processing for People in the United States

If you're in the United States, you may want to consider consular processing. While sometimes risky, consular processing can be faster than adjustment of status. Assuming you have a current priority date, consular processing takes nine months to one year. In some parts of the United States, adjustment of status takes more than 24 months. Of course, if you are not eligible to adjust status, you have no other choice than to apply for your immigrant visa at a U.S. consulate.

Applying for Adjustment of Status

- If you are age fourteen or older, you must also submit USCIS Form G-325A, biographic information, and two photographs. Note that the photos must be passport-style.

- You must pay a separate biometrics (fingerprinting) fee, and USCIS will notify you when to appear so they can take your prints and photo.

- Usually, you must also file your birth certificate with the I-485 application, along with a translation, if necessary.

- An applicant under fourteen must have a parent or a guardian sign the form.

Filing Your I-485 Adjustment of Status Application

If you are an Immediate Relative of a U.S. citizen, you may file your USCIS Form I-130 and USCIS Form I-485 applications simultaneously. You may also file petitions and I-485 applications simultaneously in Family-Based-and Employment-Based cases if your priority date is current.

The stories of Frieda, Sherman, Jeremy, and Sean illustrate when you may file your application for adjustment of status.

Frieda's Story

Frieda came to the United States on a student visa. While here, she fell in love with and married Tom, a United States citizen and a student at her college. After the wedding, Frieda filed her application for adjustment of status using USCIS Form I-485. She attached a petition signed by her husband. Although the USCIS has not approved it, she may file her application with the petition, because she is an Immediate Relative of a U.S. citizen. Since the law doesn't limit the number of Immediate Relatives of U.S. citizens who can adjust status each year, Frieda doesn't have to worry about a priority date. A visa for her is immediately available. That's why the USCIS allows her to file the I-130 petition and I-485 application simultaneously.

Sherman's Story

Sherman is an unmarried 25-year-old South African engineer whose mother recently became a U.S. citizen. Sherman came to the United States to visit his mother and decided that he wanted to stay. He is still in lawful status. When he decided to become a permanent resident of the United States, his preference category, the First Family-Based Preference, was current for South Africans. Because Sherman had a visa immediately available for him, he could file his application for adjustment of status simultaneously with his mother's petition.

Jeremy's Story

Jeremy and his wife came to the United States from their native Sweden. Once in the U.S., they began to work for a computer design firm. They liked the United States so much that they decided to make it their home. Jeremy's mother was a U.S. citizen and was willing to petition for Jeremy. At the time Jeremy decided to become a permanent resident, the Third Family-Based Preference (the preference category for the married children of U.S. citizens), was backlogged several years. Therefore, although Jeremy's mother filed a petition for him, Jeremy could not file his application for adjustment of status since no visa was immediately available in his preference category. Three months after Jeremy's mother filed the petition, the USCIS approved it. Every month, Jeremy checked the Visa Bulletin (discussed earlier in this chapter) until finally his priority date became current. He was then able to file his application for adjustment of status. He included a copy of the USCIS notice of approval of the petition his mother had filed for him. Jeremy was able to adjust his status because he had maintained his non-immigrant employment based status.

Sean's Story

Sean, from Scotland, was in the United States working in New York as an architect in H-1B temporary professional worker status. He came to the job with a master's degree and two years' experience in indoor swimming pool design. His company agreed to sponsor him for an immigrant visa and filed a labor certification application for him. A year later, the U.S. Department of Labor certified that no U.S. worker was ready, willing, and able to do the job that Sean was doing. They also certified that his employer had offered the job at the prevailing wage. Sean's immigrant visa category (Third Employment-Based Preference) had no backlog, so he could file for adjustment of status and include USCIS form I-140 with the approved labor certification attached.

Agency Check

The USCIS will send your fingerprints and one page from USCIS Form G-325A (Biographical Information) for a Federal Bureau of Investigations (FBI) "agency check." Normally, the FBI will report within 60 days as to whether you have an arrest record in the United States. However, the fingerprint clearance won't be considered late until 120 days after the USCIS sent your prints to the FBI. The USCIS will often also check with the Central Intelligence Agency (CIA) and the U.S. consul in your country of last residence and/or other countries where you have lived.

Medical Exam

Unless you had a medical exam as part of your refugee or K-1 application, you must submit a blood test, a chest X ray, and proof that you have been vaccinated against certain diseases as part of your adjustment of status application. For information on medical conditions that could result in your being denied permanent residence, see chapter 5. The X ray will sometimes be waived for pregnant women. Or sometimes a pregnant woman must wait until she gives birth and then take the X- ray. The blood tests may be waived if you have a legitimate religious objection to your blood being drawn. The vaccination requirement can be waived if getting vaccinated would be contrary to your religious beliefs or moral convictions, or if getting vaccinated would not be medically appropriate.

The Final Step: USCIS Interview for Adjustment of Status

Your final step as an applicant for adjustment of status is usually an interview with an USCIS examiner. USCIS usually waives interviews in cases involving applications for adjustment of status based on an I-140 petition (a petition based on an offer of employment) or a petition for a parent or minor unmarried child of a U.S. citizen. If your case is based on an I-130 petition filed by your spouse, and USCIS calls you for an interview, they will want your petitioning spouse to appear at the interview with you.

Sometimes you can get your immigrant visa in a marriage case without your spouse appearing, but that is highly unusual. This is different from interviews for permanent residence at U.S. consulates abroad. There, a consular officer does not expect your petitioning spouse to appear, unless the officer specifically requests your spouse to do so.

If all goes well at your adjustment of status interview, the USCIS examiner may grant you immigrant status that day. "Going well" means that your priority date is current (or you are an Immediate Relative of a U.S. citizen or a priority date is not an issue as in the case of an asylee or refugee), the agency check revealed no damaging information, and you are not found inadmissible. Keep in mind that if you have derivative beneficiaries, they can apply simultaneously with you for permanent residence.

Sometimes an USCIS examiner defers a final decision on an adjustment of status application. This is likely to happen in cases in which the USCIS examiner requests further information or documentation—for instance, a document such as a passport or birth certificate, which would normally be presented at an adjustment interview—that you forgot to bring. The examiner might like to see more evidence about whether you are inadmissible for criminal activity or as a person likely to become a public charge. Or the examiner may believe that an investigation of some aspect of your case, such as whether yours is a real marriage, is required. A deferred decision may also result from bureaucratic error, such as a lost agency check. If you have another USCIS file, sometimes the delay is due to problems locating that file.

 In cases where the USCIS waived your interview, you will get an answer by mail. If the USCIS denies your application, you may challenge that decision in deportation proceedings or on rare occasions in federal court. In that case, you will almost certainly need the help of an immigration law expert.

Adjustment of Status of Asylees and Refugees

If you were admitted as a refugee or USCIS granted you asylum, you may apply for adjustment of status after one year in refugee or asylee status. If you had a medical exam prior to admission as a refugee, USCIS will usually not require a further medical examination. If you are an asylee, a medical examination is required.

For both the asylee and refugee, certain grounds of exclusion, including the public charge exclusion, do not apply. Waivers are available for all other grounds of exclusion unless you are inadmissible as a subversive, former Nazi or Nazi collaborator, or trafficker in narcotics. If you are an asylee or refugee, your spouse and unmarried children under twenty-one are also eligible for adjustment of status. Your relationship with them must predate your becoming a refugee or asylee.

If you are an asylee, USCIS will backdate your permanent residence to one year before the adjustment application was approved. If you are a refugee, the USCIS will backdate the approval to your date of entry into the United States.

Consular Processing

As I explained earlier, immigrant visa applicants use consular processing if they are already outside the United States or if they are in the United States, but do not qualify for adjustment of status. Consular processing is similar for all consulates, although each might have its own forms and/or local procedures.

The process begins when the Department of State National Visa Center (NVC), in Portsmouth, New Hampshire **(603-334-0700)**, receives your approved I-130 or I-140 petition from USCIS. If your priority date is current or you are the Immediate Relative of a U.S. citizen, the NVC sends you (or your representative) information on how to get your immigrant visa instruction online. This includes instructions on paying visa processing fees and where appropriate how to submit an affidavit of support. The instructions will also advise what documents you must submit.

If your visa category is backlogged, the NVC will send you a notice that they have received the petition. Write down your case number (it is different from the number on your USCIS petition filing receipt) and keep it in a safe place. Check the NVC notice to make sure your immigrant visa classification (how you qualify for an immigrant visa) and your priority date are correct. The NVC will send you the information on how to get your application forms online when your priority date is three to six months of current. Submit the forms as requested and you will receive an interview notice for your immigrant visa interview at the U.S. consulate.

The Visa Application

After the consulate receives all of the necessary forms and documents and a visa becomes available, the consul will send you information on completing the visa application. This visa application package includes information concerning the medical examination and the time and location of your interview.

At your interview, a U.S. consular officer will review all the documents that make up your case, including the petition filed by your relative or employer. If the officer has any doubts about the petition, the officer may defer a decision while the consulate investigates your case. The consular officer can return your immigrant visa petition to USCIS for reconsideration or possible revocation if he believes that the underlying petition should not have been approved or is no longer approvable.

If the officer believes that you don't qualify for an immigrant visa, the officer will deny your application. Your only chance then is to ask the officer to reconsider or write to the U.S. Department of State for an Advisory Opinion asking that they reverse the officer's decision. The Department of State sometimes reverses the decision of a consular officer on a question of law, but rarely on a question of fact.

To get an advisory opinion on how a consular official applied the immigration law in a particular case, an applicant or her/his legal representative may contact the Office of Visa Services in in Washington, at **LegalNet@state.gov**.

The stories of Jeff and Mandy help us understand the review process when a consular officer denies an immigrant visa application.

Jeff's Story

Jeff's mother, a permanent resident of the United States, petitioned for him. Jeff's mother was receiving public assistance, but Jeff had an uncle from the U.S. who was very successful. His uncle and mother both signed an affidavit of support for him, but Jeff couldn't convince the U.S. consular officer who interviewed him that he was not likely to be a public charge. The officer denied Jeff's immigrant visa application.

Jeff would be wasting his time if he wrote for an Advisory Opinion from the Department of State regarding the consular officer's denial. Deciding whether Jeff is likely to become a public charge is something left to the discretion of the consular officer. Jeff must just keep trying to provide further evidence that he can support himself if he wants to become a permanent resident of the United States.

Mandy's Story

Mandy had a rough time growing up and had been in and out of trouble. She had only one criminal conviction, however, and that was for possession of a small amount of hashish when she was eighteen years old. Mandy eventually fell in love with a U.S. citizen who was traveling throughout the world, and he petitioned for her for permanent residence. Mandy was convinced that she qualified for permanent residence despite her criminal conviction because under the law of her country, the conviction had been entirely expunged. When she went to her immigrant visa interview, she admitted that she had been arrested and brought the papers from the court explaining the expungement. The consular officer's view was that under immigration laws, the expungement was not sufficient to eliminate the exclusion by drug-related offense, and the officer denied Mandy an immigrant visa.

If Mandy believes that she deserves to become a permanent resident and the consular officer disagrees, she can seek an Advisory Opinion from the Department of State. The Department of State Office of Visa Services will write to the consular officer, and the officer will abide by that decision. If Mandy is successful, the U.S. consul will issue her an immigrant visa.

Other Things to Know About Your Final Immigrant Visa Interview

Here are some other things to consider as you prepare for your immigrant visa interview.

Review of Petition

Even if USCIS has approved a petition filed by you, a relative, or your employer, the immigration examiner may review the petition as part of the USCIS review of your right to become a permanent resident. If you filed the petition at the same time as your application for adjustment of status, the USCIS examiner will certainly review it.

If an USCIS examiner or consular officer believes that the documents establishing a brother-sister, parent-child, husband-wife, or employee-employer relationship are questionable, the officer can request a field investigation. For a Family-Based Preference case, an investigator may go to the area where the beneficiary and petitioner were born, or where their relationship developed, in order to learn whether the relationship is real. In parent-child or sibling cases, the consul may request that the petitioner and beneficiary take a blood test to verify the relationship.

If you are applying for permanent residence based on marriage to a U.S. citizen or permanent resident, the consular officer or USCIS examiner may investigate the relationship or may examine previous divorces to ensure they are valid.

At the final interview, the USCIS examiner or consular officer is going to want to review all original documents. This includes birth certificate and marriage certificates, as well as job letters and other proof of income.

Do You Need a Lawyer?

Though many people get permanent residence without the help of a lawyer, I recommend that you have a lawyer or other immigration law expert help you prepare for your final visa interview. At an adjustment of status interview, you have the right to have a lawyer or accredited representative attend the interview with you. At a consular interview, while you do not have a right to have a lawyer, most consular officers will allow a lawyer to attend the interview or be available to answer your question.

Section 2
Naturalization and U.S. Citizenship

"Mom, you'll never become a citizen. You've been in this country 20 years, and you still don't speak or read English," complains Maria.

"But I don't need to speak English to live in this neighborhood," Maria's mother, Jane, a permanent resident explains. "Anyway, I don't need to become a U.S. citizen. I'm happy the way I am."

"But Mom, what if you retire back home in the old country? You may not be able to come back and visit us," Maria responds.

Maria is already a U.S. citizen and would like her family to become U.S. citizens. That way they can be assured of the right to come back to the United States even after spending time abroad. Her brother, Chris, has been a permanent resident for ten years, but he is afraid to apply for naturalization because of his criminal record. Chris was arrested for a minor shoplifting offense ten years ago when he first came to the United States. It was his first and only arrest.

Jane and Chris may both qualify for United States citizenship. As you will learn in this section, Jane may be excused from the English language requirement because of her age and her long residence here. As for Chris, since he has had a clean record for five years, he, too, has a good chance of becoming a U.S. citizen. But because of his criminal record, Chris should speak to an immigration law expert before filing his naturalization application.

This section will help you with the last step in the immigration journey: Naturalization, the process of becoming a U.S. citizen. I begin in chapter 7 by discussing the advantages of becoming a United States citizen as well as the risks and pitfalls of the naturalization process. In chapter 7, I also discuss dual citizenship. In chapter 8, I explain the requirements for naturalization. In chapter 9, I provide step-by-step instructions on how to complete USCIS Form N-400, Application for Naturalization, and provide practical hints for getting through the naturalization process. Finally, in chapter 10, I discuss children and naturalization: how a person becomes a U.S. citizen by birth and how your children may become citizens upon your naturalization.

Of course, the first step toward naturalization is to become a permanent resident. If you are not already a permanent resident, you should read section 1 to find out how you can become one.

Chapter 7 - Do You Want to Become a U.S. Citizen?

In this chapter, I discuss the advantages of becoming a U.S. citizen, consider the risks of the naturalization process, and explain dual citizenship. I also discuss whether you will need a lawyer to help you become a naturalized U.S. citizen.

Why Become a U.S. Citizen?

Let's look at the reasons why a permanent resident might want to become a U.S. citizen. As compared to a permanent resident, a U.S. citizen can:

1. Vote and hold public office. The right to vote is usually reserved for U.S. citizens. Some cities allow permanent residents to vote in local school board and community board elections, but those are rare exceptions. If you become a naturalized citizen, you can hold all public offices except President and Vice President of the United States.

2. Be employed in government jobs not available to permanent residents. Most federal jobs and some state and municipal jobs (such as firefighter and police officer) require U.S. citizenship as a condition of employment.

3. Live outside the United States without losing permanent residence. Unlike a permanent resident, a U.S. citizen does not have to worry about the right to return to the United States after a lengthy absence abroad. If you are a permanent resident and you spend too much time abroad, you may be considered to have abandoned your U.S. residence. You may lose your right to return.

John's story illustrates why a person who plans to live abroad for a long time may want to become a U.S. citizen.

John's Story

John had been a permanent resident for 20 years when he retired from his job at age 65. A native of Greece, he wanted to live out his final years at home, so he sold his house in the United States, closed his bank account, and moved to Athens.

Every Christmas, John came back to the United States to spend time with his family. Though John was not living here, he used his green card to enter the United States. For several years, he had no problem at the airport. CBP inspectors didn't question him about his permanent resident status.

Finally, five years after John had moved to Athens, the CBP inspector at JFK Airport in New York City noticed that John entered the United States every Christmas. The inspector asked John how long he was planning to stay. John told the truth, answering "one month." The inspector questioned John further and learned that he was not really living in the United States but in Athens. The inspector told John that he was ineligible to come into the United States as a permanent resident. The USCIS inspector gave him two choices: he could return home immediately to Greece and give up his permanent residence, or he could ask for a hearing and try to prove to an immigration judge that he hasn't abandoned his U.S. residence. If John had become a U.S. citizen, he could have lived in Athens as long as he liked and returned to the United States anytime without encountering a problem.

Why Become a U.S. Citizen? (Continued)

4. Avoid danger of being removed for events occurring after naturalization. If you are a U.S. citizen, you cannot be removed for violations of law or public policy that occurred after you became a U.S. citizen. A permanent resident can be removed for a number of reasons, including criminal activity, smuggling, and political activity. Once you become a U.S. citizen, you cannot be removed from the United States unless you didn't have the right to become a U.S. citizen in the first place. In that case, the USCIS will have to take your citizenship away before they can remove you.

Jean and Gary's stories illustrate this benefit of becoming a U.S. citizen.

Jean's Story

The day after Jean was naturalized as a U.S. citizen, she was on her way to a party in New York City with three of her friends. Jean was unaware that her friend Tom, who sat next to her in the back seat, had brought an ounce of cocaine with him, which he had put under the seat. When the driver of the car ran a red light, the car was stopped by the police. It turned out that the driver had an outstanding arrest warrant, and after a search of the car the police discovered the cocaine under the seat. Jean and her friend Tom were both indicted and charged with possession of cocaine with intent to sell. If Jean goes to trial, she may be able to convince the jury that she didn't know that the cocaine was there. However, if the jury doesn't believe her, they may find her guilty.

Fortunately for Jane, although she has been a U.S. citizen for only a few days, she cannot be removed even if convicted of a serious crime. The United States is her new country and while she might face jail time, she has the right to remain in the United States.

Gary's Story

When Gary applied to become a permanent resident of the United States, he stated on his application that he had never been arrested by the police either in the United States or his country of origin. That was not true. Gary had been convicted of armed robbery in his home country, but by bribing a court officer he managed to get documentation proving that he had never been arrested. He became a permanent resident. Later, when he applied for naturalization, he again lied and said that he had never been arrested.

After he became a citizen, a scandal broke out in the U.S. consulate that had processed his immigrant visa application. Every application that had been processed in the month that Gary was interviewed for his immigrant visa was carefully investigated. The investigators discovered that Gary had been arrested and convicted of a serious offense and had lied about the events on his immigrant visa application. The USCIS may try to denaturalize (take his citizenship away) Gary.

The denaturalization process is very complicated and difficult. The U.S. government will evaluate Gary's case and decide whether to try to denaturalize him. If he is denaturalized, he might be removed from the United States.

5. Get a U.S. passport. Sometimes a United States citizen can visit countries that citizens of other countries cannot. Some permanent residents become U.S. citizens so that they can travel easily to countries where previously they needed a visa or were forbidden to go.

Why Become a U.S. Citizen? (Continued)
6. Have the right to public benefits. The 1996 welfare reform law took away the right of some permanent residents to get many public benefits. If you become a U.S. citizen, you'll feel better knowing that if you need help from the government, you'll be able to get it.
7. Petition married children and siblings to come to the United States.

Risks of the Naturalization Process

When you apply for naturalization, you give the USCIS the opportunity to review your immigration history. If you have committed an act that may make you removable consult an immigration law expert before filing your application. Be especially careful if you have been convicted of a crime or if the USCIS may think that you obtained your permanent resident status improperly.

Michael's and Sharon's stories illustrate the risks of applying for naturalization.

Michael's Story

Michael had been a permanent resident for just two years when he was caught selling a small amount of cocaine in New York City. Since it was his first offense and since the cocaine was under a gram, the judge sentenced Michael to five years' probation. He did not go to jail. After his probation was over, thinking that his record was clean, Michael applied for naturalization. Not only was Michael not naturalized, but the USCIS began deportation (called "removal" as of April 1, 1997) proceedings against him, as a person convicted of a drug-related offense. He may be able to fight his removal and may ultimately get U.S. citizenship. But almost certainly, he will have to defend himself before an immigration judge.

Sharon's Story

Sharon became a permanent resident when her permanent resident mother petitioned for her. After her interview at the U.S. consulate in Trinidad, when the consul had given her an immigrant visa, Sharon decided to marry her high school boyfriend, Billy. She married Billy before she made her first entry into the United States as a permanent resident. However, when she entered the United States, she did not tell the inspector at the airport that she had married. This is considered visa fraud and is a removable offense.

Five years later, when Sharon applied for U.S. citizenship, the USCIS examiner noticed that her marriage had taken place before she entered the United States. Since a person immigrating as the daughter of a permanent resident must be unmarried, Sharon didn't legally qualify to become a permanent resident. Fortunately, in the meantime her mother had become a U.S. citizen. Her mother then petitioned for her as the married child of a United States citizen. Sharon got a new immigrant visa and began the wait for citizenship all over again.

Dual Citizenship: If You Naturalize, Can You Keep Foreign Citzenship?

If you naturalize, must you give up your citizenship in other countries? That depends on the laws of the other country. When you become a U.S. citizen, the U.S. government asks you to renounce all other citizenships. Many countries do not hold that renunciation against you, allowing you to become a U.S. citizen while keeps your previous citizenship. For information about many country's dual citizenship policies, see Appendix C. If you are worried that naturalization will mean that you lose citizenship in another country, visit that country's website or call the country's consulate before you naturalize.

Chapter 8 - Requirements for Naturalization

If you are a permanent resident, you can become a U.S. citizen through the process called **naturalization**. To be naturalized, most applicants must meet the following requirements:

1. You have resided in the United States as a permanent resident continuously for five years. (You can qualify after only three years of permanent residence if you were married to, and living with, the same U.S. citizen spouse during those three years. Even less if you qualify under the special rules for military service members and veterans.

2. You have been physically present in the United States for half of the five- (or three-) year period.

3. You are a person of good moral character.

4. You have a basic knowledge of United States government and history (the civic knowledge requirement).

5. You are able to read, write, and speak simple English (with exceptions for some older, longtime or disabled permanent residents).

6. You are at least eighteen years of age.

7. You express your allegiance to the U.S. government.

As you will learn, the law provides exceptions to many of these requirements.

Continuous Residence Requirement

In order to be naturalized, you must have resided continuously in the United States as a lawful permanent resident for at least five years before being naturalized. If you are the spouse of a U.S. citizen, you may be naturalized three years after you become a permanent resident if you have been married to and living in marital union with a U.S. citizen for the entire three years. The USCIS says that you must be married to and living with your U.S. citizen spouse both at the time you file your naturalization application and at the time of your naturalization interview. The five or three years required is sometimes referred to as the statutory period. You may file your application ninety days before you have met the continuous residence requirement. If you file your application more than ninety days before you have the necessary five or three years, the USCIS will deny your application as prematurely filed.

The three-year rule for the spouse of a permanent resident is illustrated by the stories of Angelo, Joseph, Louisa, and Karen.

Angelo's Story

Angelo became a permanent resident on January 2, 2007, when his mother sponsored him. On January 1, 2014, he married John, a U.S. citizen. Angelo will first become eligible to become a U.S. citizen on January 1, 2017. At that time, he will have been married to and living in marital union with a U.S. citizen for three years while a permanent resident.

Joseph's Story

On January 2, 2014, Joseph became a conditional permanent resident when his wife, Susan, a U.S. citizen, sponsored him. If Joseph and Susan stay married and living together, Joseph can become a U.S. citizen on January 2, 2017. If they divorce, Joseph must wait until 2019 to qualify for citizenship.

Louisa's Story

Louisa became a permanent resident when her U.S. citizen husband sponsored her. She was married on January 2, 1998, and became a permanent resident on January 2, 1999. Two-and-a-half years after she became a permanent resident, she and her husband separated. Louisa could not become a U.S. citizen using the three-year rule because she was no longer living with her husband, although she is still married to him. To take advantage of the three-year rule, Louisa has to have been married to and living with a U.S. citizen for three years. Louisa had to wait until January 2, 2004, when she has five years of permanent residence, to qualify for citizenship.

Karen's Story

Karen was sponsored by her brother, and she became a permanent resident on January 2, 2001. Four years later, on January 2, 2005, Karen married Tom, a U.S. citizen. Karen became eligible for U.S. citizenship on January 2, 2006, five years after she became a permanent resident. Marrying a United States citizen did not speed up her eligibility for naturalization; she qualified after acquiring five years of continuous residence separate and apart from marrying a U.S. citizen.

Continuous residence doesn't mean that you must have been in the United States without ever leaving for the statutory period. It does mean, however, that during the five (or three) years before naturalization:

1. You did not abandon your permanent residence.
2. The United States was your principal residence.
3. And, most important, you have not been out of the country for more than one year at a time, or 365 consecutive days straight. An absence of more than a year breaks the continuity of your residence. This is true even if you reentered the United States with a USCIS reentry permit.

The permit is valid for reentry after up to two years abroad. The advantage of the reentry permit is that it is a way of telling immigration authorities that your long period abroad does not reflect an intention to abandon your residence. If you break your continuous residence, the USCIS gives you one full year for the first day of your return. Then you need four more years (two more if you are married to and living with a U.S. citizen) before you can file for naturalization.

If you are going abroad on business, to do religious work, or to work for the U.S. government, you may be absent for more than a year without breaking your continuous residence if you get approval to do so from the USCIS (see "Exceptions to the Continuous Residence Requirement," in chapter 8).

Sonia's story illustrates how absence abroad for more than one year breaks the period for continuous residence.

Sonia's Story

Sonia was sponsored by her mother, and became a permanent resident on January 1, 2009. On January 1, 2010, Sonia left the United States to study for two years in Spain. Because Sonia was going to be out of the United States for an extended period, she applied for a reentry permit. (See chapter 1 for more on reentry permits.) The USCIS granted the reentry permit, and when Sonia completed her studies, she entered the United States on January 2, 2011.

Because Sonia was out of the United States for more than one continuous year, she had to wait four years and one day from her last entry—or until January 3, 2015—before she could become a U.S. citizen. If she had been married to and living with a U.S. citizen, she would have been granted citizenship after two years and one day.

If you have been outside the United States for more than six months, but less than a year in several of the years just prior to your applying to be naturalized, the USCIS examiner may think that you have abandoned your residence. Much will depend on the reason or reasons you left the country. If you have a reasonable explanation for having spent so much time outside the United States, the examiner can be convinced that you kept your residence here. Common reasons why people spend a lot of time abroad are illness in the family, attendance at a school or university, or business affairs. Trips abroad of less than six months are usually not a problem unless you have so many of them that it looks like you are living outside the United States.

Overcoming Breaks in Continuous Residence

Sometimes USCIS will ignore trips abroad of more than one year if they occurred more than five years ago (or three years ago under the special rules for the spouse of a U.S. citizen). Still, it is best to get advice from an immigration law expert if you have traveled abroad from more than a continuous year and you did not return with a valid reentry permit. That's because you want to have a defense to removal should USCIS decide to follow a more restrictive policy in your case.

Melissa's story illustrates how sometimes the USCIS will ignore a break in continuous residence.

Melissa's Story

Melissa became a permanent resident in 2000. In 2006, she travelled home to Brazil to visit her family, intending to return to the United States in three weeks. While in Brazil, a former employer offered Melissa a high-paying, high tech job so she decided to stay in Brazil for longer than planned. A little over two years later, Melissa returned to live in the United States. She flew into JFK airport, showed her green card to the immigration inspector and was admitted into the United States. Since then, she has made only short vacation trips abroad.

Melissa wants to become a U.S. citizen. USCIS form N-400, Application for Naturalization, asks for an applicant's travel history for the past five years only. So, it's possible that the USCIS naturalization examiner who interviews Melissa will not know that she had been outside the United States for two consecutive years. Even if the examiner becomes aware of Melissa's lengthy time abroad, the examiner may nevertheless approve her application. After all, if Melissa applies to naturalize in 2016, she will have lived continuously in the United States for eight years—a good indication that she never abandoned her U.S. residence.

Exceptions to the Continuous Residence Requirement

Certain business people, religious workers, government employees, researchers for a United States research institution recognized by the USCIS, and sea men and women may be out of the United States for more than one year and still meet the continuous residence requirement. To apply for this exception, you must file USCIS Form N-470, Application to Preserve Residence for Naturalization Purposes. Special continuous residence rules also apply to applicants who have served in the U.S. military (see "Special Naturalization Qualifications—Veterans and Those in Military Service," on the following page.) Your spouse and dependent children residing abroad in your household are also entitled to this benefit.

Business Workers

To qualify for the exception for business workers, you must have been physically present in the United States for an uninterrupted period of at least one year after becoming a permanent resident. You must be employed by, or under contract with, the government of the United States; an American institution of research recognized by the Attorney General; a U.S. firm or corporation, or a subsidiary of a U.S. firm or corporation (more than fifty percent of the subsidiary must be owned by the American company), engaged in developing the trade and commerce of the United States; or a public international organization of which the United States is a member. The USCIS publishes lists of research institutes and public international organizations whose employees qualify under Title 8 of the Code of Federal Regulations (CFR).

Unless you are employed by or are under contract with the U.S. Government, a business worker whom the USCIS grants an exemption from the continuous residence requirement is not exempt from the physical presence requirement discussed below.

Religious Workers

Religious workers, like people abroad on business, must have been physically residing in the United States after being granted permanent residence for at least one year before the applicant files for the exemption using USCIS Form N-470.

In order to qualify for a religious worker exemption, you must be authorized by a United States religious denomination to perform ministerial or priestly functions or be engaged solely as a missionary, brother, nun, or sister by a U.S. religious denomination or an interdenominational missionary organization.

Unlike business workers, religious workers whose Form N-470 applications are approved may count periods outside the United States performing religious duties toward satisfaction of the physical presence requirement (discussed below) for naturalization.

Sea Men and Women

You may be exempted from both the continuous residence and physical presence (see the next section) requirements if you have served on a U.S. vessel. A U.S. vessel is one that is operated by the U.S. government or whose home port is the United States. This rule applies as well to those who work on vessels registered in the United States or owned by U.S. companies. You must have been a permanent resident for the statutory five- (or three-) year period, but time spent outside the United States won't be held against you.

Physical Presence Requirement

In order to be naturalized, you must have been physically present in the United States for half of the required five- (or three-) year statutory period of continuous residence. The USCIS counts back from the day they receive your naturalization application.

Tom and Marie Jean's stories illustrate the physical presence requirement.

Tom's Story

Tom became a permanent resident on January 2, 2008. On a trip to the Dominican Republic, he fell in love with a college student named Sandra. Tom was a professor at the University of Miami, and he took advantage of every school break to spend time with Sandra in the Dominican Republic. He spent every January, June, July, and August in the Dominican Republic with her.

Tom's Story (Continued)

Tom will have no trouble becoming a U.S. citizen once he has five years' permanent residence. Since he was out of the United States for only four months out of every 12 months, Tom will have met the physical presence requirement. He also maintained his residence in the United States as shown by his continuous employment at the university.

Marie Jean's Story

Marie Jean became a permanent resident on January 1, 2008. On January 1, 2009, she began traveling regularly to France as part of her job as an international financial advisor to a U.S. bank. While she maintained a home in the United States, she only spent one week out of every month in the country, spending the other three weeks in France. She will not lose her permanent residence status as long as she maintains an apartment, a bank account, her employment by a U.S. company, and other ties to the United States. If she continues to spend a large portion of her time in France however, she will never fulfill the physical presence requirement. If on January 2, 2013, she had five years' continuous residence, but she had not spent half of her time in the United States during the five-year period.

Good Moral Character Requirement

Good moral character does not mean moral excellence. If you have a record of criminal activity; have failed to pay required family support; have had problems with alcohol or drugs; have been involved in illegal gambling, prostitution, or procuring prostitutes; have failed to pay your taxes; have failed to register with the selective service; or have lied to the USCIS to gain immigration benefits, you may fail the good moral character requirement. Parking tickets, disorderly conduct convictions, and many other minor offenses usually will not prevent you from proving that you have good moral character. However, the USCIS may say that you don't have good moral character if you have repeated convictions for minor violations.

The question of who has "good moral character" under U.S. laws is not easy to answer. If you have any doubts, particularly regarding a criminal record, you should speak to an immigration law expert before filing your naturalization application.

Generally, good moral character must be shown only for the statutory period of five (or three) years. Except for aggravated felonies, which are explained below, crimes committed before the statutory period, either in the United States or abroad, will not affect your right to become a citizen unless they reflect on your present character. Although, if your criminal case was conditionally discharged or you are still on probation or parole for a crime, the USCIS may deny your naturalization until your criminal case is discharged or your parole or probation has ended.

An aggravated felon convicted on or after November 29, 1990, is permanently barred from naturalizing. An aggravated felon is a person who has been convicted of one of several serious crimes, especially crimes involving drugs and violence. (For a clearer idea of what constitutes an aggravated felony, see appendix B, "List of Aggravated Felonies.")

The 1996 immigration law expanded the definition of aggravated felony. If you were convicted of an aggravated felony before November 29, 1990, you may be able to show good moral character, but at the same time you may be deportable. If you have ever been convicted of a crime, even a minor one, you would be foolish to apply for naturalization without speaking to an immigration law expert.

The stories of Sam, Tim, and Jane show the complexity of the good moral character requirement.

Sam's Story

Sam had been involved in a number of illegal gambling operations. He had been arrested several times, and each time he pled guilty to minor gambling charges. Since a person who makes a living from illegal gambling cannot be naturalized, when Sam went to his interview, he was questioned about whether he had continued to gamble. Although he had not been arrested at any time during the last five years, the USCIS naturalization examiner noted that Sam lived in an expensive neighborhood and wore expensive clothes.

Sam had been employed during the last five years as a clerk in a small neighborhood store. The examiner wanted to know how Sam could afford his high lifestyle on his low salary; he suspected that perhaps Sam was still involved in illegal gambling. Fortunately for Sam, he had inherited two million dollars from a wealthy relative about five years before his interview. He was able to convince the examiner that he was not involved in criminal activity despite his newfound wealth.

Tim's Story

Tim became a permanent resident on January 1, 2000. He had been arrested on numerous occasions for illegal horse race bookmaking. His last arrest was back in 2004 but, nevertheless, Tim was denied naturalization as a U.S. citizen in 2010. When he went for his interview, the USCIS examiner noticed that although he had not been employed for the last five years, he lived in a mansion in Beverly Hills, traveled to Europe regularly and wore a gold watch. The examiner denied the application on the assumption that Tim earned a living from illegal gambling—an activity that is precluded from establishing good moral character. The examiner's decision was based on Tim's many arrests and the fact that he had no visible means of support.

Jane's Story

Jane became a permanent resident in January 1995. In January 1999, she was caught stealing a purse from a fancy boutique. She pled guilty to a theft in February 2000 and was placed on probation. Her crime was not an aggravated felony. In February 2005 when her probation ended, she was interviewed regarding her naturalization as a U.S. citizen. During those five years, she had led an average life and had no run-ins with the law. Jane was able to establish good moral character for the previous five years and had no problem becoming a U.S. citizen.

Good Moral Character and Criminal Activity

You cannot prove good moral character if, during the five- (or three-) year period prior to your naturalization, you have been convicted in the United States or abroad of one or more of the following:

- A crime involving moral turpitude.
- Two or more gambling offenses.
- A narcotics offense.
- Two or more nonpolitical offenses for which you were sentenced to five years' imprisonment or more.
- Any crime for which you were confined to prison for more than 180 days.
- Any aggravated felony.

You can also be denied naturalization if you have admitted committing a crime involving moral turpitude or the USCIS believes that you have been involved in drug trafficking, even if you have never been convicted of these crimes.

Not all criminal activity, even where a felony conviction is involved, will necessarily result in the USCIS denying your naturalization application. An example of a conviction that may not be a bar to naturalization would be a conviction for vehicular manslaughter.

Because conviction of a single crime involving moral turpitude can be a bar to naturalization, let's consider how the law defines these terms. Moral turpitude is conduct or behavior that is reprehensible in its own right. It is an indication of inherent baseness or depravity of character.

Good people may break the law, but good people don't commit crimes involving moral turpitude.

A crime involving fraud or dishonesty will usually be considered to involve moral turpitude. Among crimes considered by the immigration laws to involve moral turpitude are arson; assault with intent to kill, commit rape, rob, or inflict serious bodily harm with a dangerous or deadly weapon; bigamy; blackmail; bribery; bad check convictions; burglary; counterfeiting; embezzlement; forgery; larceny; manslaughter; murder; pandering; perjury; prostitution; receiving stolen goods; robbery; and sexual offenses.

Crimes not generally considered to involve moral turpitude include simple assault, breaking the peace, drunkenness, disorderly conduct, a single gambling offense, or violations of government regulations that do not require intent to defraud as an element of the crime.

Child Support

If you willfully fail to meet your child support obligations, you do not have good moral character for naturalization purposes. Child support refers to financial support that you provide your children when they are not living with you.

How does the USCIS know whether you are meeting your child support obligations? On USCIS Form N-400, you are asked whether you are separated or divorced and whether you are living with or apart from your spouse. Sometimes an interview notice will advise you to bring in your divorce decree and any papers relating to the divorce. At the interview, the USCIS examiner may ask you about the child support obligation and whether it has been met. You may be required to produce documentation that you have met your obligations, such as canceled checks. The USCIS may check with the person caring for your children or ask you to get a letter from them confirming that you are supporting your children.

Selective Service Registration

Immigration law views failure to register for selective service as a reflection on your moral character and your adherence to the U.S. Constitution. The United States is not presently drafting men or women into the armed forces. Still, U.S. Selective Service laws require that all men, U.S. citizens, permanent residents, and undocumented immigrants register with Selective Service.

The registration requirement applies to men only if they were in the United States between the ages of eighteen to twenty-five and were born after January 1, 1960. The requirement ends once you reach the age of twenty-six. Persons born before January 1, 1960, are not required to register. The registration requirement does not apply to men here in lawful nonimmigrant status, such as with F-1s student or H-1Bs temporary worker visas.

If you are not yet twenty-six years old, you can register late with the Selective Service. You can get a registration form at your local post office or you can register online at **sss.gov**. You can bring proof of your late registration with you to your naturalization interview, and the USCIS examiner may excuse your failure to register.

Some men were unaware of their obligation to register and didn't get a notice to register from either the Selective Service or any other agency. If this describes your situation, try submitting an affidavit (a sworn statement) to the USCIS examiner explaining that you didn't willfully and knowingly fail to register. The examiner may approve your application. If the examiner denies your application, you can apply again once you have the required five (or three) years of good moral character.

If you are found to have knowingly and willfully failed to register, you must wait until you are at least thirty-one, five years after your obligation to register ended, before you can become a United States citizen.

If you're married to and living with a U.S. citizen, you can be naturalized when you reach the age of twenty-nine, three years after your obligation to register ended.

 If you did register with Selective Service, but you don't know your registration number, you may call Selective Service toll free at **(847) 688-6888**. Have your date of birth and social security number ready when you call. You may also write to the Selective Service asking for your number at **Selective Service, P.O. Box 94636, Palatine, IL 60094-4636**. Include your name, date of birth, and social security number. You can also usually obtain your selective service registration number online at **sss.gov**.

Taxes

If you were required to file a federal tax return but failed to do so, your naturalization application can be denied. Many people are not required to file tax returns because their income is less than the amount for which filing is required. Don't be afraid to answer "No" to this question if you earned so little money in a particular year or years that you were not required to file a return. Usually, the USCIS will want to see your last five years' tax returns, or they will want an explanation as to why you didn't file returns.

Richard's story illustrates how a person may be naturalized without having filed tax returns.

 Richard's Story

Richard always had a hard time making money. Ever since his mother got him an immigrant visa, he has worked only part-time, if at all. Sometimes he survived on welfare. Never did he make more than $4,000 in a single year. In 2006, Richard applied to become a U.S. citizen. He can truthfully answer that he never failed to file a federal tax return—because he earned so little, filing a return wasn't required. At his naturalization interview, he presented an affidavit from his mother explaining that she had supported him for the last five years. He also brought proof he was receiving public benefits (welfare). Richard became a United States citizen.

If you filed improper returns, for instance claiming dependents you didn't have the right to claim, you can apply for naturalization and file corrected returns. If you provide the correct returns at your interview, USCIS will approve your application. The same is true if you failed to file returns. Just make sure you file before your naturalization interview.

Other Common Indications of a Lack of Good Moral Character

A habitual drunkard or a user or dealer of drugs is not a person of good moral character. The same is true if you earn income from illegal gambling, prostitution, or drug dealing. If you have been arrested for one of these activities and currently have no visible means of support, the USCIS examiner may wonder if you are still engaging in illegal activity.

If you are a polygamist or have ever smuggled aliens into the United States for economic gain, you will fail to meet the good moral character requirement.

 ## Civics Knowledge Requirement

In order to be naturalized, you must have a basic understanding of the history and government of the United States. You must correctly answer questions from a list of one hundred questions provided by the USCIS. If you are sixty-five years of age and you have been a permanent resident for twenty years, you need to answer only six out of ten simple questions from a list of twenty-five. You can find these lists at the end of this chapter.

English Language Requirement

With limited exceptions, every naturalization applicant must pass an English speaking, reading, and writing test. If you can answer orally the questions on the application form (such as "Where do you live?" and "Where were you born?"), you can probably pass the English oral comprehension and speech test.

If a question arises at the interview that needs to be discussed in detail—for instance, whether you made required child support payments—you have the right to have that discussion in your native language.

You are exempt from the English language requirement if you have been a permanent resident for twenty years or more and you are at least fifty years old or you have been a permanent resident for fifteen years or more and you are at least fifty-five years old. If you qualify for this exemption, you must still pass a civics and history test, but you can be tested in your native language.

If you are incapable of writing, reading, or speaking because of a documented mental or physical disability, you may apply to be exempted from the English language requirement.

You are also exempt from taking an English language test if you take a similar test as part of the process of getting permanent residence through the amnesty program.

Finally, Hmong immigrants who fought in the CIA's war in Laos during the Vietnam War era are exempt from the English language requirement. To be eligible for this exemption, Hmong veterans must have served with a special guerrilla unit or irregular force operating in Laos in support of the U.S. military anytime between February 28, 1961, and September 18, 1978.

Age Requirement

In order to be naturalized, you must be at least eighteen years old. You may not file your application prior to your eighteenth birthday. Children of applicants for naturalization who are under eighteen years of age sometimes may acquire citizenship through their parents (see chapter 10).

Competency Requirement

At one time, to naturalize, you must have been legally competent. That is, you must have had the mental capacity to take an oath of allegiance to the United States. Under current law, the USCIS will waive the oath requirement if the applicant is unable to understand, or communicate an understanding of, the oath's meaning because of a physical or developmental disability or mental impairment. Even severely disabled people, unable to understand the oath, qualify for naturalization.

Allegiance to the U.S. Government

To become a U.S. citizen, you must express your allegiance to the United States and our form of government. As part of the naturalization process, you must take an oath of allegiance to the United States. You can find the Oath of Allegiance in appendix D. You must be willing to either bear arms on behalf of the United States or perform some form of military service or civilian work of national importance. As mentioned under "Competency Requirement," the USCIS can waive the oath for the disabled.

You may be denied naturalization if you are, or have been, a member of or were connected to a communist party or a similar organization during the ten years prior to filing your naturalization application. You may also be barred from naturalization if you have been connected with an organization that believes in anarchy, the overthrow of organized government, sabotage, injury, or assassination of U.S. government officers.

If your membership in the communist party was more than ten years prior to your filing for naturalization you may still be naturalized. Your political activity may be forgiven as well, if your membership in the organization ended before you were sixteen years of age or if your membership was involuntary. Involuntary means compelled by law or for the purposes of getting the necessities of life.

Special Naturalization Qualifications: Veterans and Those in Military Service

If you are a United States military veteran or someone in the Army, Navy, Air Force, Marine Corps, Coast Guard, or in certain components of the National Guard or the Selected Reserve of the Ready Reserve, you may be able to naturalize without meeting the normal residence and physical presence requirements. You are also exempt from paying the application and biometrics fees.

Individuals presently serving in the U.S. military during time of war, qualify for naturalization regardless of immigration status.

 For the purposes of this rule, the country has been at war since September 11, 2001.

Service members who recently separated from service qualify for naturalization even if they don't meet the Continuous Residence and Physical Presence and the three month state residency requirements if they:

- Have served honorably, in active duty or reserve service, for a period or periods adding up to one year or more.

- Are permanent residents, and...

- Apply during service or within six months of the termination of service.

Under Section 329 of the Immigration and Nationality Act (INA), any person who has served honorably as a member of the Selected Reserve of the Ready Reserve or in an active-duty status in the military, air, or naval forces of the United States may qualify for naturalization, even if they are not lawful permanent residents, if:

- They are veterans who serve(d) in active duty or are (were) in the Selected Reserve of the Ready Reserve during one of the following designated periods of conflict:
    - April 6, 1917 – November 11, 1918
    - September 1, 1939 – December 31, 1946
    - June 25, 1950 – July 1, 1955
    - February 28, 1961 – October 15, 1978
    - September 11, 2001 – Present

- At the time of enlistment, reenlistment, extension of enlistment, or induction they are/were physically present in the United States or a qualifying area, whether or not they have been lawfully admitted to the United States for permanent residence, or at any time subsequent to enlistment or induction they are/were lawfully admitted to the United States for permanent residence.

 N-400, the Application for Naturalization submitted by a member of the military must also be accompanied by Form N-426, the Request for Certification of Military or Naval Service, a copy of the permanent resident card (if applicable), and two passport-style photos. **No fees are required**. More information for members of the military and their families is available on the USCIS website at **www.uscis.gov/military** or by calling the USCIS military helpline at **877-CIS-4MIL (877-247-4645)**.

List of 100 Questions Used by
USCIS Naturalization Examiners

American Government:
Principles of American Democracy

1. What is the supreme law of the land?
A. The Constitution

2. What does the Constitution do?
A. Sets up the government; defines the government; protects basic rights of Americans

3. The idea of self-government is in the first three words of the Constitution. What are these words?
A. We the people

4. What is an amendment?
A. A change (to the Constitution); an addition (to the Constitution)

5. What do we call the first ten amendments to the Constitution?
A. The Bill of Rights

6. What is one right or freedom from the First Amendment?
A. Speech; religion; assembly; press; petition the government

7. How many amendments does the Constitution have?
A. Twenty-seven (27)

8. What did the Declaration of Independence do?
A. Announced our independence (from Great Britain); declared our independence (from Great Britain); said that the United States is free (from Great Britain)

9. What are two rights in the Declaration of Independence?
A. Life; liberty; pursuit of happiness

10. What is freedom of religion?
A. You can practice any religion, or not practice a religion.

11. What is the economic system in the United States?
A.Capitalist economy; market economy

12. What is the "rule of law"?
A. Everyone must follow the law; Leaders must obey the law; Government must obey the law; No one is above the law.

American Government:
Systems of Government

13. Name one branch or part of the government.
A. *Congress; legislative; President; executive; the courts; judicial*

14. What stops one branch of government from becoming too powerful?
A. *Checks and balances; separation of powers*

15. Who is in charge of the executive branch?
A. *The President*

16. Who makes federal laws?
A. *Congress; Senate and House (of Representatives); (U.S. or national) legislature*

17. What are the two parts of the U.S. Congress?
A. *The Senate and House (of Representatives)*

18. How many U.S. Senators are there?
A. *One hundred (100)*

19. We elect a U.S. Senator for how many years?
A. *Six (6)*

20. Who is one of your state's U.S. Senators now?
A. *Your U.S. Senators*

21. The House of Representatives has how many voting members?
A. *Four hundred thirty-five (435)*

22. We elect a U.S. Representative for how many years?
A. *Two (2)*

23. Name your U.S. Representative.
A. *[Answers will vary. You can identify your U.S. Representative at **www.house.gov** or by calling the U.S. House of Representatives at **202-224-3121**.]*

24. Who does a U.S. Senator represent?
A. *All people of the state*

25. Why do some states have more Representatives than other states?
A. *(Because of) the state's population; (because) they have more people; (because) some states have more people*

26. We elect a President for how many years?
A. *Four (4)*

27. In what month do we vote for President?
A. *November*

28. What is the name of the President of the United States now?
A. *Barack Obama*

29. What is the name of the Vice President of the United States now?
A. *Joseph R. Biden, Jr.*

American Government:
Systems of Government (Continued)

30. If the President can no longer serve, who becomes President?

A. The Vice President

31. If both the President and the Vice President can no longer serve, who becomes President?

A. The Speaker of the House

32. Who is the Commander in Chief of the military?

A. The President

33. Who signs bills to become laws?

A. The President

34. Who vetoes bills?

A. The President

35. What does the President's Cabinet do?

A. Advises the President

36. What are two Cabinet-level positions?

A. Secretary of Agriculture;
Secretary of Commerce;
Secretary of Defense;
Secretary of Education;
Secretary of Energy;
Secretary of Health and Human Services;
Secretary of Homeland Security;
Secretary of Housing and Urban Development;
Secretary of the Interior;
Secretary of State;
Secretary of Transportation;
Secretary of the Treasury;
Secretary of Veterans Affairs;
Secretary of Labor;
Attorney General;
Vice President

37. What does the judicial branch do?

A. Reviews laws; explains laws; resolves disputes (disagreements); decides if a law goes against the Constitution.

38. What is the highest court in the United States?

A.The Supreme Court

39. How many justices are on the Supreme Court?

A. Nine (9)

40. Who is the Chief Justice of the United States now?

A. John Roberts

American Government:
Systems of Government (Continued)

41. Under our Constitution, some powers belong to the federal government. What is one power of the federal government?
A. *To print money; to declare war; to create an army; to make treaties*

42. Under our Constitution, some powers belong to the states. What is one power of the states?
A. *Provide schooling and education; provide protection (police); provide safety (fire departments); give a driver's license; approve zoning and land use.*

43. Who is the Governor of your state now?
A. *[Governor from your state].*

44. What is the capital of your state?
A. *Albany [For New York the answer is Albany. Other answers will vary.]*

45. What are the two major political parties in the United States?
A. *Democratic and Republican*

46. What is the political party of the President now?
A. *Democratic (Party)*

47. What is the name of the Speaker of the House of Representatives now?
A. *(Paul) Ryan*

American Government:
Rights and Responsibilities

48. There are four amendments to the Constitution about who can vote. Describe one of them.
A. *Citizens eighteen (18) and older (can vote); You don't have to pay (a poll tax) to vote; Any citizen can vote. (Women and men can vote.); A male citizen of any race (can vote)*

49. What is one responsibility that is only for United States citizens?
A. *Serve on a jury; vote in federal election*

50. Name one right only for United States citizens?
A. *Vote in federal election, run for federal office*

51. What are two rights of everyone living in the United States?
A. *Freedom of expression; freedom of speech; freedom of assembly; freedom to petition the government; freedom of worship; the right to bear arms*

52. What do we show loyalty to when we say the Pledge of Allegiance?
A. *The United States; the flag*

American Government:
Rights and Responsibilities (Continued)

53. What is one promise you make when you become a United States citizen?
A. Give up loyalty to other countries; defend the Constitution and laws of the United States; obey the laws of the United States; serve in the U.S. military (if needed); serve (do important work for) the nation (if needed); be loyal to the United States

54. How old do citizens have to be to vote for President?
A. Eighteen (18) and older

55.What are two ways that Americans can participate in their democracy?
A. Vote; join a political party; help with a campaign; join a civic group; join a community group; give an elected official your opinion on an issue; call Senators and Representatives; publicly support or oppose an issue or policy; run for office; write to a newspaper

56. When is the last day you can send in federal income tax forms?
A. April 15

57. When must all men register for the Selective Service?
A. At age eighteen (18); between eighteen (18) and twenty-six (26)

American History:
Colonial Period and Independence

58. What is one reason colonists came to America?
A. Freedom; political liberty; religious freedom; economic opportunity; practice their religion; escape persecution

59. Who lived in America before the Europeans arrived?
A. Native Americans; American Indians

60. What group of people was taken to America and sold as slaves?
A. Africans; people from Africa

61. Why did the colonists fight the British?
A. Because of high taxes (taxation without representation); because the British army stayed in their houses (boarding, quartering); because they didn't have self-government.

62. Who wrote the Declaration of Independence?
A. (Thomas) Jefferson

63. When was the Declaration of Independence adopted?
A. July 4, 1776

64. There were 13 original states. Name three.
A. New Hampshire; Massachusetts; Rhode Island; Connecticut; New York; New Jersey; Pennsylvania; Delaware; Maryland; Virginia; North Carolina; South Carolina; Georgia

American History:
Colonial Period and Independence (Continued)

65. What happened at the Constitutional Convention?

A. The Constitution was written; The Founding Fathers wrote the Constitution

66. When was the Constitution written?

A. 1787

67. The Federalist Papers supported the passage of the U.S. Constitution. Name one of the writers.

A. (James) Madison; (Alexander) Hamilton; (John) Jay; Publius

68. What is one thing Benjamin Franklin is famous for?

A. U.S. diplomat; oldest member of the Constitutional Convention; first Postmaster General of the United States; writer of "Poor Richard's Almanac"; started the first free libraries

69. Who is the "Father of Our Country"?

A. (George) Washington

70. Who was the first President?

A. (George) Washington

American History:
The 1800s

71. What territory did the United States buy from France in 1803?

A. The Louisiana Territory; Louisiana

72. Name one war fought by the United States in the 1800s.

A. War of 1812; Mexican-American War; Civil War; Spanish-American War

73. Name the U.S. war between the North and the South.

A. The Civil War; the War between the States

74. Name one problem that led to the Civil War.

A. Slavery; economic reasons; states' rights

75. What was one important thing that Abraham Lincoln did?

A. Freed the slaves (Emancipation Proclamation); saved (or preserved) the Union; led the United States during the Civil War

76. What did the Emancipation Proclamation do?

A. Freed the slaves; freed slaves in the Confederacy; freed slaves in the Confederate states; freed slaves in most Southern states

77. What did Susan B. Anthony do?

A. Fought for women's rights; fought for civil rights

American History:
Recent American History & Other Important Historical Information

78. Name one war fought by the United States in the 1900s.
A. World War I; World War II; Korean War; Vietnam War; (Persian) Gulf War

79. Who was President during World War I?
A. (Woodrow) Wilson

80. Who was President during the Great Depression and World War II?
A.(Franklin) Roosevelt

81. Who did the United States fight in World War II?
A. Japan, Germany, and Italy

82. Before he was President, Eisenhower was a general. What war was he in?
A. World War II

83. During the Cold War, what was the main concern of the United States?
A. Communism

84. What movement tried to end racial discrimination?
A. Civil rights (movement)

85. What did Martin Luther King, Jr. do?
A. Fought for civil rights; worked for equality for all Americans

86. What major event happened on September 11, 2001 in the United States?
A. Terrorists attacked the United States.

87. Name one American Indian tribe in the United States
A. Cherokee; Navajo; Sioux; Chippewa; Choctaw; Pueblo; Apache; Iroquois; Creek; Blackfeet; Seminole; Cheyenne; Arawak; Shawnee; Mohegan; Huron; Oneida; Lakota; Crow; Teton; Hopi; Inuit

88. Name one of the two longest rivers in the United States.
A. Missouri (River); Mississippi (River)

89. What ocean is on the West Coast of the United States?
A. Pacific (Ocean)

90. What ocean is on the East Coast of the United States?
A. Atlantic (Ocean)

91. Name one U.S. territory.
A. Puerto Rico; U.S. Virgin Islands; American Samoa; Northern Mariana Islands; Guam

92. Name one state that borders Canada.
A. Maine; New Hampshire; Vermont; New York; Pennsylvania; Ohio; Michigan; Minnesota; North Dakota; Montana; Idaho; Washington; Alaska

93. Name one state that borders Mexico.
A. California; Arizona; New Mexico; Texas

94. What is the capital of the United States?
A. Washington, D.C.

American History:
Recent American History & Other Important Historical Information (Continued)

95. Where is the Statue of Liberty?

A. *New York (Harbor); Liberty Island [Also acceptable are New Jersey, near New York City, and on the Hudson (River)]*

96. Why does the flag have 13 stripes?

A. *Because there were 13 original colonies; because the stripes represent the original colonies*

97. Why does the flag have 50 stars?

A. *Because there is one star for each state; because each star represents a state; because there are 50 states.*

98. What is the name of the national anthem?

A. *The Star-Spangled Banner*

Holidays

99. When do we celebrate Independence Day?

A. *July 4*

100. Name two national U.S. holidays.

A. *New Year's Day; Martin Luther King, Jr. Day; Presidents' Day; Memorial Day; Independence Day; Labor Day; Columbus Day; Veterans Day Thanksgiving; Christmas*

65/20 Questions and Answers

These are citizenship questions for applicants sixty-five or older who have been permanent residents for twenty years or more. You must answer six out of ten questions selected by an USCIS examiner.

Civic Knowledge Questions and Answers for the Elderly

If you are sixty-five years of age or older and you have been a permanent resident for at least twenty years at the time you submit your application for naturalization, you will answer ten questions from a list of only twenty questions when you are tested on your basic understanding of U.S. history and government (civics). You must answer at least six of the ten questions correctly to pass. You also qualify to take the civics test in the language of your choice. On this page you will find the list of twenty questions.

1. What is one right or freedom from the First Amendment?
A. *Speech; religion; assembly; press; petition the government*

2. What is the economic system in the United States?
A. *Capitalist economy; market economy*

3. Name one branch or part of the government.
A. *Congress; Legislative; President; executive; the courts; judicial*

4. What are the two parts of the U.S. Congress?
A. *The Senate and House (of Representatives)*

5. Who is one of your state's U.S. Senators now?
A. *Senators from your state.*

6. In what month do we vote for President?
A. *November*

7. What is the name of the President of the United States now?
A. *Barack Obama; Obama*

8. What is the capital of your state?
A. *[For New York the answer is Albany. Other answers will vary.]*

9. What are the two major political parties in the United States?
A. *Democratic and Republican*

10. What is one responsibility that is only for United States citizens?
A. *Serve on a jury; vote in a federal election*

11. How old do citizens have to be to vote for President?
A. *Eighteen (18) and older*

12. When is the last day you can send in federal income tax forms?
A. *April 15*

13. Who was the first President?
A. *(George) Washington*

14. What was one important thing that Abraham Lincoln did?

A. Freed the slaves (Emancipation Proclamation); saved (or preserved) the Union; led the United States during the Civil War

15. Name one war fought by the United States in the 1900s.

A. World War I; World War II; Korean War; Vietnam War; (Persian) Gulf War

16. What did Martin Luther King, Jr. do?

A. Fought for civil rights; worked for equality for all Americans

17. What is the capital of the United States?

A. Washington, D.C.

18. Where is the Statue of Liberty?

A. New York (Harbor); Liberty Island [Also acceptable are New Jersey, near New York City, and on the Hudson (River).]

19. Why does the flag have 50 stars?

A. Because there is one star for each state; because each star represents a state; because there are 50 states

20. When do we celebrate Independence Day?

A. July 4

English Reading Vocabulary for the Naturalization Test

People

Abraham Lincoln

George Washington

Civics

American flag
Bill of Rights
capital
citizen
city
Congress
country
Father of Our Country
government
President
right
Senators
state/states
White House

Places

America
United States
U.S.

Holidays

Presidents' Day
Memorial Day
Flag Day
Independence Day
Labor Day
Columbus Day
Thanksgiving

Question Words

How
What
When
Where
Who
Why

Verbs

can
come
do/does
elects
have/has
is/are/was/be
lives/lived
meet
name
pay
vote
want

Other (Function)

a
for
here
in
of
on
the
to
we

Other (Content)

colors
dollar bill
first
largest
many
most
north
one
people
second
south

English Reading Vocabulary for the Naturalization Test

People	Civics	Places	Holidays
Adams	American Indians	Alaska	February
Lincoln	capital	California	May
Washington	citizens	Canada	June
	Civil War	Delaware	July
	Congress	Mexico	September
	Father of Our Country	New York City	October
	flag	United States	November
	free	Washington	
	freedom of speech	Washington, D.C.	
	President		
	right		
	Senators		
	state/states		
	White House		

Holidays	Verbs	Other (Function)	Other (Content)
Presidents' Day	can	and	blue
Memorial Day	come	during	dollar bill
Flag Day	elect	for	fifty/50
Independence	have/has	here	first
Day	is/was/be	in	largest
Labor Day	lives/lived	of	most
Columbus Day	meets	on	north
Thanksgiving	pay	the	one
	vote	to	one hundred/100
	want	we	people
			red
			second
			south
			taxes
			white

Chapter 9 - Getting Naturalized

USCIS form N-400: Getting Help With Your Application, Answering the Difficult Questions, Filing for Naturalization, Getting USCIS to Waiver the Fee, Preparing for the Final Interview, Your Right to Appeal

Most of USCIS Form N-400 is very straightforward, but some questions require care in answering. Answer the questions truthfully. Lying on the form or at your naturalization interview is grounds for denying your application. If you think your answer will lead to USCIS denying your application, consult and immigration law expert before submitting your application. In addition to truthfulness, consistency is important, because your N-400 will be compared to all other immigration forms you previously filed with USCIS. In this chapter, you will find images of the various parts of form N-400 followed by step-by-step instructions for all questions.

 You can get USCIS Form N-400 and other USCIS forms by calling **800-870-3676** or from the USCIS Web site, **http://uscis.gov/**. The Web version is available in an easy-to-use "fillable" format. You can complete the form on your computer, print it out with your information, and mail it to USCIS. You can't yet file online, but hopefully that's coming in the future. You can find a sample form in appendix ??.

Tips on Completing USCIS Form N-400

- Print clearly using black ink, type your answers, or complete the form online.

- If extra space is needed to answer a question or if you cannot answer a question because you do not have the information or you do not know the answer, attach a separate sheet of paper with an explanation. On the sheet, indicate the application part and question number, write the date, and include your signature, name and "A" number.

- If a question is not applicable, write 'N/A'. If the answer is none, write 'none'.

- Write dates in the order month/day/year using eight digits (mm/dd/yyyy).

Enter Your 9 Digit A-Number:
► A-

- Write your "A" number on the top right hand corner of each page where indicated. You can find your "A" number on your Permanent Resident Card (formerly known as the Alien Registration Card or green card). The "A" number is the seven to nine digit number on your card (the number of digits will depend on when your card was created). If your "A" number is fewer than nine digits, write enough zeroes before the first number to make your "A" number a nine digit number.

- If you are completing this form on a computer, the data you enter will be captured and saved using the 2D barcode at the bottom of each page. This technology is intended to help the accuracy and processing of the N-400. Do not damage the 2D barcode by stapling, writing or using white correction fluid on it.

- Avoid highlighting, crossing out, or writing outside the area that has been provided for a response.

A. Part 1 – Information About Your Eligibility

Part 1. Information About Your Eligibility *(Check only one box or your Form N-400 may be delayed)*

You are at least 18 years old **and**

1. ☐ Have been a Permanent Resident of the United States for at least 5 years.

2. ☐ Have been a Permanent Resident of the United States for at least 3 years. In addition, you have been married to and living with the same U.S. citizen spouse for the last 3 years, **and** your spouse has been a U.S. citizen for the last 3 years at the time of filing your Form N-400.

3. ☐ Are a Permanent Resident of the United States, and you are the spouse of a U.S. citizen, **and** your U.S. citizen spouse is regularly engaged in specified employment abroad. *(Section 319(b) of the Immigration and Nationality Act)*

4. ☐ Are applying on the basis of qualifying military service.

5. ☐ Other (explain): _____

Check the box that best applies to your case:

- **Check "1."** if you qualify because you have been a permanent resident for five or more years.

- **Check "2."** if you have been married to, and living with the same U.S. citizen for three years while a permanent resident. (If you check this option, at the naturalization interview you must provide a marriage certificate and documentation of your spouse's U.S. citizenship, and proof that you are living together, and that you have been living together for the entire time that you have had your green card.) Note that if you are applying based on marriage to a citizen, you must remain married until you are sworn-in as a U.S. citizen. Death of a U.S. citizen spouse, even if it occurs after having filed the application, ends eligibility to naturalize based on marriage.

- **Check "3."** if you are a permanent resident married to a U.S. citizen and your spouse is working abroad for the United States Government, certain American research institutions and companies engaged in foreign trade or commerce, an international organization, such as the United Nations, or you are working as a minister or missionary of a religious organization. Special, less restrictive rules may apply.

- **Check "4."** if you are applying for naturalization based on military service (see "Exceptions to the Requirements: Veterans and Those in Military Service" in Chapter 8).

- **Check "5."** if you are applying for naturalization on another basis, and explain. Speak with an immigration law expert if you think you qualify based on other factors.

B. Part 2 – Information About You

Part 2. Information About You *(Person applying for naturalization)*		
1. **Your Current Legal Name** *(**do not** provide a nickname)*		
Family Name *(Last Name)*	Given Name *(First Name)*	Middle Name *(if applicable)*

Your legal name is on your birth certificate, or, if it was changed through marriage or divorce, it is on your marriage certificate or divorce judgment.

2. **Your Name Exactly As It Appears on Your Permanent Resident Card** *(if applicable)*		
Family Name *(Last Name)*	Given Name *(First Name)*	Middle Name *(if applicable)*

Even if your name is misspelled on your Permanent Resident Card (green card), write it exactly that way here. This is important to identify you. USCIS will use your correct name from Part 2, Question 1 for your naturalization certificate.

3. **Other Name(s) You Have Used Since Birth** *(include nicknames, aliases, and maiden name if applicable)*		
Family Name *(Last Name)*	Given Name *(First Name)*	Middle Name *(if applicable)*

Include nicknames, aliases, your maiden name and any other names you may have ever used. Also, write down misspelled names, if any. If there are none, write "N/A".

4. **Name Change** *(optional)*		
Read the Form N-400 Instructions before you decide whether or not you would like to legally change your name.		
Would you like to legally change your name?		☐ Yes ☐ No
If "Yes," print the new name you would like to use in the space below.		
Family Name *(Last Name)*	Given Name *(First Name)*	Middle Name *(if applicable)*

You can use the citizenship process to legally change your name. To do so, in Part 2, Question 4 check 'Yes' and in the box below write the new name you want to use. At your naturalization interview, you should confirm with the USCIS officer that if your naturalization application is approved you will be sworn in by a Federal Judge or Magistrate rather than by a USCIS officer. Only a Federal Judge or Magistrate can change your name and a name change becomes final only when you are naturalized in court. If you do not want to change your name, in Question 4 check "No" and in the box below write "N/A".

5. **U.S. Social Security Number** (*if applicable*)	6. **Date of Birth** (*mm/dd/yyyy*) ▶	7. **Date You Became a Permanent Resident** (*mm/dd/yyyy*) ▶
8. **Country of Birth**		9. **Country of Citizenship or Nationality**

- **For "5."** print your social security number. If you do not have a U.S. Social Security number write "N/A".

- **For "6."** be sure to write your date of birth as month/day/year using eight digits (mm/dd/yyyy).

- **For "7."** write the official date your lawful permanent residence began. You can find this date on your Permanent Resident Card (green card.)

- **For "8."** write the name of your country of birth, even if it no longer exists.

- **For "9."** write the country where your passport is from. If you are stateless, write the name of the country where you were last a citizen or national. If you are a citizen or national of more than one country, write the name of the country that issued your last passport.

10. **Are you requesting an accommodation(s) to the naturalization process because of a disability and/or an impairment?** (*See Form N-400 Instructions for accommodation examples*)	☐ Yes ☐ No

If "Yes," check the box(es) below that applies:

☐ Deaf or hard of hearing and need an interpreter who uses the following sign language (e.g., American Sign Language):

☐ Use a wheelchair or other device that assists with mobility.

☐ Blind or low vision.

☐ Require another type of accommodation. (explain):

Question 10 is where you let USCIS know that you will need special accommodations. If you are unable to fully participate in the naturalization process because of a disability, USCIS will make every reasonable effort to ensure special accommodations on a case-by-case basis. Such accommodations may include sending an officer to your house or rest home to interview you if you are housebound. Check the appropriate box to describe the accommodation you need.

11. **Do you have a physical or developmental disability or mental impairment that prevents you from demonstrating your knowledge and understanding of the English language and/or civics requirements for naturalization?**	☐ Yes ☐ No

If "Yes," submit a completed Form N-648, Medical Certification for Disability Exceptions, when you file your Form N-400.

You must be able to speak, read, and write basic English and answer questions about United States government and history, unless you qualify for a medical exemption or an exemption based on your age and longtime permanent residence. The exemption and exceptions are described in Chapter 8.

12.	**Exemptions from the English Language Test**		
A.	Are you **50** years of age or older **and** have you lived in the United States as a Permanent Resident for periods totaling at least **20** years at the time of filing your Form N-400?	☐ Yes	☐ No
B.	Are you **55** years of age or older **and** have you lived in the United States as a Permanent Resident for periods totaling at least **15** years at the time of filing your Form N-400?	☐ Yes	☐ No
C.	Are you **65** years of age or older **and** have you lived in the United States as a Permanent Resident for periods totaling at least **20** years at the time of filing your Form N-400? *(If you meet this requirement, you will also be given a simplified version of the civics test.)*	☐ Yes	☐ No

If you qualify to be interviewed in your native language as discussed in Chapter 8, check the box that corresponds to your age and the length of time you have lived in the United States as a permanent resident. By checking one of these boxes you will be exempt from the English reading and writing requirement but you will still have to pass the civics portion of the exam in your native language. USCIS will provide an interpreter for your interview.

C. Part 3 – Information to Contact You

Part 3. Information to Contact You

1.	**Daytime Phone Number** (___) ___ - ___	2.	**Work Phone Number** *(if any)* (___) ___ - ___	3.	**Evening Phone Number** (___) ___ - ___
4.	**Mobile Phone Number** *(if any)* (___) ___ - ___	5.	**E-mail Address** *(if any)*		

By including your telephone numbers and e-mail address, USCIS can more quickly contact you about your application, though phone contact from the USCIS is rare. If you are hearing impaired and use a TDD telephone connection, indicate this by writing 'TDD' after the telephone number.

D. Part 4 – Information About Your Residence

Part 4. Information About Your Residence

1. **Where have you lived during the last 5 years?** Begin with where you live now and then list every location where you have lived during the last 5 years. **If you need more space, use an additional sheet(s) of paper.**

   Date of Residence   From *(mm/dd/yyyy)* ▶ [ ]   To *(mm/dd/yyyy)* ▶ [Present]

   Street Number and Name [ ]   Apt. ☐ Ste. ☐ Flr. ☐ Number [ ]

   City [ ]   County [ ]   State [▼]   ZIP Code + 4 [ ] - [ ]

   Province or Region *(foreign address only)* [ ]   Country *(foreign address only)* [ ]   Postal Code *(foreign address only)* [ ]

USCIS asks you to list both your home address and your mailing address. Answer this question with your current physical address, regardless of whether you receive mail there. Do not put a post office (P.O.) box number here. If your address includes a space or lot number, enter this information in the "Street Number and Name" field.

If you have been living at a shelter, you do not have to provide that address if it is confidential. Instead, you can provide a different address where you can receive mail OR write that the address is "confidential" and provide only the city and state. If you live at a location that does not have a formal postal address, write the address the best way you can. If you do not know the zip code plus the extra four numbers, leave this space blank.

A. **Mailing Address** *(if different from the address above)*

   C/O *("In Care Of" Name, if applicable)* [ ]

   Street Number and Name [ ]   Apt. ☐ Ste. ☐ Flr. ☐ Number [ ]

   City [ ]   State [▼]   ZIP Code + 4 [ ] - [ ]

   Province or Region *(foreign address only)* [ ]   Country *(foreign address only)* [ ]   Postal Code *(foreign address only)* [ ]

Your mailing address is where USCIS will send your notice to appear for fingerprinting (biometrics) and for the naturalization interview. If your mailing address is the same as your home address, write 'same'. If it is different, write your mailing address. If you think you will be moving while your application is being processed, use the mailing address of a friend or relative. This is important because mail from USCIS will not be forwarded to your new address when you move. Not receiving your mail from USCIS may result in you missing your biometrics and interview appointment notices and having your application denied. If you use the mailing address of a friend or relative, in the "Care of" box write the name of the person who will be receiving the mail for you.

2. Date of Residence   From *(mm/dd/yyyy)* ▶ [   ]   To *(mm/dd/yyyy)* ▶ [   ]

Street Number and Name   Apt. Ste. Flr. Number

[   ]   ☐   ☐   ☐   [   ]

City   County   State   ZIP Code + 4

[   ]   [   ]   [▼]   [   ] - [   ]

Province or Region *(foreign address only)*   Country *(foreign address only)*   Postal Code *(foreign address only)*

[   ]   [   ]   [   ]

Be sure to write your addresses starting with where you live now and going backward. List every address where you have lived during the last five years Note that you do not need to re-write your current address since you already wrote it in Part 4, Section 1. Simply write in the "From" column the date on which you moved to your current address. If you got your green card through marriage, expect USCIS to compare the addresses listed with those on taxes and bank accounts.

If you do not know your additional four digit zip code you may write "0000" in the box. If you need additional space to list all of your residences, attach a separate sheet of paper or use the form on page 87 of this guide. Make sure to sign and date the sheet.

E. Part 5 – Information About Your Parents

Part 5. Information About Your Parents

1. Were your parents married before your 18th birthday? ☐ Yes ☐ No

2. Is your mother a U.S. citizen? ☐ Yes ☐ No

If "Yes," complete the following information.

A. Current Legal Name of U.S. Citizen Mother

Mother's Family Name *(Last Name)*	Mother's Given Name *(First Name)*	Mother's Middle Name *(if applicable)*

B. Mother's Country of Birth   **C. Mother's Date of Birth** *(mm/dd/yyyy)*

	▶

3. Is your father a U.S. citizen? ☐ Yes ☐ No

If "Yes," complete the information below.

A. Current Legal Name of U.S. Citizen Father

Father's Family Name *(Last Name)*	Father's Given Name *(First Name)*	Father's Middle Name *(if applicable)*

B. Father's Country of Birth   **C. Father's Date of Birth** *(mm/dd/yyyy)*

	▶

If one or both of your parents became U.S. citizens before you turned eighteen, you may already be a U.S. citizen. See an authorized immigration law expert if this applies to you.

Complete Part 5. if one or both of your biological or legally adoptive parents is a U.S. Citizen. Check "No" if your mother and father are not U.S. Citizens.

In Part 5, Question 2, Part A, current legal name of U.S. Citizen mother is her name on her birth certificate unless it was changed through marriage or divorce, in which case, it is the name on the marriage certificate or divorce judgment.

In Part 5, Question 3, Part A, current legal name of U.S. Citizen father is the name on his birth certificate unless it was changed through marriage or divorce, in which case, it is the name on the marriage certificate or divorce judgment.

F. Part 6 – Information For Criminal Records Check

USCIS conducts an investigation of each applicant upon filing for naturalization consisting of a criminal and security check. These background and security checks include collecting fingerprints (unless the applicant is seventy-five years or older) and a "name check" from the Federal Bureau of Investigations (FBI).

Part 6. Information for Criminal Records Check

1. **Gender** ☐ Male ☐ Female   2. **Height** Feet ☐ Inches ☐

3. **Ethnicity** *(Select one)*
   ☐ Hispanic or Latino   ☐ Not Hispanic or Latino

4. **Race** *(Select one or more)*
   ☐ White ☐ Asian ☐ Black or African American ☐ American Indian or Alaska Native ☐ Native Hawaiian or Other Pacific Islander

5. **Hair color**
   ☐ Black ☐ Brown ☐ Blonde ☐ Gray ☐ White ☐ Red ☐ Sandy ☐ Bald (No hair)

6. **Eye color**
   ☐ Brown ☐ Blue ☐ Green ☐ Hazel ☐ Gray ☐ Black ☐ Pink ☐ Maroon ☐ Other

---

For each question, check the box or boxes that best describe your natural features. The categories are those used by the FBI. You can select one or more.

The FBI will use the information in this section, together with your fingerprints, to search for criminal records and in some instances, for federal employment or military service. Although the results of this search may affect your eligibility for naturalization, USCIS does not make naturalization decisions based on gender, race, or physical description. If you have had any encounters with the police or other governmental authorities, speak with an authorized immigration law expert before filing a naturalization application.

If you have had any encounters with the police or other government authorities, it might be helpful for you to obtain a copy of your Identity History Summary also known as the FBI RAP sheet detailing your criminal history. See below on how you can obtain a copy of your Identity History Summary. After you obtain it, bring it to an authorized immigration law expert to seek legal advice as to whether your criminal history might lead you to being placed in removal (i.e. deportation) proceedings or lead to other negative consequences if you file an application with the USCIS.

How to Request a Copy of Your Identity History Summary (Also known as "FBI RAP Sheet")

There are two ways to obtain a copy of your Identity History Summary. You can either submit a request directly through the FBI, or you can have a third party "FBI-approved Channeler" obtain it for you. You can also request proof that a record does not exist.

To submit a request to the FBI, you must first complete the "Applicant Information Form." This form is available on the FBI website by visiting **www.fbi.gov**, clicking on "Stats & Services," and selecting "Identity History Summary Checks" See under "How to Request a Copy of Your Record" and click the link "Submit a request directly to the FBI". You will also need to obtain an original rolled-ink set of all ten fingerprints. You can often get your prints taken at a local police station. Mail the completed and signed form, your fingerprints, and an $18 money order or certified check made payable to the "Treasury of the United States" to **FBI CJIS Division – Summary Request, 1000 Custer Hollow Road, Clarksburg, WV 26306.**

Please note that you must enclose $18 for each Identity History Summary that you are requesting.

G. Part 7 – Information About Your Employment and Schools You Attended

Part 7. Information About Your Employment and Schools You Attended

1. Employer or School Name

Street Number and Name · Apt. · Ste. · Flr. · Number

City · State · ZIP Code + 4

Province or Region *(foreign address only)* · Country *(foreign address only)* · Postal Code *(foreign address only)*

Date From *(mm/dd/yyyy)* · Date To *(mm/dd/yyyy)* · Your Occupation

Make sure you list your places of employment or study full-time or part-time starting with your current job/school and going backward, for the last five years. Also include military service, if applicable.

If you worked for yourself, write "self-employed".

If you were not employed over the last five years, write "unemployed," in the box "Your Occupation." Enter "N/A" in all other boxes. You will not be kept from naturalizing just because you were not employed, but the officer may look more closely at how you support yourself to make sure you have not been receiving income from an illegal source. If you are receiving public benefits, that is not a bar to naturalization. You can still become a U.S. citizen, as long as you did not make a misrepresentation that you were a U.S. Citizen or lied to obtain a this benefit.

If you have been employed, USCIS will ask that you present your federal tax returns. Failure to report income may be grounds for denying you U.S. citizenship. Unless you earned so little income that you were not required to pay taxes, USCIS may not naturalize you until you have complied with Internal Revenue Service (IRS) regulations.

.gov For more information about whether you were required to file taxes visit **www.irs.gov/filing**.

If you obtained your permanent residence through employment and you left that employment shortly after becoming a permanent resident, the USCIS officer may ask why you left the job with your sponsor. If you worked only a short period of time for your sponsor after obtaining your permanent residence, talk to an authorized immigration law expert.

If you need additional space to list all of your places of employment and study, attach a separate sheet of paper and provide all the information requested. Make sure to sign and date the sheet.

GETTING NATURALIZED   113

H. Part 8 – Time Outside the United States

Information on trips outside the United States is particularly important. Many people have traveled and or have been absent from the United States. If you have long absences from the United States, or if you have traveled a great deal, USCIS will want to make sure that you meet the continuous residence and physical presence requirements. During your naturalization interview, USCIS might ask you questions about trips outside the United States from before your five (or three) years of continuous residence in the United States even though the naturalization form only asks about the last five years.

If you were outside of the United States for more than one continuous year (365 consecutive days) during the statutory period, you have broken your continuous residence. You must wait until you have accrued the five (or three) years of continuous residence before you can apply for citizenship.

If you were outside of the United States for more than six consecutive months, but less than one year, the USCIS officer will want to know why you were abroad for so long. You must attach additional proof that you did not intend to abandon your residence.

You must have also been physically present in the United States for at least half of the time during the statutory period. That means you must have been physically present at least 913 days in the last five years (or 548 days in the last three years.) The law allows exceptions for some religious workers, seamen, people serving in the military, and people working for the U.S. government abroad.

Part 8. Time Outside the United States

1.	How many **total days (24 hours or longer)** did you spend outside the United States during the last 5 years? [_____] days

Write the total number of days you spent outside of the United States during the last five years (this may be easiest to do once you have completed Part 8, Question 3 of the N-400). Count the days of every trip that lasted 24 hours or longer. Do not count days spent outside of the United States on military service.

2.	How many trips of **24 hours or longer** have you taken outside the United States during the last 5 years? [_____] trips
3.	List below all the trips of **24 hours or longer** that you have taken outside the United States during the last 5 years.
	Begin with your most recent trip and work backwards. **If you need more space, use an additional sheet(s) of paper.**

Date You Left the United States (mm/dd/yyyy)	Date You Returned to the United States (mm/dd/yyyy)	Did Trip Last 6 Months or More?	Countries to Which You Traveled	Total Days Outside the United States
		☐ Yes ☐ No		
		☐ Yes ☐ No		
		☐ Yes ☐ No		
		☐ Yes ☐ No		
		☐ Yes ☐ No		
		☐ Yes ☐ No		

Write the number of trips you have taken outside the United States during the last five years. Count every trip that lasted 24 hours or longer in the last five years (this may be easiest to do once you have completed Part 8, Question 3). Do not count trips taken while on military service.
[Part 8 Question 3 Image]

Make your best effort to provide the requested information for every trip that you have taken outside the United States during the last five years. Begin with your most recent trip and work back in time. Use the stamps in your passport to help you. If you are not sure about the dates or duration of a trip, say so by writing 'approximately'. If you do not know all your trip dates because you travel outside of the United States frequently, attach a separate sheet of paper with a statement explaining where you travel and how often.

Include the estimated number of days you were outside the United States. If you need additional space to list all of your trips, attach a separate sheet of paper and provide all the information requested. Make sure to write the Application Part and question number you are responding to as well as the date, your full name and A number and sign the sheet.

I. Part 9 – Information About Your Marital History

As mentioned before, if you are applying under the three-year rule as the spouse of a U.S. citizen, you must be currently married to and living with your U.S. citizen spouse. If you obtained your permanent residence based on a spousal petition, and you divorced or separated from your spouse shortly after you obtained permanent residence, USCIS may question whether yours was a bona fide (real) marriage, or if it was simply to obtain immigration benefits. The USCIS officer may also be interested in your marital status to make sure you have been honest in applying for public benefits and/or completing tax returns.

Part 9. Information About Your Marital History

1.	What is your current marital status?
	☐ Single, never married ☐ Married ☐ Separated ☐ Divorced ☐ Widowed ☐ Marriage annulled

Select the option that best applies to you.

2.	If you are married, is your spouse a current member of the U.S. Armed Forces?	☐ Yes ☐ No

If your spouse is currently a member of the U.S. Armed Forces indicate "Yes" here.

3.	How many times have you been married *(including annulled marriages and marriage(s) to the same person)*?	
	*If you are single and have **never** been married, indicate "0" and go to **Part 10**.*	

Write the number of times you have been married. Include any annulled marriages. If you were married to the same spouse more than one time, count each time as a separate marriage. If you have never been married indicate it by writing the number "0".

4. **If you are married now, provide the following information about your current spouse.**

A. Legal Name of Current Spouse

Family Name *(Last Name)*	Given Name *(First Name)*	Middle Name *(if applicable)*

B. Previous Legal Name of Current Spouse

Family Name *(Last Name)*	Given Name *(First Name)*	Middle Name *(if applicable)*

C. Other Names Used by Current Spouse *(include nicknames, aliases, and maiden name, if applicable)*

Family Name *(Last Name)*	Given Name *(First Name)*	Middle Name *(if applicable)*

D. Current Spouse's Date of Birth
(mm/dd/yyyy) ▶

E. Date You Entered into Marriage with Current Spouse
(mm/dd/yyyy) ▶

F. Current Spouse's Present Home Address

Street Number and Name

Apt. ☐ Ste. ☐ Flr. ☐ Number

City	County	State ▾	ZIP Code + 4 -

Province or Region *(foreign address only)*	Country *(foreign address only)*	Postal Code *(foreign address only)*

G. Current Spouse's Present Employer

If you have never been married, this section is not applicable to you. Go to Part 10. If you have been married but are not currently married, this part is also not applicable to you, so go to Part 9, Question 9.

If you are now married, provide information about your current spouse. Include this information even if you are separated but not divorced, or if your spouse lives outside of the United States.

5. **Is your current spouse a U.S. citizen?**   ☐ Yes ☐ No

If "Yes," answer **Item Number 6.**
If "No," go to **Item Number 7.**

Check the appropriate box to indicate whether your current spouse is a U.S. citizen.

6. **If your current spouse is a U.S. citizen, complete the following information.**

    A. **When did your current spouse become a U.S. citizen?**

        ☐ At birth - *Go to **Item Number 8.***   ☐ Other - *Complete the following information.*

    B. **Date your current spouse became a U.S. citizen**

        (mm/dd/yyyy) ▶ [_____]

If your spouse is not a U.S. citizen, this section is not applicable to you. Go to Part 9, Question 7. If your spouse is a U.S. citizen through naturalization, give the date of naturalization.

7. **If your current spouse is not a U.S. citizen, complete the following information.**

    A. **Current Spouse's Country of Citizenship or Nationality**   **B.** **Current Spouse's A-Number** *(if applicable)*

    [_____]   ▶ A- [_____]

    C. **Current Spouse's Immigration Status**

        ☐ Permanent Resident   ☐ Other (explain): [_____]

If your spouse is a U.S. citizen, this section is not applicable to you. If your spouse is not a U.S. citizen, complete this section. In Question B, if your spouse does not have an "A" number, write "N/A". In Question C, if your spouse is a permanent resident, check the box that says "Permanent Resident." If your spouse is not a permanent resident, check the box that says "Other" and list his/her status. If your spouse does not have immigration status in the United States, write "N/A" after "Other". Write "Lives Abroad" instead of listing his/her status if your spouse does not live in the United States.

8. How many times has your current spouse been married *(including annulled marriages and marriage(s) to the same person)*? If your current spouse has been married before, provide the following information about your current spouse's prior spouse.

If your current spouse has had more than one previous marriage, use an additional sheet(s) of paper to provide the information requested in Items A. - H. below for each marriage.

A. Prior Spouse's Family Name *(Last Name)*   Given Name *(First Name)*   Middle Name *(if applicable)*

B. Prior Spouse's Immigration Status
☐ U.S. Citizen   ☐ Permanent Resident   ☐ Other (explain):

C. Prior Spouse's Date of Birth
(mm/dd/yyyy) ▶

D. Prior Spouse's Country of Birth

E. Prior Spouse's Country of Citizenship or Nationality

F. Date of Marriage with Prior Spouse
(mm/dd/yyyy) ▶

G. Date Marriage Ended with Prior Spouse
(mm/dd/yyyy) ▶

H. How Marriage Ended with Prior Spouse
☐ Annulled   ☐ Divorced   ☐ Spouse Deceased   ☐ Other (explain):

Information on all prior marriages of the applicant's current spouse is required. If your current spouse was never previously married, then write the number "1" and go to Part 9, Question 9. If your current spouse was previously married, write the number of times and give information about his/her prior spouses. Make your best attempt to contact his/her prior spouse(s), to obtain the necessary information. If the prior spouse(s) cannot be contacted, include as much information as you have. This is especially important if your current spouse obtained immigration benefits from his/her prior spouse.

- **For Question B**, if the prior spouse was not a U.S. citizen or a permanent resident during your spouse's marriage to that individual, check "Other" and list his/her status at the time. If the prior spouse did not live in the United States, write "Lived Abroad" instead of listing his/her status here.

- **For Question H**, if the marriage was otherwise legally terminated, check "other" and explain.

- **For more than one prior marriage of your spouse**, use a separate sheet of paper to provide answers to questions A through H for each marriage and provide all the information requested. Make sure to write the date and sign the sheet. If your spouse was married to the individual more than one time, write about each marriage separately.

9.   If you were married before, provide the following information about your prior spouse. **If you have more than one previous marriage, use an additional sheet(s) of paper to provide the information requested in Items A. - H. below for each marriage.**

A.   **Your Prior Spouse's Family Name** *(Last Name)*   **Given Name** *(First Name)*   **Middle Name** *(if applicable)*

B.   **Your Prior Spouse's Immigration Status When Your Marriage Ended**
☐ U.S. Citizen   ☐ Permanent Resident   ☐ Other (explain):

C.   **Your Prior Spouse's Date of Birth**
(mm/dd/yyyy) ▶   D.   **Your Prior Spouse's Country of Birth**

E.   **Your Prior Spouse's Country of Citizenship or Nationality**

F.   **Date of Marriage with Your Prior Spouse**
(mm/dd/yyyy) ▶   G.   **Date Marriage Ended with Your Prior Spouse**
(mm/dd/yyyy) ▶

H.   **How Marriage Ended with Your Prior Spouse**
☐ Annulled   ☐ Divorced   ☐ Spouse Deceased   ☐ Other (explain):

Information on all prior spouses of the applicant is required. If you were never married before, this section is not applicable to you. Go to 10. If you were married before or are a widow/widower, give information about your former spouse(s). Make your best attempt to contact your prior spouse(s), if necessary, to obtain this information. If your prior spouse(s) cannot be contacted, include as much information as you have.

- **For Question B**, if your prior spouse was not a U.S. citizen or a permanent resident during your marriage, check "Other" and list his/her status. If your prior spouse did not have an Immigration Status when your marriage ended, check "other" and write "N/A" in the space provided. If the prior spouse did not live in the United States, write "Lived Abroad" instead of listing his/her status here.

- **For Question H**, if the marriage was otherwise legally terminated, check "other" and explain.

- **For more than one prior marriage**, use a separate sheet of paper to provide answers to questions A through H for each marriage and provide all the information requested. Make sure to write the date and sign the sheet. If you were married to the same spouse more than one time, write about each marriage separately.

J. Part 10 – Information About Your Children

Part 10. Information About Your Children

---

1. **Indicate your total number of children.** (*All children should be indicated, including: A. Children who are alive, missing, deceased; B. Children born in the United States or in other countries; C. Children under 18 years of age or older; D. Children who are currently married or unmarried; E. Children living with you or elsewhere; F. Current stepchildren; G. Legally adopted children; and H. Children born when you were not married.*)

Count all sons and daughters alive, missing, deceased, adopted or stepchildren, even if they are U.S. citizens, adults, born out of wedlock, born outside the United States, or live outside the United States. This is not an application for them; USCIS is simply requesting information about them. This information may assist USCIS in determining matters of good moral character and your obligation to pay child support. Be prepared to show evidence that you support your children who are minors especially if they reside apart from you. If you file a petition for your child in the future, USCIS will want to see that you claimed the child as your own at the time you applied for citizenship. Failure to answer this question accurately may lead to problems later.

 NOTE: Children of an applicant for naturalization may automatically derive (obtain) citizenship through that parent when the parent naturalizes. The child must be a permanent resident, unmarried, under eighteen years of age at the time that the parent naturalizes, and living in the United States in that parent's legal and physical custody. Speak with an authorized immigration law expert if you think that your child may receive this benefit when you naturalize. The expert can assist you with identifying the documents you will need to prove that your child has derived citizenship.

---

2. Provide the following information about **all your children** *(sons and daughters)* **listed in Item Number 1.**, regardless of age. Use an additional sheet(s) of paper to list any additional children.

A.1. Child's Current Legal Name

Family Name *(Last Name)*   Given Name *(First Name)*   Middle Name *(if applicable)*

A.2. Child's A-Number *(if applicable)*   **A.3. Child's Date of Birth**

▶ A-   *(mm/dd/yyyy)* ▶

A.4. Child's Country of Birth

A.5. Child's Current Address

Street Number and Name   Apt. Ste. Flr. Number

City   County   State   ZIP Code + 4

Province or Region *(foreign address only)*   Country *(foreign address only)*   Postal Code *(foreign address only)*

A.6. What is your child's relationship to you? *(e.g., biological child, stepchild, legally adopted child)*

Provide all of the requested information for each son and daughter alive, missing, deceased, adopted or stepchild, even if they are U.S. citizens, adults, or live outside the United States. Failure to answer these questions accurately may lead to problems later.

In question A5, titled "Child's Current Address," write: "With me" - if the son or daughter is currently living with you. If your children are not living with you then write the address including state and county where they are currently living. If the son or daughter is not currently living with you but is missing or deceased indicate such by writing 'Missing' or 'Deceased'. If you need space to list additional sons and daughters, attach a separate sheet of paper and provide all the information requested. Make sure to write the date and sign the sheet.

K. Part 11 – Additional Information

In order for you to be naturalized, you must be a person of good moral character and you must be committed to the principles of the United States. Part 11 is designed to help USCIS determine whether you meet these criteria. Answer these questions carefully. If any part of a question applies to you, you must answer 'Yes'. If you answer 'Yes', make sure that you consult an authorized immigration law expert before you submit your naturalization application. You will need to attach your written explanation and any additional information or documentation that helps explain your answer. Your 'Yes' answer may negatively affect your eligibility for citizenship.

! Do not lie. USCIS takes the position that if you make a statement that is not true, even if it is meaningless, it is grounds for denying your application.

Part 11. Additional Information

1.	Have you **ever** claimed to be a U.S. citizen *(in writing or any other way)*?	☐ Yes ☐ No
2.	Have you **ever** registered to vote in any Federal, State, or local election in the United States?	☐ Yes ☐ No
3.	Have you **ever** voted in any Federal, State, or local election in the United States?	☐ Yes ☐ No

These questions are designed to determine whether you have ever made a false claim to U.S. citizenship or improperly registered for or voted in an election. Only U.S. citizens can register to vote and vote in national and local elections in the United States. Making a false claim to U.S. citizenship by voting in such an election, or even by filling out a voter registration card, can make you deportable. Speak with an authorized immigration law expert if this applies to you.

In some cities, even undocumented immigrants can vote in school board and community elections. If a local law allowed you to vote in a particular election, your having voted in that election will not make you deportable and will not affect your ability to naturalize.

4.	Do you now have, or did you **ever** have, a hereditary title or an order of nobility in any foreign country?	☐ Yes ☐ No

A title of nobility is considered inconsistent with U.S. citizenship. If you hold a title of nobility, you must renounce the title before becoming a citizen.

5.	Have you **ever** been declared legally incompetent, or been confined to a mental institution?	☐ Yes ☐ No

USCIS asks if you have been ever declared legally incompetent or confined to a mental institution to decide whether you are capable of understanding the Oath of Allegiance to the United States. In 2000, a law went into effect allowing USCIS to waive the oath requirement for applicants who are mentally impaired or physically disabled. Answering 'Yes' to this question will not bar you from naturalizing.

6.	Do you owe any overdue Federal, State, or local taxes?	☐ Yes ☐ No

Owing taxes is not an absolute bar to becoming a U.S. citizen; it is a factor that may be taken into consideration by the USCIS officer. If you do owe taxes, at the interview USCIS will want to see (1) a signed agreement from the Internal Revenue Service (IRS) showing that you have filed a tax return and arranged to pay the taxes you owe, and (2) documentation from the IRS showing the current status of your repayment program.

7.	**A.** Have you **ever** not filed a Federal, State, or local tax return since you became a Permanent Resident?	☐ Yes ☐ No
	B. If *"Yes,"* did you consider yourself to be a "non-U.S. resident"?	☐ Yes ☐ No
8.	Have you called yourself a "non-U.S. resident" on a Federal, State, or local tax return since you became a Permanent Resident?	☐ Yes ☐ No

If you were required to file a federal tax return but failed to do so, your naturalization application may be denied. Many people are not required to file tax returns because their income is less than the amount for which filing is required. For more information about whether this applies to you, visit www.irs.gov/filing. Do not be afraid to answer 'Yes' to Question 7A if you did not file tax returns because you were not required to. You must provide a written explanation with your application.

NOTE: Usually USCIS asks you to bring to your interview tax returns from the statutory five (or three) year period, or they will want to know why you did not file tax returns.

If you answer 'Yes' to either Question 7B or 8, you may be ineligible for naturalization because calling yourself a "non-U.S. resident" after becoming a Legal Permanent Resident can be considered abandoning your permanent residence. Speak with an authorized immigration law expert if this applies to you.

9. A. Have you **ever** been a member of, involved in, or in any way associated with, any organization, association, fund, foundation, party, club, society, or similar group in the United States or in any other location in the world? ☐ Yes ☐ No

    B. If *"Yes,"* provide the information below. **If you need more space, attach the names of the other group(s) on an additional sheet(s) of paper and provide any evidence to support your answer.**

Name of Group	Purpose of the Group	Dates of Membership	
		From *(mm/dd/yyyy)*	To *(mm/dd/yyyy)*

If you do not have any of the affiliations mentioned in Question 9A, you should answer "No." If that is not the case, answer "Yes" and in Question 9B list the names of the organizations that you have ever been a member of or associated with, including religious, social, and athletic clubs. List the purpose of each group and the dates of membership or association with each group. This question is designed to help USCIS determine whether you are ineligible for naturalization because of certain political activities, such as membership in communist or pro-communist organizations.

10. Have you **ever** been a member of, or in any way associated *(either directly or indirectly)* with:
    A. The Communist Party? ☐ Yes ☐ No
    B. Any other totalitarian party? ☐ Yes ☐ No
    C. A terrorist organization? ☐ Yes ☐ No

Having been associated with a communist or totalitarian party or terrorist organization may affect your ability to naturalize. Speak with an authorized immigration law expert if you answer "Yes" to any of these questions.

11. Have you **ever** advocated *(either directly or indirectly)* the overthrow of any government by force or violence? ☐ Yes ☐ No

Having ever advocated the overthrow of a government may affect your ability to naturalize. Speak with an authorized immigration law expert if you answer "Yes" to this question.

12. Have you **ever** persecuted *(either directly or indirectly)* any person because of race, religion, national origin, membership in a particular social group, or political opinion? ☐ Yes ☐ No

Persecutors are generally not eligible for admission as permanent residents. Answering "Yes" to this question may lead USCIS to question if your permanent residence was obtained by fraud. Speak with an authorized immigration law expert if you answer 'yes' to this question.

13. Between March 23, 1933 and May 8, 1945, did you work for or associate in any way *(either directly or indirectly)* with:

    A. The Nazi government of Germany? ☐ Yes ☐ No

    B. Any government in any area (1) occupied by, (2) allied with, or (3) established with the help of the Nazi government of Germany? ☐ Yes ☐ No

    C. Any German, Nazi, or S.S. military unit, paramilitary unit, self-defense unit, vigilante unit, citizen unit, police unit, government agency or office, extermination camp, concentration camp, prisoner of war camp, prison, labor camp, or transit camp? ☐ Yes ☐ No

Former Nazis may not naturalize no matter how much time has elapsed since party membership. They are permanently barred from demonstrating good moral character required for naturalization. Responding falsely to these particular questions can also lead to your naturalization being revoked (this is called "denaturalization").

14. Were you **ever** involved in any way with any of the following:

    A. Genocide? ☐ Yes ☐ No

    B. Torture? ☐ Yes ☐ No

    C. Killing, or trying to kill, someone? ☐ Yes ☐ No

    D. Badly hurting, or trying to hurt, a person on purpose? ☐ Yes ☐ No

    E. Forcing, or trying to force, someone to have any kind of sexual contact or relations? ☐ Yes ☐ No

    F. Not letting someone practice his or her religion? ☐ Yes ☐ No

If you are the victim of one of the crimes listed in 14 A-F, you can answer "No." If you committed one of the acts listed in 14 A-F, then you must answer "Yes." You must also answer "Yes" if any action you took, even if under duress, contributed or enabled another person to carry out these acts against others. Acting under duress means being pressured or forced to act against your will. If you respond "yes" to this question, you must submit a written explanation with your application.

People who have ever engaged in genocide, torture, extrajudicial killing are generally not admissible as permanent residents and are permanently barred from demonstrating good moral character required for naturalization. If you lie on the naturalization application about your involvement with this activity and the government discovers your involvement, it can be a basis for the government to take away your U.S. citizenship (denaturalization) and deport you.

If you have ever tried to hurt or kill another person or have badly hurt or killed another person, then you might be prevented from demonstrating good moral character for naturalization and you might be deportable. Please speak with an authorized immigration law expert.

If you ever either forced or tried to force someone to have any kind of sexual contact or sexual relations (e.g., molestation, attempted rape, rape, etc.), then you might be deportable. Speak with an authorized immigration law expert.

Certain people who have ever engaged in severe violations of religious freedom are not admissible as permanent residents and are permanently barred from demonstrating good moral character required for naturalization. Not letting someone practice his/her religion might occur when a person persecutes or tortures another person (or threatens to do so) because of her or his religious beliefs.

If you lie on the naturalization application about your involvement with this activity and the government discovers your involvement, it can be a basis for the government to take away your U.S. citizenship (i.e., denaturalization) and deport you.

15. Were you **ever** a member of, or did you **ever** serve in, help, or otherwise participate in, any of the following groups:

The government wants to prevent people, who have engaged in acts of genocide, terrorism, torture and other prohibited conduct, from obtaining U.S. citizenship. Toward that end, the USCIS asks the above questions to determine whether you have been involved with any groups that have been involved in genocide, terrorism, torture, or other prohibited conduct.

Being a member of, or serving in, or helping, or otherwise participating in one of the groups listed in Question 15A through 15I does not automatically mean that you will be denied naturalization. Speak with an immigration law expert if you answer 'yes' to these questions.

There are legitimate reasons for serving in the military or in the police, such as compulsory military service requirements in some countries. If you respond "yes" to any of the questions asked in 15A through 15I, then you must provide with your application a written explanation of your involvement with the group.

A. Military unit?   ☐ Yes ☐ No

If you have ever been a member of a military unit, or ever served in a military unit, or ever helped or participated in a military unit, then you must respond "yes" to Question 15A and provide with your naturalization application a written explanation about your involvement. Common examples of membership in a military unit include serving in the army, navy, air force, marines, national guard, or coast guard.

B. Paramilitary unit? *(a group of people who act like a military group but are not part of the official military)*   ☐ Yes ☐ No

If you have ever been a member of a paramilitary unit, or ever served in a paramilitary unit, or ever helped or participated in a paramilitary unit, then you must respond "yes" to Question 15B and provide with the naturalization application a written explanation of your involvement. A paramilitary unit is a group of people who act like a military group but are not part of the official military. A paramilitary group is often structured like the military, but is not authorized by the government. It is made up of private individuals who come together on a voluntary basis.

C. Police unit?   ☐ Yes ☐ No

If you have ever been a member of a police unit, or ever served in a police unit, or ever helped or participated in a police unit, then you must respond "yes" to Question 15C and provide with your naturalization application a written explanation of your involvement. Common examples of a police unit include serving in the state police, the local police, the sheriff's or constable's office.

D.   Self-defense unit?   ☐ Yes ☐ No

If you have ever been a member of a self-defense unit, or ever served in a self-defense unit, or ever helped or participated in a self-defense unit, then you must respond "yes" to Question 15D and provide with your naturalization application a written explanation of your involvement. A self-defense unit is formed by private individuals who are acting without authority of the government and who are responding to crime or violence occurring in their communities. The self-defense unit is usually formed to help defend the community from the crime or violence.

E.   Vigilante unit? *(a group of people who act like the police, but are not part of the official police)*   ☐ Yes ☐ No

If you have ever been a member of a vigilante unit, or ever served in a vigilante unit, or ever helped or participated in a vigilante unit, then you must respond "Yes" to Question 15E and provide with your naturalization application a written explanation of your involvement. A vigilante unit is a group of people who act like the police, but are not part of the official police. People who take the law into their own hands without the authority of the government are acting as vigilantes.

F.   Rebel group?   ☐ Yes ☐ No

If you have ever been a member of a rebel group, or ever served in a rebel group, or ever helped or participated in a rebel group, then you must respond "yes" to Question 15F and provide with your naturalization application a written explanation of your involvement. Rebel groups are individuals who voluntarily associate through their common opposition and resistance to authority, usually the government.

G.   Guerrilla group? *(a group of people who use weapons against or otherwise physically attack the military, police, government, or other people)*   ☐ Yes ☐ No

If you have ever been a member of a guerrilla group, or ever served in a guerrilla group, or ever helped or participated in a guerrilla group, then you must respond "Yes" to Question 15G and provide with your naturalization application a written explanation of your involvement. Guerrilla groups are a group of people who use weapons against or otherwise physically attack the military, police, government, or other people.

H.   Militia? *(an army of people, not part of the official military)*   ☐ Yes ☐ No

If you have ever been a member of a militia, or ever served in a militia, or ever helped or participated in a militia, then you must respond "yes" to Question 15H and provide with your naturalization application a written explanation of your involvement. A militia is an army of people who are not part of the official military of a country.

I. Insurgent organization? *(a group that uses weapons and fights against a government)*	☐ Yes ☐ No

If you have ever been a member of an insurgent organization, or ever served in an insurgent organization, or ever helped or participated in an insurgent organization, then you must respond "yes" to Question 15-I and provide with your naturalization application a written explanation of your involvement. An insurgent organization is a group that uses weapons and fights against a government.

16. Were you **ever** a worker, volunteer, or soldier, or did you otherwise **ever** serve in any of the following:	
A. Prison or jail?	☐ Yes ☐ No
B. Prison camp?	☐ Yes ☐ No
C. Detention facility? *(a place where people are forced to stay)*	☐ Yes ☐ No
D. Labor camp? *(a place where people are forced to work)*	☐ Yes ☐ No
E. Any other place where people were forced to stay?	☐ Yes ☐ No

Questions 16A through 16E look to identify people who worked at detention facilities where human rights violations occurred. If you worked at a detention facility where human rights violations occurred, the government may investigate your application further to see whether you were involved in the human rights violations, such as forced labor. If you were involved in human rights violations or other illegal activity while working at or serving in one of the facilities mentioned above, then you might be prevented from demonstrating good moral character required for naturalization and you might be deportable. Please speak to an authorized immigration law expert if you were involved in such activity.

If you have ever worked at or served in a prison, jail, prison camp, detention facility, labor camp, or any other place where people were forced to stay, then you must answer "yes" to question 16 as applicable and you must provide a written explanation of your work and service with your application.

It is not against the law to work at or serve in a prison, jail, or detention facility. Therefore, answering "Yes" to questions 16A through 16E does not automatically mean that you will be denied naturalization and placed in deportation (removal) proceedings.

17. Were you **ever** a part of any group, or did you **ever** help any group, unit, or organization that used a weapon against any person, or threatened to do so?	☐ Yes ☐ No
A. If *"Yes,"* when you were part of this group, or when you helped this group, did you ever use a weapon against another person?	☐ Yes ☐ No
B. If *"Yes,"* when you were part of this group, or when you helped this group, did you ever tell another person that you would use a weapon against that person?	☐ Yes ☐ No

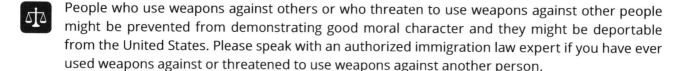

People who use weapons against others or who threaten to use weapons against other people might be prevented from demonstrating good moral character and they might be deportable from the United States. Please speak with an authorized immigration law expert if you have ever used weapons against or threatened to use weapons against another person.

18.	Did you **ever** sell, give, or provide weapons to any person, or help another person sell, give, or provide weapons to any person?	☐ Yes ☐ No
	A. If *"Yes,"* did you know that this person was going to use the weapons against another person?	☐ Yes ☐ No
	B. If *"Yes,"* did you know that this person was going to sell or give the weapons to someone who was going to use them against another person?	☐ Yes ☐ No

If you ever sold, gave, or provided weapons to any person or you ever helped another person to sell, give, or provide weapons to another person, then you must respond "yes" to Question 18. The government is looking to prevent people, who were or are involved in the unlawful sale or trade in weapons, from naturalizing. If you were lawfully engaged in this activity, respond "Yes" to Question 18 and provide an explanation of your activity. If you knew that the person to whom you gave, sold, or provided the weapons was going to use them against another person or was going to give them to another person to use against another person, then you might not be able to demonstrate good moral character and depending on the circumstance you might be deportable. Please speak with an authorized immigration law expert if you engaged in this activity.

- **If you responded "no" to Question 18**, leave Questions 18A and 18B blank.

- **If you responded "yes" to Question 18**, then you must answer Questions 18A and 18B.

| 19. | Did you **ever** receive any type of military, paramilitary *(a group of people who act like a military group but are not part of the official military)*, or weapons training? | ☐ Yes ☐ No |

If you ever received any type of military or paramilitary or weapons training, then respond "yes" to Question 19. Paramilitary refers to a group of people who act like a military group but are not part of the official military.

The government is looking for people who were or are involved in terrorist activity. It is not automatically against the law to have received military, paramilitary, or weapons training. If you have received military, paramilitary, or weapons training, then provide an explanation of this training with your naturalization application.

| 20. | Did you **ever** recruit *(ask)*, enlist *(sign up)*, conscript *(require)*, or use any person under age 15 to serve in or help an armed force or group? | ☐ Yes ☐ No |
| 21. | Did you **ever** use any person under age 15 to do anything that helped or supported people in combat? | ☐ Yes ☐ No |

 If you ever asked, signed-up, required, or used any person under the age of fifteen to serve in or help an armed force or group or ever used any person under the age of fifteen to help or support people in combat, then you might be deportable from the United States for recruiting or using child soldiers. Please speak with an authorized immigration law expert if you have engaged in this activity.

22.	Have you **ever** committed, assisted in committing, or attempted to commit, a crime or offense for which you were **not** arrested?	☐ Yes ☐ No

23.	Have you **ever** been arrested, cited, or detained by any law enforcement officer *(including any and all immigration officials or the U.S. Armed Forces)* for any reason?	☐ Yes ☐ No

24.	Have you **ever** been charged with committing, attempting to commit, or assisting in committing a crime or offense?	☐ Yes ☐ No

25.	Have you **ever** been convicted of a crime or offense?	☐ Yes ☐ No

26.	Have you **ever** been placed in an alternative sentencing or a rehabilitative program *(e.g., diversion, deferred prosecution, withheld adjudication, deferred adjudication)*?	☐ Yes ☐ No

27.	A. Have you **ever** received a suspended sentence, been placed on probation, or been paroled?	☐ Yes ☐ No
	B. If *"Yes,"* have you completed the probation or parole?	☐ Yes ☐ No

28.	A. Have you **ever** been in jail or prison?	☐ Yes ☐ No
	B. If *"Yes,"* how long were you in jail or prison? Years [ ] Months [ ] Days [ ]	

29. If you answered *"Yes"* to **Item Numbers 23. - 28.**, complete the following table. **If you need more space, use an additional sheet(s) of paper and provide any evidence to support your answer.** If you answered *"No"* to *all* **Item Numbers 23. - 28.**, go to **Item Number 30.**

Why were you arrested, cited, detained, or charged?	Date arrested, cited, detained, or charged. *(mm/dd/yyyy)*	Where were you arrested, cited, detained, or charged? *(City, State, Country)*	Outcome or disposition of the arrest, citation, detention or charge *(no charges filed, charges dismissed, jail, probation, etc.)*

If you have ever committed certain criminal acts, even if you were never convicted of a crime, you might be ineligible for naturalization. Talk to an authorized immigration law expert if you have criminal history.

For Question 28.B, if you were detained in jail for less than 24 hours, write "1" in the "Days" field. On a separate sheet of paper, write an explanation that includes the actual number of hours you were detained.

USCIS takes the position that if you were arrested and never charged with a crime, or if your record was entirely expunged, sealed, or otherwise cleared, you must still answer "Yes" to the relevant questions on the application even if you were told otherwise by a judge, law enforcement officer, or attorney. If you answer "yes" to any question, you must provide a written explanation as well as any evidence to support your answer with your application. Refer to the definitions on the next page to help you answer the questions in this section.

- **Being cited** means to be notified of legal proceedings against one and be required to appear.
- **Detained** means to be kept in police custody.
- **Charged** means to have a legal statement made against one listing the crime of which one is accused.
- **Convicted** means to be found guilty of, or pled guilty to the crime charged.
- **Alternative sentencing** is a collection of programs in which individuals may participate as an alternative to serving time in jail.
- **Suspended sentence** is when an individual convicted of a crime is given a sentence in which execution has been or is withheld by the court if the defendant performs certain services.
- **Probation** is when an individual found guilty of a crime is released by the court without imprisonment and subject to conditions imposed by the court, under the supervision of a probation officer. Violation of probation terms will usually result in the person being sent to jail for the term he/she would have served without probation.
- **Parole** is the conditional release of a convicted criminal after he/she has completed part of his/her prison sentence and demonstrated good conduct. The criminal receiving parole can serve the remainder of the term outside the prison if he/she complies with the terms and conditions connected with his/her release.

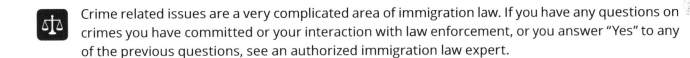 Crime related issues are a very complicated area of immigration law. If you have any questions on crimes you have committed or your interaction with law enforcement, or you answer "Yes" to any of the previous questions, see an authorized immigration law expert.

> Answer **Item Numbers 30. - 46. If you answer _"Yes"_ to any of these questions, except Item Numbers 37. and 38.**, include a written explanation on an additional sheet(s) of paper and provide any evidence to support your answer.

If you answer "yes" to any items from Questions 30 through 46 (except questions 37 and 38), you might not be able to prove good moral character required for naturalization. USCIS might deny your naturalization application. If you answer "yes" to any of these questions, provide a written explanation and provide any evidence to support your answer.

! **If the act occurred prior to the statutory five (or three) year period, you may still be able to show good moral character.**

30.	Have you **ever**:	
	A. Been a habitual drunkard?	☐ Yes ☐ No

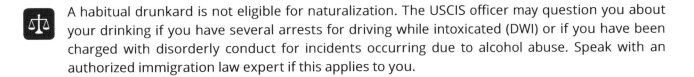 A habitual drunkard is not eligible for naturalization. The USCIS officer may question you about your drinking if you have several arrests for driving while intoxicated (DWI) or if you have been charged with disorderly conduct for incidents occurring due to alcohol abuse. Speak with an authorized immigration law expert if this applies to you.

B. Been a prostitute, or procured anyone for prostitution? ☐ Yes ☐ No

Having been convicted of a single act of prostitution will not necessarily make a person ineligible for naturalization. However, a person with prostitution arrests may be ineligible to naturalize if the events occurred during the three or five year continuous residence period needed to naturalize. Procuring a person for prostitution refers to providing a prostitute's services to others, such as owning a brothel or "pimping." Soliciting a prostitute for personal services is not procuring. If you were arrested for soliciting you need not answer "yes" to this question.

C. Sold or smuggled controlled substances, illegal drugs, or narcotics? ☐ Yes ☐ No

Selling or smuggling controlled substances may make a person removable/deportable and therefore, ineligible for naturalization. Talk to an authorized immigration law expert if this applies to you.

D. Been married to more than one person at the same time? ☐ Yes ☐ No

This question seeks to identify individuals who practice or advocate polygamy. USCIS takes the position that a person who has practiced polygamy in the past is barred from establishing good moral character. Still, if you have practiced polygamy in the past outside the United States and you did not come to the United States to practice or advocate polygamy, you might qualify for naturalization. Talk to an authorized immigration law expert if this applies to you.

E. Married someone in order to obtain an immigration benefit? ☐ Yes ☐ No

Marrying someone in order to obtain a green card is a deportable offense. When you apply for naturalization, USCIS will review your entire immigration history to see how you obtained your green card. If they determine that you received your green card through a marriage that was not "bona fide" or real, USCIS will deny your naturalization application and initiate removal (deportation) proceedings against you.

F. Helped anyone to enter, or try to enter, the United States illegally? ☐ Yes ☐ No

Even without a conviction, you may be barred from naturalizing if you helped smuggle someone into the United States. An example of smuggling is paying someone, such as a coyote, to smuggle a family member across the U.S.-Mexican border.

G. Gambled illegally or received income from illegal gambling? ☐ Yes ☐ No

Gambling illegally may make you ineligible for naturalization. This clearly does not apply to a person involved in legal gambling activities, such as an employee at a Las Vegas casino. Nor should you be barred from naturalizing simply because you were convicted of a single act of illegal gambling, though that act must have occurred prior to the statutory five (or three) year period.

H. Failed to support your dependents or to pay alimony?	☐ Yes ☐ No

Failure to support your dependents or to pay alimony may make you ineligible for naturalization. If you have children who are not living with you or a spouse who is not living with you, be prepared to answer questions as to whether you are required to support them and whether you are doing so. Particularly, if you have children who are not living with you, be prepared to establish to the satisfaction of the USCIS officer that you are contributing to the support of your children. If you are not required to support your children, you will need to prove that to the officer with sufficient documentation.

I. Made any misrepresentation to obtain any public benefit in the United States?	☐ Yes ☐ No

If you lied, including providing false information or false documentation, or omitted information in order to obtain any public benefit in the United States regardless of whether you intended to misrepresent yourself, answer "Yes" and provide a written explanation on a separate sheet of paper. If you respond "Yes" to this question, and the misrepresentation occurred in the five year statutory period (or three years if you are applying under the special rules for the spouse of a U.S. citizen), you might not be able to demonstrate good moral character required for naturalization.

Some common examples of public benefits are Medicaid, food stamps, Supplemental Security Income (SSI), and cash assistance. If you answer "Yes" to this question, speak with an authorized immigration law expert.

31. Have you **ever** given any U.S. Government official(s) **any** information or documentation that was false, fraudulent, or misleading?	☐ Yes ☐ No

Certain false statements or false documents made/submitted to any United States government official might make you removable/deportable (which may result in the government trying to take away your permanent resident status). Other false statements or false documentation might prevent you from establishing good moral character and might be only a temporary bar to naturalization. If you answer 'Yes' to this question, speak with an authorized immigration law expert.

NOTE: If the false statements were made prior to getting permanent residence and INS (Immigration and Naturalization Service) or USCIS were aware of these facts, the false statement or documentation should not be a bar to naturalization.

32. Have you **ever** lied to any U.S. Government official to gain entry or admission into the United States or to gain immigration benefits while in the United States?	☐ Yes ☐ No

This question is seeking information that will make you ineligible under the same rules that apply to Question 31 above and can also make you removable (deportable).

NOTE: If the false statements were made prior to getting permanent residence and INS or USCIS were aware of these facts, the false statement should not be a bar to naturalization.

33.	Have you **ever** been removed, excluded, or deported from the United States?	☐ Yes ☐ No
34.	Have you **ever** been ordered removed, excluded, or deported from the United States?	☐ Yes ☐ No
35.	Have you **ever** been placed in removal, exclusion, rescission, or deportation proceedings?	☐ Yes ☐ No
36.	Are removal, exclusion, rescission, or deportation proceedings *(including administratively closed proceedings)* **currently** pending against you?	☐ Yes ☐ No

If you are presently in removal proceedings, USCIS will put off a decision on your naturalization application until an immigration judge decides your case. If you were ordered removed, excluded or deported from the United States before getting permanent residence and INS or USCIS were aware of these facts, this should not be a bar for naturalization. If you answer "Yes" to any of the questions in this section, speak with an immigration law expert. Refer to the definitions below to help you answer the questions:

- **Removal proceedings** are initiated by a Notice to Appear. This occurs when the Department of Homeland Security (DHS), formerly known as the Immigration and Naturalization Service (INS), believes that an individual is inadmissible (cannot be allowed entry) to the United States, or entered the country illegally, or entered the country legally but then violated conditions of his/her visa.

- **Exclusion proceedings** occurred prior to April 1, 1997 and were initiated with a Form I-122, Notice To Applicant for Admission Detained for Hearing Before Immigration Judge.

- **Rescission proceedings** are started by a Notice of Intent to Rescind issued by DHS. This occurs when, within five years of granting adjustment of status, DHS discovers that the individual was not entitled to permanent residence status when it was granted.

- **Deportation proceedings** occurred prior to April 1, 1997 and were initiated by an Order to Show Cause. This type of proceeding occurred when INS believed that an individual entered the country illegally or entered the country legally but then violated conditions of his/her visa.

37.	Have you **ever** served in the U.S. Armed Forces?	☐ Yes ☐ No

If you served in the U.S. Armed Forces, USCIS will check your Armed Services records as part of their investigation into your background and character. You will need to submit Form N-426, Request for Certification of Military or Naval Service with your naturalization application. There is no extra fee for these forms. For further assistance, contact the Military Helpline at **1-877-CIS-4MIL (1-877-247-4645)** or visit **www.uscis.gov/military**.

38.	Are you **currently** a member of the U.S. Armed Forces?	☐ Yes ☐ No
39.	If you are **currently** a member of the U.S. Armed Forces, are you scheduled to deploy overseas, including to a vessel, within the next 3 months? *(Refer to the* **Address Change** *section within the Form N-400 Instructions on how to notify USCIS if you learn of your deployment plans after you file your Form N-400.)*	☐ Yes ☐ No
40.	If you are **currently** a member of the U.S. Armed Forces, are you **currently** stationed overseas?	☐ Yes ☐ No

There are special naturalization provisions for people who are currently on active duty in the U.S. armed forces even if serving overseas. Speak with an authorized immigration law expert if this applies to you.

41.	Have you **ever** been court-martialed, administratively separated, or disciplined, or have you received an other than honorable discharge, while in the U.S. Armed Forces?	☐ Yes ☐ No

There are special naturalization provisions for people who served honorably in the U.S. armed forces. The USCIS will look to see if you separated from the U.S. armed forces through other than an honorable discharge.

42.	Have you **ever** been discharged from training or service in the U.S. Armed Forces because you were an alien?	☐ Yes ☐ No

If you obtained a discharge from training or service in the U.S. armed forces because you were a foreign national, then you might be barred from applying for U.S. citizenship.

43.	Have you **ever** left the United States to avoid being drafted in the U.S. Armed Forces?	☐ Yes ☐ No

People who left the United States to avoid being drafted into the U.S. Armed Forces are permanently barred from naturalizing. However there are a number of exceptions. For example, Vietnam War era "draft dodgers" may naturalize because of a pardon granted by U.S. President Jimmy Carter. The pardon benefits men who left the country to avoid being drafted into the U.S. Armed Forces between August 4, 1964, and March 28, 1973. This is a complicated area of immigration law. If you answer "Yes" to this question, speak with an authorized immigration law expert.

44.	Have you **ever** applied for any kind of exemption from military service in the U.S. Armed Forces?	☐ Yes ☐ No

Men who applied for an exemption from military service based on being a non-citizen (alienage) may be permanently barred from naturalizing. Applying for an exemption is not the same as making a claim for conscientious objector status. This is a complicated area of immigration law. If you answer "Yes" to this question, speak with an authorized immigration law expert.

45. Have you **ever** deserted from the U.S. Armed Forces? ☐ Yes ☐ No

 To desert means to be absent without leave from the military for longer than thirty days. Wartime deserters may be permanently barred from naturalization. However some exceptions exist. Military deserters from the Vietnam era, between August 4, 1964, and March 28, 1973, may naturalize because of a pardon granted by U.S. President Jimmy Carter. This is a complicated area of immigration law. If you answer "Yes" to this question, speak with an authorized immigration law expert.

46. **A.** Are you a male who lived in the United States at any time between your 18th and 26th birthdays? ☐ Yes ☐ No
(This does not include living in the United States as a lawful nonimmigrant.)

B. If *"Yes,"* when did you register for the Selective Service? Provide the information below.

Date Registered *(mm/dd/yyyy)* ▶ [ ]   Selective Service Number [ ]

C. If *"Yes,"* but you **did not register** with the Selective Service System and you are:

1. Still under 26 years of age, you must register before you apply for naturalization, and complete the Selective Service information above; **OR**

2. Now 26 years of age or older but you did not register with the Selective Service, you must attach a statement explaining why you did not register, and a status information letter from the Selective Service.

Males living in the United States who have reached their eighteenth birthday but not yet reached their twenty-sixth birthday must register with the Selective Service System. This includes undocumented individuals, permanent residents, and citizens. The requirement ends once the applicant reaches the age of twenty-six. The registration requirement does not apply to men here in lawful nonimmigrant status, such as F-1 student or H-1B temporary worker.

If you registered with the Selective Service System, but you do not know your registration number, you can get your number online or by calling or writing to Selective Service. Call their toll-free number at **847-688-6888** or check their website at **www.sss.gov**. Be sure to have your date of birth and Social Security number on hand. To reach a Selective Service representative, call **847-688-6888**. To find out your registration number, write to the **National Archives and Records Administration, Attn: Archival Programs, P.O. Box 28989, St. Louis, MO 63132-0989**. Men born between March 29, 1957 and December 31, 1959 will not have Selective Service registration numbers because the Selective Service was suspended when they would have reached age eighteen.

Though the United States is not presently drafting men or women into the Armed Forces, it is USCIS's view that failing to register reflects negatively on the applicant's moral character and adherence to the U.S. Constitution.

 If you did not register with the Selective Service System, and you are not yet age twenty-six, you must register before you file your naturalization application. You can get a Selective Service registration form at your local post office, or you can register online at **www.sss.gov**.

If you are thirty-one or older at the time you file form N-400 (or twenty-nine or older under the rules for the spouse of a U.S. citizen), you can naturalize even if you failed to register. Though form N-400 says that you must submit documentation about your failure to register, USCIS does not require it from applicants who have turned thirty-one (or twenty-nine).

If you have reached your twenty-sixth birthday but have not yet reached your thirty-first birthday (or twenty-ninth birthday if married to a U.S. citizen) you can nevertheless sometimes naturalize despite a failure to register. You must prove that your failure to register was not "knowing and willful." You must submit a letter explaining why you did not register. If you are claiming that you are unaware of your obligation to register, you must also submit a Status Information Letter from Selective Service stating that the agency never contacted you. You can submit the explanation letter and the Status Information Letter either with the naturalization application or at the time of the naturalization interview. Instructions for requesting the Status Information Letter are online at **www.sss.gov/instructions.html**.

Answer Item Numbers 47. - 53. If you answer *"No"* to any of these questions, include a written explanation on an additional sheet(s) of paper and provide any evidence to support your answer.

Questions 47 to 53 ask about your willingness to swear allegiance to the United States, and question you regarding your understanding of the Oath. Be sure to read the full text of the Oath and confirm that you understand its meaning.

If you answer "No" to any of the Questions 47 through 52, attach your written explanation of why the answer was "No" and any additional information or documentation that helps to explain your answer. You may want to speak with an authorized immigration law expert. Question 53 asks about whether you are willing to give up any inherited titles or orders of nobility. You must relinquish any inherited titles or orders of nobility in order to become a U.S. citizen.

---

47. Do you support the Constitution and form of government of the United States?   ☐ Yes ☐ No

---

To naturalize, you must believe in the U.S. form of government and its Constitution. If you advocate totalitarianism or the overthrow of the U.S. government, you may be ineligible for naturalization. The law allows no exemption from the requirement that you believe in the U.S. form of government.

---

48. Do you understand the full Oath of Allegiance to the United States?   ☐ Yes ☐ No

---

This question may be used to determine whether you have the mental capacity to take the oath. If a physical or developmental disability or mental impairment prevents you from understanding the meaning of the oath, you can apply for a waiver of the oath requirement.

49.	Are you willing to take the full Oath of Allegiance to the United States?	☐ Yes ☐ No

Some individuals object to parts of the oath based on their deeply held beliefs.

- Some applicants may have deeply held beliefs that prohibit them from bearing arms against another. These individuals may qualify to take an abbreviated form of the Oath that omits the part related to bearing arms.

- Some individuals may hold beliefs that prevent them from performing any type of service in the U.S. Armed Forces. These applicants will not be required to say the words "to perform noncombatant service in the Armed Forces of the United States when required by law."

- Other applicants may be unable to swear the Oath using the words "on oath," and may replace these words with "and solemnly affirm."

- Some individuals are unable to use the words "so help me God" because of their beliefs, and may not be required to say these words.

If you object to any part of the oath, answer "No" to Question 49 and attach a written explanation of why the answer was "No" as well as any additional information or documentation that helps explain your answer. In the case of an objection due to religious beliefs, it is recommended that you include a letter from your religious or spiritual leader that supports your written explanation.

50.	If the law requires it, are you willing to bear arms on behalf of the United States?	☐ Yes ☐ No
51.	If the law requires it, are you willing to perform noncombatant services in the U.S. Armed Forces?	☐ Yes ☐ No
52.	If the law requires it, are you willing to perform work of national importance under civilian direction?	☐ Yes ☐ No

You must be willing to either bear arms, perform some form of military service, or perform civilian work of national importance in order to naturalize. So, you must answer 'Yes' to at least one of the above questions. As explained before, if you have certain deeply held beliefs you may not need to be willing to bear arms. Follow the directions in Question 49 if this applies to you, but you must answer "yes" to at least one of the above questions.

NOTE: Answer the next question **ONLY** if you answered *"Yes"* to **Part 11., Item Number 4.** of Form N-400.	
53. At your naturalization ceremony, are you willing to give up any inherited title(s) or order(s) of nobility that you have in a foreign country?	☐ Yes ☐ No

Question 53 asks about whether you are willing to give up any inherited titles or orders of nobility. You must relinquish any inherited titles or orders of nobility in order to become a U.S. citizen. If you answer "Yes" to Part 11, Question 4, then you must answer question 53.

L. Part 12 – Your Signature

Part 12. Your Signature *(USCIS will reject your Form N-400 if it is not signed)*

Your Statement

I certify, under penalty of perjury under the laws of the United States of America, that this application, and the evidence submitted with it, are all true and correct. I authorize the release of any information USCIS needs to determine my eligibility for naturalization.

Your Signature   **Date** *(mm/dd/yyyy)*

If you are physically able to write, you must sign your name here. If you cannot sign your name in English, sign your name in your native language. If you are unable to write in any language, sign your name with an "X". USCIS will not accept a photocopy or a scan of your signature.

NOTE: By signing this you are indicating that the information on this application and the documents you submitted are correct to the best of your knowledge.

M. Part 13 – Signature and Contact Information of the Person Who Prepared This Form, If Other Than the Applicant

Part 13. Signature and Contact Information of the Person Who Prepared This Form, If Other Than the Applicant

By my signature, I certify, swear or affirm, under penalty of perjury, that I prepared this form on behalf of, at the request of, and with the express consent of the applicant. I completed the form based only on responses the applicant provided to me. After completing the form, I reviewed it and all of the applicant's responses with the applicant, who agreed with every answer he or she provided for each question on the form and, when required, supplied additional information to respond to a question on the form.

Part 13. Signature and Contact Information of the Person Who Prepared This Form, If Other Than the Applicant *(continued)*

A-

Preparer's Printed Name

Family Name *(Last Name)*

Given Name *(First Name)*

Middle Name *(if applicable)*

Preparer's Signature

Date *(mm/dd/yyyy)*

Preparer's Firm or Organization Name *(if applicable)*

Preparer's Daytime Phone Number
( ) -

Preparer's Address

Street Number and Name

Apt. Ste. Flr. Number

City

County

State

ZIP Code + 4

Province or Region *(foreign address only)*

Country *(foreign address only)*

Postal Code *(foreign address only)*

Preparer's E-mail Address

Preparer's Fax Number
( ) -

If you are physically unable to write, the person who helped you complete the application signs here. Others who helped an individual complete an application may sign as well.

When completing this section, the preparer must provide her or his complete name, organization name (if applicable), address, daytime phone number, email address, fax number, and then sign and date this section.

By signing this section, the person who helped you prepare the naturalization application is affirming that she or he prepared the application with your express consent and based only on the responses that you provided. By signing, the preparer is also affirming that she or he reviewed the completed application with you and that you agreed with all the answers on the form.

N. Part 14 – Statement of Applicants Who Used an Interpreter

Part 14. Statement of Applicants Who Used an Interpreter

NOTE: If you answered "*Yes*" to **Part 2., Item Numbers 11.** or **12.** of this form **and** during the completion of the form used an interpreter to interpret the questions on the form, then **you and your interpreter** must complete this section.

Applicant's Statement

Each and every question and instruction on this form, as well as my answer to each question, has been read to me by the interpreter named below in [ ], a language in which I am fluent.

(language used)

I understand each and every question and instruction on this form, as translated to me by my interpreter, and have provided true and correct responses in the language indicated above.

Your Signature | **Date** *(mm/dd/yyyy)*

Part 14. Statement of Applicants Who Used an Interpreter *(continued)* | A- [ ][ ][ ][ ][ ][ ][ ][ ][ ]

Your Interpreter's Statement

I certify that I am fluent in English and [ ].

(language used)

I further certify that I have read each and every question and instruction on this form, as well as the answer to each question, to this applicant in the above-mentioned language, and the applicant has informed me that he or she has understood each and every instruction and question on the form, as well as the answer to each question.

Interpreter's Printed Name

Family Name *(Last Name)* | Given Name *(First Name)* | Middle Name *(if applicable)*

Interpreter's Signature | **Date** *(mm/dd/yyyy)*

Telephone Number

([ ]) [ ] - [ ]

If you answered "Yes" to Part 2, Question 11 or 12 of the naturalization application, because you are eligible for a waiver of the English literacy requirements and you used an interpreter to help you complete the application, then you and the interpreter must complete, sign, and date this section.

O. Part 15, Part 16, and Part 17 – Signature at Interview, Renunciation of Foreign Titles, and Oath of Allegiance

Do not complete Parts 15, 16, and 17 until a USCIS officer instructs you to do so. You will be instructed to sign these parts at your interview if your application for citizenship is approved. You will only complete and sign Part 16 if you answered "yes" to Part 11 Questions 4 and 53 and you are going to renounce inherited titles or orders of nobility.

NOTE: Do not complete Parts 15., 16., and 17. until the USCIS Officer instructs you to do so at the interview.

Part 15. Signature at Interview

I swear *(affirm)* and certify under penalty of perjury under the laws of the United States of America that I know that the contents of this Form N-400, Application for Naturalization, subscribed by me, including corrections number 1 through _____, are true and correct. The evidence submitted by me on numbered pages 1 through _____ is true and correct.

Subscribed to and sworn to *(affirmed)* before me

USCIS Officer's Printed Name or Stamp   **Date** *(mm/dd/yyyy)*

Applicant's Signature   **USCIS Officer's Signature**

Part 16. Renunciation of Foreign Titles   A- [ ][ ][ ][ ][ ][ ][ ][ ]

If you answered *"Yes"* to **Part 11., Item Numbers 4.** and **53.**, then you must affirm the following before a USCIS officer:

I further renounce the title of _____ **which I have heretofore held; or**
(list title(s))

I further renounce the order of nobility of _____ **to which I have heretofore belonged.**
(list order of nobility)

Applicant's Printed Name   **Applicant's Signature**

USCIS Officer's Printed Name   **USCIS Officer's Signature**

Part 17. Oath of Allegiance

If your application is approved, you will be scheduled for a public oath ceremony at which time you will be required to take the following Oath of Allegiance immediately prior to becoming a naturalized citizen. By signing below you acknowledge your willingness and ability to take this oath:

I hereby declare on oath, that I absolutely and entirely renounce and abjure all allegiance and fidelity to any foreign prince, potentate, state, or sovereignty, of whom or which I have heretofore been a subject or citizen;

that I will support and defend the Constitution and laws of the United States of America against all enemies, foreign and domestic;

that I will bear true faith and allegiance to the same;

that I will bear arms on behalf of the United States when required by the law;

that I will perform noncombatant service in the Armed Forces of the United States when required by the law;

that I will perform work of national importance under civilian direction when required by the law; and

that I will take this obligation freely, without any mental reservation or purpose of evasion, so help me God.

Applicant's Printed Name

Family Name *(Last Name)*   Given Name *(First Name)*   Middle Name *(if applicable)*

Applicant's Signature

Submitting Form N-400 to USCIS

Gathering All Documents to Send with Your Form N-400

Below you will find the USCIS checklist of documents to send with your Form N-400

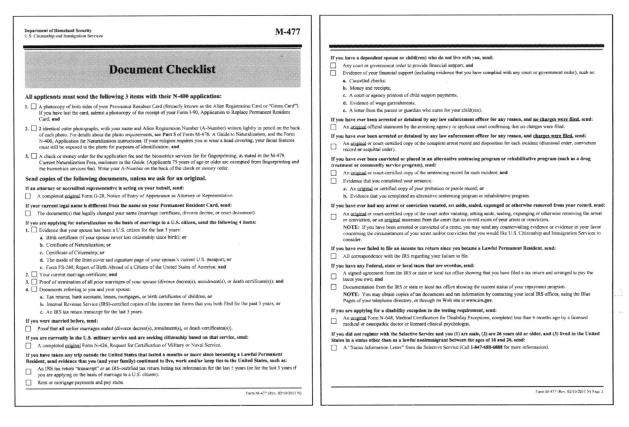

Requesting a Fee Waiver for Your Application

When you submit your N-400, you must submit the correct filing fee of $680 or you must submit a fee waiver request. If you submit an incorrect fee, the USCIS will reject your application. If you are unable to pay the $680 filing fee to apply for naturalization you can request USCIS to waive it. To qualify, you must document your "inability to pay." If you apply for a fee waiver and USCIS rejects your request, USCIS will send your application back to you instructing you to submit the filing fee.

A few years ago, USCIS introduced Form I-912, Request for Fee Waiver, to make this process easier for those who are eligible and "to bring clarity and consistency" to the process. While the use of Form I-912 is not required, it is strongly encouraged. It reflects the factors USCIS considers when making a decision on the request. Form I-912 is available to download at **www.uscis.gov/forms** and can be requested by telephone at **800-870-3676**.

USCIS will determine if you qualify for a fee waiver using the three main criteria:

1. **Receipt of a means-tested public benefit from a State or Federal agency.** This means a benefit awarded on the basis of a person's income and resources, for example, Supplemental Security Income (SSI), Food Stamps, and Temporary Assistance for Needy Families (TANF). If the recipient of the benefit has a spouse, or is the head of household, then their spouse and dependents may also qualify. Evidence that you are currently receiving a means-tested benefit should be in the form of a letter, notice, and/or other official document(s) containing the name of the agency granting you the benefit and the name of the recipient of the benefit.

2. **The applicant's household income is at or below the 150 percent of the Federal Poverty Guidelines at the time of filing.** Refer to USCIS Form I-912P, HHS Poverty Guidelines for Fee Waiver Requests, to establish whether household income is at or below 150% level. This form can be found at www.uscis.gov/forms. The poverty guidelines are revised annually by the Secretary of Health and Human Services and can also be found at **www.aspe.hhs. gov/poverty**. A household may include the spouse, parents, and unmarried children under twenty-one (or twenty-four if the child is a full-time student and living with you when attending school). To establish that the household income is at or below the 150% level, an applicant may submit pay stubs, IRS Form W2 and tax return Transcripts for the most recent tax year, if employed, and proof of any other income such as child support, alimony, Social Security) or financial support from family members.

3. **The applicant has financial hardship due to extraordinary expenses or other circumstances which makes him/her unable to pay the fee.** The financial hardship must be the result of an "unexpected situation that could not normally be anticipated," for example, a sudden illness that leaves the applicant unable to work. The applicant must submit proof of all assets owned or controlled by the applicant and his/her dependents (for example real estate, bank accounts, stocks or bonds but not pension plans or IRA's) as well as evidence of any liabilities and expenses.

While USCIS suggests establishing any one of the above three criteria will lead to a grant of a fee waiver, an applicant should feel free to submit any additional documentation that he/she believes will be relevant to proving an inability to pay.

If you are applying for a fee waiver, include a cover sheet with your application with the words "FEE WAIVER REQUEST INCLUDED" in red letters.

Photos and Fingerprints

You must also submit two photographs with your application. Print your name on the back of each, and below your name, write your "A" number—the number on your permanent residence card. You do not submit fingerprints with your application. The USCIS will notify you when to appear at a fingerprinting center.

File Your FORM N-400

You can find the correct filing address at uscis.gov, or by calling the USCIS National Service Center at: 1 (800) 375-5283. File Form N-400 Application for Naturalization with a check or a money order in the amount of $680* ($595 application fee plus $85 biometrics fee) made out to: "U.S. Department of Homeland Security." Write your "A" number on the front of the check or money order.

 *All fees listed as of June, 2015. For updated fees, check www.uscis.gov/forms

Naturalization applicants seventy-five years of age or older are exempt from having to pay the fingerprinting fee of $85. These applicants need only to submit a check or money order in the amount of $595.

- There is no filing fee for applicants currently serving in the U.S. Armed Forces. You can locate the USCIS address with jurisdiction zip code at www.uscis.gov or by calling **800-375-5283.**

- You may file your application as early as three months before you meet the continuous residence requirement of five years (or three years, but note that you must have been married to and living with the U.S. citizen spouse for a full three years.

- Keep a copy of everything you send to USCIS, your postal receipts, and the receipts for the money order, if you sent one.

 To determine how long USCIS expects it to take to make a decision on your application, you can check the USCIS website for N-400 processing times. Do this by visiting **www.uscis.gov**, clicking on "Check Processing Times."

After Submitting Form N-400 to USCIS

Biometrics Appointment

After mailing your application, USCIS will send you a receipt notice and notification advising you to appear for biometrics (fingerprinting) and photographs. Only a USCIS designated Application Support Center can do fingerprinting for naturalization purposes. After the biometrics appointment, you will receive a notice for an interview with a USCIS officer.

The USCIS Interview

At this interview you will be expected to prove your eligibility for naturalization and you will be tested on your basic knowledge of English and United States civics, unless you qualify for an exemption.

All individuals should bring the following original documents to the interview:

- Permanent Resident Card (green card). You may attend even if you have lost your green card or it has expired.

- Valid government issued photo identification.

- All Passport(s) and any travel documents since receiving your permanent residence.

- All tax returns filed during the five or three year statutory period, including any correspondence relating to payment arrangements.

- All marriage certificates and divorce judgments/decrees.

- Any additional documents requested by USCIS in the interview notice and copies of any documentation submitted with the naturalization application.

Applicants are also advised to bring to the interview an extra copy of all documents, in case the USCIS officer requests to keep them on file.

Males between the ages of eighteen and thirty-one should bring proof of registration with the Selective Service System. Individuals unable to take the full oath of allegiance because of religious reasons should bring a letter from their church or other religious institution explaining how their religious beliefs prevent them from taking the full oath. Individuals who have ever been arrested should bring the original certificate of disposition for each arrest, ticket or citation, including arrests that may have been sealed or expunged, or that occurred in another country. Individuals with minor children residing outside the home should bring evidence of their payment of financial support, such as cancelled checks, money order receipts and bank drafts, along with copies of any court orders relating to required payments.

If you are applying under the three year rule as the spouse of a U.S. citizen should bring proof that their spouse has been a citizen of the United States for over three years, such as a birth certificate, naturalization certificate, certificate of citizenship, or U.S. passport; marriage certificate; proof of termination of any and all prior marriages of both the applicant and the spouse; and evidence of living with the U.S. citizen spouse for the last three years, such as lease agreements, home ownership documents, or tax returns.

 All documents must be originals or certified copies. Any documents in a foreign language must be accompanied by a certified translation in English. The translator must certify that he/she is competent to translate and that the translation is accurate.

At the start of your interview, the USCIS officer will ask you to swear that all the information you are about to give is true. After you have taken this oath, the USCIS officer will review your application to make sure that the statements you made in it are accurate. The officer will update your file with any changes that may have occurred since you submitted your application, such as marriage, travel abroad, or change in employment.

Your ability to speak and understand English is determined during this interview based on the way you answer the questions the USCIS officer asks you. The officer will also assess your English reading and writing ability and civics knowledge, during the interview. He/she will do so by asking you to read up to three sentences in English, to write up to three dictated sentences in English, and by testing you orally with up to ten questions on civics. Applicants will be asked ten questions and must correctly answer six. As discussed earlier, some older, long-time resident applicants and some disabled residents are not required to read, write, and speak basic English in order to become U.S. citizens. USCIS has designed many online materials to provide an overview of the naturalization interview and test.

Witnesses—No Longer Required

Up until 1981, the USCIS required naturalization applicants to bring two character witnesses to the naturalization interview. This is no longer the case. You can bring a witness if you need a witness to help you prove that you are eligible to be naturalized.

An applicant who fails the English or civics tests will be scheduled for another appointment to retake that test within ninety days, and will not have to pay another fee. If the applicant fails the test a second time, the application will be denied. However, there is no limit to how often you can re-apply for citizenship. Keep in mind that each time you apply, you will be required to pay the filing fee or submit a new fee waiver request.

After the Interview

The USCIS officer will usually decide your case at the interview, but not always. The law requires USCIS make a decision within 120 days of the date of the interview. If your case is not decided within this amount of time, you have the right to file a petition with the federal district court to get your case resolved.

If USCIS approves your naturalization application during the interview, the USCIS officer should give you the choice of **(1)** waiting in the office to be given a swearing in ceremony notice, or **(2)** having USCIS mail the notice.

At the time of the swearing-in ceremony, you will take the Oath of Allegiance to the United States and become a naturalized citizen. The USCIS ceremony is usually faster but if you want to legally change your name as part of the naturalization process, you may need to request a court ceremony. You can discuss this with the USCIS naturalization officer who interviews you. If your name was previously changed through marriage or divorce, you can be sworn in by a USCIS officer and your Certificate of Naturalization will be issued in this new name. You become a U.S. citizen when you complete the swearing-in ceremony.

Request for a Hearing on a USCIS Denial of Naturalization

If USCIS denies your application, the USCIS officer must inform you that you have thirty days to request a hearing before an immigration officer. A request for a hearing is made by filing Form N-336 along with a $650 filing fee.

 *All fees listed as of June, 2015. For updated fees, check www.uscis.gov/forms

If you are unsuccessful at that hearing, you may seek a review of the decision in federal court.

How to Handle Changes During the Naturalization Process

Address Changes

If you are likely to change your address while you have an application pending with USCIS, use a post office box or the mailing address of a friend or relative, as your mail may not get to your new residence. If you do move, you must update your address. To do so, do all of the following:

- Complete Form AR-11, Change of Address, and mail it Certified Mail, Return Receipt Requested, to:

    U.S. Department of Homeland Security
    Citizenship and Immigration Services
    Attn: Change of Address
    1344 Pleasants Drive
    Harrisonburg, VA 22801

- Send a letter listing your old address and your new address to the USCIS address listed on your N-400 receipt notice. Attach a copy of your receipt notice. If you have not yet received a receipt notice, submit the change of address to the USCIS office where you filed. Be sure to include your A number or file number on your letter.

- Report your change of address by phone, by calling **800-375-5283**, or online at **www.uscis. gov.** To do this you will need your receipt number. If you have not yet received a receipt notice with a receipt number for your naturalization application, you can still submit a change of address. To do so, if you paid for your application by check, look at the back of the submitted check that was returned to you through your bank. On the back is your 13-digit USCIS receipt number. If you paid for your application by money order, you can change your address without a receipt number, by calling the National Customer Service Center at **800-375-5283**.

- Inform the post office that you have moved. You can do this online at **www.usps.com** or by visiting your local post office.

The law requires all individuals who are not U.S. Citizens, or in A or G status to report a change of address to USCIS within 10 days of moving.

Completing the necessary USCIS Form AR-11, Alien's Change of Address Card to abide by this legal requirement does not update an address on any applications pending with USCIS. Individuals with pending cases must follow all the steps listed above. Also note that one of the residence requirements for naturalization is that you must reside in the state or USCIS District for 90 days prior to filing your application.

If you obtained your permanent residence based on a spouse petition, and you divorced or separated from your spouse shortly after you received permanent residence, the USCIS may question whether yours was a "real," or bona fide, marriage. For more on spouse petitions, see chapter 2. The USCIS examiner may be interested in your marital status also to make sure you were honest in applying for public benefits and/or completing tax returns.

Jeremy's story illustrates one reason why an USCIS examiner may carefully question a naturalization applicant about marital history.

Jeremy's Story.

Jeremy got his green card by marrying Jenny, a U.S. citizen. He and his wife were married for three years. Jeremy had been married once before, to Rachel. Just two months after Jeremy got his permanent residence, he and Jenny divorced. Jeremy then married Rachel for a second time and petitioned for her for a green card. The fact that Jeremy remarried his ex-wife doesn't prove that his marriage to Jenny was a green card marriage. After all, the actress Elizabeth Taylor married Richard Burton twice. However, to become a U.S. citizen, Jeremy may have to present proof to the USCIS naturalization examiner that he didn't marry Jenny just to get a green card.

Do You Need a Lawyer in Order to Naturalize?

Most people become citizens without the help of a lawyer. Of course, if you can afford a private lawyer, you may want to hire one to help you. You may just want someone to help you feel comfortable throughout the process. Some naturalization cases are complicated and require the assistance of an immigration law expert. If you cannot afford a lawyer, there are many organizations throughout the United States that help people with naturalization applications for little or no cost.

Consider consulting with an immigration law expert if you are concerned that the USCIS may discover that you have done something that makes you removable. (See "Risks of the Naturalization Process" in chapter 7.) If you believe that you will have a problem at your interview, you may want an attorney to attend the interview with you.

Chapter 10 - How Children Become U.S. Citizens

Birth in the United States, Birth Abroad, and Naturalization

You may not know it, but you may already be a U.S. citizen. You may have been born a U.S. citizen either because you were born in the United States or because you were born to a United States citizen abroad. Or you may have become a U.S. citizen at the time of one of your parents' naturalization.

Birth in the United States

Unless your parents were foreign diplomats, if you were born in the United States, you are a U.S. citizen. Even if your parents were undocumented immigrants, you are still a U.S. citizen. You are also a U.S. citizen if you were born in Puerto Rico, the U.S. Virgin Islands, Guam, or the Mariana Islands. If you were born in American Samoa or Swain's Island, you are a U.S. national and you are eligible for a U.S. passport. François's story shows how a person can be a U.S. citizen and not even know it.

François's Story

François was 25 years old when he tried to get a visa to leave Haiti for the United States. He loved a young woman named Marcia, who was a U.S. citizen. Marcia had met François while in Haiti on business. When François was fired from his job, he decided to visit Marcia, so he applied for a visitor's visa. The U.S. consular officer denied his application because François could not establish that he had not abandoned his residence in Haiti.

François and Marcia wrote letters to each other regularly, and he was anxious to join her in the United States. Marcia loved François but did not want to marry him until they had spent time together. She was desperate to find a way to get him to America and even considered arranging for a smuggler to bring him in with phony papers. Finally, she visited an immigration lawyer who discussed the many options, including a K-1 fiancé visa. Finally, near the end of the meeting with the lawyer, Marcia mentioned that François had been born in the United States but had never bothered filing for citizenship. His parents had been studying at New York University when François was born. He and his family left the United States when he was nine months old. François and Marcia had not known until she talked to the lawyer that his U.S. birth meant he was a U.S. citizen.

Marcia obtained François's birth certificate and sent it to him. He came to the United States the next day, using the birth certificate as proof of his U.S. citizenship.

Birth Abroad To A U.S. Citizen Parent Or Parents

If you were born outside the United States and one of your parents was a U.S. citizen, you may have automatically become a U.S. citizen at birth. A child born abroad today to U.S. parents is a U.S. citizen if one of the following requirements is met:

- Both parents were U.S. citizens, the parents were married, and one parent had resided in the United States.

- The parents were not married and the U.S. citizen mother had been physically present in the United States for at least one year before the child's birth.

- The parents were not married and the U.S. citizen father **(1)** legitimated the child before the child's eighteenth birthday or acknowledges paternity in writing under oath, **(2)** agreed in writing to provide financial support until the child reaches the age of eighteen (unless the father is deceased), or **(3)** had been present in the United States for at least one continuous year before the child's birth.

- The parents were married but only one parent was a U.S. citizen, and the U.S. citizen parent had been physically present in the United States or a U.S. possession for five years prior to the child's birth, at least two of which were after the parent turned fourteen.

Citizenship Charts for Children Born Abroad

The current rules I just described apply to children of U.S. citizens born abroad on or after November 14, 1986. The rules may be different if you were born before November 14, 1986. To help you figure out if you are a U.S. citizen, I've provided charts that outline the citizenship rules which apply to births outside the United States. Which rule applies to you depends on the date of your birth. The charts at the end of this chapter will help you to decide if you became a U.S. citizen at the time of your birth.

Michelle's story gives us an example of how the charts can help us determine whether a child born abroad is a U.S. citizen at birth.

Michelle's Story

Michelle was born in Italy in 1960, and lived in Italy her entire life. Michelle had never been to the United States. Her father, Frank, was a twenty-year-old U.S. citizen who had grown up in New York City. He left New York for his first trip abroad when he was nineteen, travelling to Italy to study Italian architecture. Michelle's mother was an Italian citizen. Michelle's mother and father were married at the time of her birth. Shortly after Michelle was born, her parents separated and Frank returned to the United States. They divorced two years later.

Michelle is a U.S. citizen. Since she was legitimate at birth, we look to Chart A under the section for children born on or after December 24, 1952. We see that a child born abroad to one citizen with five years of prior physical presence in the United States, at least two of which are after age fourteen, is a U.S. citizen at birth. Frank had lived more than ten years in the United States, five of those years after age fourteen.

The chart also shows no retention requirement (a requirement that the child had to reside, or be physically present, in the United States for a certain number of years before attaining a specific date) for Michelle, a child born in 1960. Michelle is a U.S. citizen though she has never set foot in the United States.

If you are a U.S. citizen at birth because you were born abroad and one or both of your parents were U.S. citizens, you don't need to claim your U.S. citizenship by any specific time. If you are a citizen but were not born in the United States, you can apply for a U.S. passport at a post office, passport office, or U.S. consulate. Or you may apply to the USCIS for a certificate of citizenship using USCIS Form N-600, Application for Certificate of Citizenship. Applying for a U.S. passport is usually easier and faster.

Derivative Citizenship

If one of your parents is a citizen of the U.S., you may be a derivative citizen. Derivative citizenship happens automatically by what we call operation of law. That means that if certain acts occur, you get U.S. citizenship, whether you know it or not. You don't fill out an application, it just happens.

On February 27, 2001, a law went into effect that changed the rules for who gets derivative citizenship. The law applies to natural born children and adopted children. It does not apply to stepchildren unless the stepparent legally adopts the child. Under this law, called the Child Citizenship Act of 2001, a child born outside the United States automatically becomes a U.S. citizen when all of the following conditions have been fulfilled:

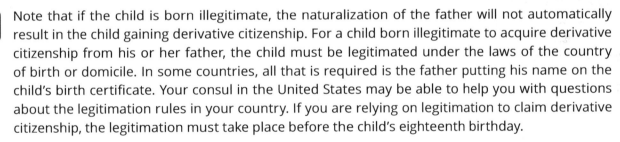

1. At least one parent of the child is a citizen of the United States whether by birth or by naturalization.
2. The child is under the age of eighteen years.
3. The child is residing in the United States in the legal and physical custody of the citizen parent.
4. The child is a permanent resident, pursuant to a lawful admission for permanent residence.

Note that if the child is born illegitimate, the naturalization of the father will not automatically result in the child gaining derivative citizenship. For a child born illegitimate to acquire derivative citizenship from his or her father, the child must be legitimated under the laws of the country of birth or domicile. In some countries, all that is required is the father putting his name on the child's birth certificate. Your consul in the United States may be able to help you with questions about the legitimation rules in your country. If you are relying on legitimation to claim derivative citizenship, the legitimation must take place before the child's eighteenth birthday.

The order of events makes no difference. If your child is a permanent resident, under eighteen, and then you naturalize, your child gets automatic citizenship. If you naturalize and then your child gets permanent residence, the child becomes a U.S. citizen the moment he or she becomes a permanent resident, so long as that happens before the child is eighteen.

The stories of Suki and Yoichi, Carina, and Sofia illustrate derivative naturalization under the new law.

Suki and Yoichi's Story

Suki, Yoichi and their parents moved to the United States from Japan in 1990 when Suki was ten and Yoichi was twelve. The whole family came to the United States with immigrant visas. In 1997 their parents naturalized. At the age of seventeen, Suki became a U.S. citizen upon the naturalization of her parents.

Suki can get a United States passport. To get the passport, she must take her parents' naturalization certificate, her parents' marriage certificate, her birth certificate, and her foreign passport showing legal permanent resident entry or a resident alien card to a U.S. passport office.

Suki and Yoichi's Story (Continued)

The birth certificate and marriage certificate must also have an English translation. Yoichi had already reached the age of eighteen at the time her parents were sworn in as U.S. citizens. To become a U.S. citizen, Yoichi must file her own naturalization application.

Carina's Story

Carina was born in France in 1990 and was the child of Jean-Pierre, a French citizen. Jean-Pierre wasn't married to Carina's mother. When Carina was still an infant, her father came to work in the U.S. as a chef in a gourmet French restaurant. Carina and Jean-Pierre lived together in the United States. The restaurant sponsored Jean-Pierre for a permanent resident visa. Carina got her permanent residence when her father did because she was a derivative beneficiary of a preference petition. If Jean-Pierre becomes a U.S. citizen before Carina's eighteenth birthday, Carina will automatically become a U.S. citizen. French law considers children born out of wedlock to be legitimate at birth. Jean-Pierre need not take any action to make Carina a U.S. citizen, other than to be naturalized, before Carina turns eighteen years old.

Suppose Jean-Pierre naturalizes when Carina is seventeen, and the next month Carina returns to France, not knowing that she is a U.S. citizen. She can return to the United States as a U.S. citizen anytime. If she presents her birth certificate identifying Jean-Pierre as her father with a copy of his naturalization certificate to a U.S. consular officer, Carina can get a U.S. passport. The fact that she didn't know she was a U.S. citizen and left the United States so soon after her father's naturalization is irrelevant.

Sofia's Story

Sofia's parents, Juan and Carmen, were living in Venezuela when Sofia was born. They were citizens of Venezuela. When Sofia was four years old, her parents decided to move to the United States and became permanent residents. They left Sofia in Venezuela with her grandmother while they established themselves in the United States. When Sofia was twelve years old, her mother naturalized. When Sofia was thirteen, her father petitioned for her and she came to the United States as a permanent resident. Since Sofia's mother is a U.S. citizen, upon entering the United States with an immigrant visa, Sofia automatically got derivative naturalization. She may immediately apply for a U.S. passport.

Children who are automatically naturalized don't have to pass any tests. If you want proof that your child was automatically naturalized, you may get a certificate of citizenship or U.S. passport for your child. To get a certificate of citizenship, file USCIS Form N-600. Getting a U.S. passport is faster, cheaper, and easier.

Children Who Turned Eighteen Before February 27, 2001

Prior to February 27, 2001, permanent resident children derived citizenship under rules different from those that apply today. Children who turned eighteen prior to this date automatically became U.S. citizens only if one of the following conditions is met: **(1)** a parent naturalized before the child turned eighteen, **(2)** the child became a permanent resident before turning eighteen, or **(3)** the child was unmarried, and one of the following requirements was met:

- The other parent was or became a U.S. citizen.
- The child was born out of wedlock and the parent naturalized was the mother.
- The child's other parent was deceased.
- The parents were divorced or separated and the parent being naturalized had legal custody of the child following the divorce or separation.

Citizenship by Application for Children Born Abroad

Some children born abroad who do not acquire citizenship at birth or who do not acquire derivative citizenship may get U.S. citizenship through an application by a parent. The parent must apply for a certificate of citizenship for the child using USCIS from N- 600K. To qualify, one parent must be a U.S. citizen, the child must be legally present in the United States, the child must be under eighteen, and the child must be in the legal and physical custody of a U.S. citizen parent who has been in the U.S. five years, two of which were after his or her fourteenth birthday.

If the child is adopted, the child must have been adopted prior to age sixteen (unless the child was a natural sibling of an adopted child and was adopted while under eighteen) and must meet all the requirements for an adopted child or orphan. A citizen parent who has not been physically present in the U.S. for five years, two of which were after his/her fourteenth birthday, may also obtain a certificate for his or her child if the child is under eighteen, is present in the U.S. pursuant to a lawful admission, and a grandparent (parent of the USC parent) has been physically present in the U.S. for five years, two of which are after the grandparent's fourteenth birthday.

Chart A
Birth Outside of U.S. to Citizen Parent(s)—Legitimate Births

Date of Birth of Child	Residence Required of Parent(s) to Transmit Citizenship	Residence Required of Child to Retain Citizenship
Before 5/24/34	Either your father or your mother is a citizen who resided in the U.S. before birth.	None
On or after 5/24/34 and before 1/13/41	**a.** Both parents are citizens, one with prior residence. **b.** One parent is citizen with prior residence.	None
On or after 1/13/41 and before 12/24/52	**a.** One parent is a citizen with ten years of prior residence in the U.S., at least five of which were after age sixteen. (If citizen parent had honorable military service between 12/7/41 and 12/31/46, sufficient if the five years were after age twelve. If military service was between 12/31/46 and 12/24/52, parent needs ten years of physical presence, at least five years of which were after age fourteen.)	Two years continuous presence in U.S. between ages fourteen and twenty-eight except no retention requirement if born on or after 10/10/52. (**Exception**: No retention requirements if citizen parent was employed by certain U.S. organizations at time of birth. This exception does not apply if citizenship is transmitted under military service exemptions in column to the left.
	b. Both parents are cititzens, one with prior residence in the U.S.	Same as immediately above.
On or after 12/24/52	**a.** Both parents are citizens, one with prior residence in the U.S.	None
	b. One citizen parent with ten years of prior physical presence in the U.S., at least five of which were after age fourteen (for births 12/24/52 to 11/13/86.) **OR** One citizen parent with five years of prior physical presence in the U.S., at least two of which were after age fourteen (for births on or after 11/14/86.)	None. The retention requirement was abolished effective 10/10/78. Persons still citizens on that date have no retention requirements.

Chart B
Birth Outside of U.S. to Citizen Parent(s)—Illegitimate Births

Child Not Legitimated

Date of Birth of Child	Requirements for Transmission of Citizenship
Before 12/24/52	Mother was a U.S. citizen who had resided in the U.S. or its outlying possessions before birth of child. A child born after 5/24/34 acquired U.S. citizenship when the Nationality Act of 1940 bestowed citizenship retroactive to date of birth.
On or after 12/24/52	Mother was a U.S. citizen who had ben physically present in the U.S. or its outlying possessions for a continuous period of one year at any time before birth of child.

Child Legitimated by Alien Father

The general rule is that citizenship acquired by an illegitimate child through its citizen mother is not affected by later legitimation by an alien father. The only exception is that citizenship is not transmitted by a U.S. citizen mother if an illegitimate child is legitimated by an alien father and all three of these conditions are met: **(1)** the child was born before May 24, 1934, **(2)** the child was legitimated before age twenty-one, and **(3)** the legitimation was before January 13, 1941.

Child Legitimated by U.S. Citizen Father

Legitimation makes a child legitimate at birth. Therefore, the transmission and retention requirements applicable to legitimate children born outside the U.S. **(Chart A)** apply. In other words, if the child did not acquire citizenship through the mother but was legitimated by a U.S. citizen father under the following condition, apply the appropriate provisions of **Chart A**. No legitimation at all is required for children of certain veterans of World War II.

Date of Birth of Child	Requirements for Transmission of Citizenship
Before 1/13/41	1. Child legitimated at any time after birth under law of father's domicile. 2. Father had the required residence at time of child's birth. 3. No residence required for child to retain U.S. citizenship.
On or after 1/13/41	1. Child legitimated before age twenty-one under law of father's domicile and before December 24, 1952. 2. Father had the required residence at time of child's birth. 3. Child complies with residence requirements for retention.
On or after 12/24/52	1. Child legitimated before age twenty-one under law of father's domicile. 2. Father had the required residence at time of child's birth. 3. Child must be unmarried.

Chart B (Continued)
Birth Outside of U.S. to Citizen Parent(s)—Illegitimate Births

Child Legitimated or Acknowledged by U.S. Citizen Father

Date of Birth of Child

Requirements for Transmission of Citizenship

Child born on or after 11/15/68 and relationship established on or after 11/14/86

1. Child-father blood relationship established.
2. Father, unless deceased, must provide written statement under oath that he will provide financial support for child until child reaches age eighteen.
3. Child must be legitimated under law of child's residence or domicile, or father must acknowledge paternity of child in writing under oath or paternity must be established by competent court.
4. Father must have been a U.S. citizen and met the required residence requirements at time of child's birth.
5. Child must be under age eighteen when legitimated or acknowledged. (Child of age fifteen to eighteen on November 14, 1986 may elect to acquire citizenship under prior law.)

Section 3
Nonimmigrant Visas

"Andrew, cousin Jerry just called. He won't be coming this summer. He didn't get his visitor's visa." Emily was upset that her favorite cousin wouldn't be coming to her son's high school graduation ceremony.

"Did he do what I told him? Did he show the U.S. consul the bank statement, the title to his house and the letter from his employer?" asked Andrew.

"No, he just attached our invitation to the application. He thought that would be enough. I guess it wasn't enough," Emily said, disappointed.

"Don't worry, Emily," Andrew responded. "Jerry can still get the visa if he does what I told him. He still has enough time to get here for the graduation ceremony, and while he's here, let's talk to him about going back to college. I spoke to the foreign student advisor at State Technical College. Jerry might qualify for a student visa."

Most foreign nationals come to the United States as nonimmigrants. Examples of nonimmigrants are tourists, students, temporary workers, and business visitors. A nonimmigrant visa limits what you, as a nonimmigrant, can do in the United States and, in most cases, it limits the length of your stay.

A nonimmigrant visa is a stamp put in your passport, usually by a U.S. consular officer, that allows you to enter the United States for a nonimmigrant purpose. Nonimmigrant status refers to your legal status while in the United States on a nonimmigrant visa. Nonimmigrants from some countries may enter the United States without first getting a visa. I discuss this option in the Chapter 12 on Visitor's visas and Chapter 14 on temporary professional visas.

In chapter 11, I provide a list, with a brief explanation, of all nonimmigrant visas. In chapters 12, 13, 14, 15, and 16, I provide detailed information and practical advice about the most common types of nonimmigrant visas. In chapter 12, I discuss the B-1/B-2 visitor's visa (and the Visa Waiver Program, which allows some visitors to enter without a visa).

I devote chapter 13 to the F-1 student visa, used by more than 500,000 people every year. In chapter 14, I explain the H-1B visa for temporary professional workers and the special rules for Canadian and Mexican professionals based on the North American Free Trade Agreement (NAFTA). In Chapter 14, I also briefly discuss the H-1B1 visa for professional workers from Chile, Singapore and E-3 status for Australian professional workers. In chapter 15, I discuss the K visa for the spouse or fiancé(e) of a U.S. citizen. In chapter 16, I review general concepts that apply to nonimmigrants coming to the United States. I also provide hints on how to make a successful nonimmigrant visa application, including how to prove nonimmigrant intent.

Chapter 11 - Types of Nonimmigrant Visas

Here's a list, with short explanations, of all nonimmigrant visas.

A   **A-1: Ambassador, Public Minister, Career Diplomat, or Consular Officer and Members of Immediate Family**

A-2: Other Foreign Government Official or Employee and Members of Immediate Family

A-3: Attendant, Servant, or Personal Employee of A-1 and A-2 Classes and Members of Immediate Family

Applications for A-1, A-2, and A-3 visas are handled on a country-to-country basis through the U.S. Department of State.

B   **B-1: Temporary Visitor for Business**

B-2: Temporary Visitor for Pleasure

B-1 visas are for individuals coming to the United States for business purposes. Examples include setting up a new enterprise, taking orders, or providing other services for a foreign company, or attending a professional conference. A B-1 business visitor cannot receive a salary from a United States employer.

B-2 visas are for individuals coming to the United States on vacation, to attend a family event such as a wedding or funeral, and for other noncommercial activities. They also are available to prospective students coming to the United States to investigate colleges or universities for possible future attendance.

The B-1/B-2 visas do not allow you to work for a U.S. employer, but you may be able to change to an employment status. (For more on B-1/B-2 status, see chapter 12.)

C   **C-1: Continuous Transit**
The C-1 visa is for entry into the United States in transit to another country or, if a crew member, to join a ship. It is for people passing through the United States with a stopover of no more than 29 days.

C-2: Travel to UN Headquarters
The C-2 visa is for travel to the United Nations in New York. C-2 visa holders may travel only within the 25-mile radius of Columbus Circle, New York, New York.

CW-1: Workers in the Mariana Islands
Requires sponsorship by employers in the Mariana Islands, with strict requirements including considering qualified U.S. workers for the position.

D   **D-1: Crewman's Visa**
The D-1 visa is for crew members landing temporarily in the United States, who will depart on a vessel from the same transportation line.

D-2: Crewman's Visa
The D-2 visa is for ship crew members intending to depart on a vessel from a different company than the one used to travel to the United States.

E   **E-1: Treaty Trader**

E-2: Treaty Investor

E-3: Temporary Professional Workers from Australia

E-1 and E-2 visa status is based on treaties between the United States and a foreign national's country of nationality. Not all foreign countries have trader or investor agreements with the United States that qualify their nationals for E-1 or E-2 status. Some countries have either E-1 or E-2 eligibility, but not both.

E-1 treaty status is for managers and essential employees of foreign companies. The company must be engaged in trade with the United States. The trade must represent at least fifty-one percent of the company's business activities. To get an E-1 visa, the company must be at least half owned by nationals of the treaty country. You, the treaty trader, must be a national of the same treaty country. To get an E-1 visa, you must be entering the United States to serve as a manager or your work must involve skills essential to the company's operations.

E-2 investor status requires an investment by one or more nationals of a treaty investor country. As with the E-1, the U.S. organization must be at least half owned by nationals of the treaty country. The investment cannot be passive (for example, bank accounts or undeveloped land). An investment that only supports you and your family is considered marginal and will not qualify you for E-2 status. E-2 status is available to the investor to direct and develop the enterprise. It is also available to essential employees of the investor, who will function in a managerial capacity or who have special skills necessary to the development of the investment.

Presently, E-1 treaty trader status is available to nationals of Argentina, Australia, Austria, Belgium, Bolivia, Bosnia-Herzegovina, Brunei, Chile, Canada, China (Taiwan), Colombia, Costa Rica, Croatia, Denmark, Estonia, Ethiopia, Finland, France, Germany, Greece, Honduras, Iran, Ireland, Israel, Italy, Japan, Jordan, Korea, Latvia, Liberia, Luxembourg, Macedonia, Mexico, Montenegro, the Netherlands, Norway, Oman, Pakistan, Paraguay, the Philippines, Poland, Serbia, Singapore, Slovenia, Spain, Suriname, Sweden, Switzerland, Thailand, Togo, Turkey, and the United Kingdom.

E-2 treaty investor status is available to nationals of Albania, Argentina, Armenia, Australia, Austria, Azerbaijan, Bangladesh, Belgium, Bolivia, Bosnia-Herzegovina, Bulgaria, Cameroon, Canada, Chile, China (Taiwan), Colombia, Congo (formerly Zaire), Costa Rica, Croatia, Czech Republic, Denmark, Ecuador, Egypt, Estonia, Ethiopia, Finland, France, Georgia, Germany, Grenada, Honduras, Iran, Ireland, Italy, Jamaica, Japan, Jordan, Kazakhstan, Korea, Kosovo, Kyrgyzstan, Latvia, Liberia, Lithuania, Luxembourg, Macedonia, Mexico, Moldova, Mongolia, Montenegro, the Netherlands, Norway, Oman, Pakistan, Panama, Paraguay, the Philippines, Poland, Romania, Serbia, Senegal, Slovakia, Slovenia, Spain, Sri Lanka, Suriname, Sweden, Switzerland, Thailand, Togo, Tunisia, Turkey, Ukraine and the United Kingdom.

The spouse of an E-1 or E-2 status holder is eligible for USCIS employment authorization.

E-3: Professional Workers

For nationals of Australia, this visa is similar to the H-1B category. It is available in two-year intervals for professional temporary workers.

F   F-1: Status for Students

You can get F-1 status to attend school at any level, from grade school to graduate school. The USCIS must have accredited the school to issue Form I-20, a document you use to prove that the school has accepted you. Under limited circumstances, an F-1 student may work. (For more on F-1 student status, see chapter 13.)

G   G-1, G-2, G-3, G-4: Individuals Coming to Work for International Organizations and Their Employees and Families

G visas allow United Nations (UN) employees, World Bank employees, employees of other international organizations, and members of nongovernmental organizations affiliated with the UN to work in the United States.

H   H-1A: Professional Nurses

H-1A status, which was a category exclusively for licensed nurses, was eliminated September 1, 1995. Nonimmigrant, professional nurses must now meet the qualifications for H-1B, H-1C, or TN status (see the following list).

H-1B: Professional Workers

H-1B status is for the temporary professional worker. I devote chapter 14 to this popular status.

H-1B status allows a specialty worker (defined as a person doing a job for which the employer requires at least a four-year college degree or the equivalent) to live and work in the United States for up to six years straight. Unlike some nonimmigrant categories, to get H-1B status, you need not prove that you have a residence abroad. Nor must you show that it would be hard to find a U.S. worker to do your job.

H-1B1: Professional Workers

This status, similar to H-1B1, is available only to nationals of Chile and Singapore. I discuss these visas in Chapter 14.

H-1C: Nurses in Health Professional Shortage Areas (HPSAs)

H-1C status is available for nurses working in Health Professional Shortage Areas (HPSAs) for a period of three years. This law sunsets (automatically ended) in 2009. Nurses with bachelor's degrees working in jobs that normally require a bachelor's degree in nursing can get H-1B status.

H-2A: Temporary Agricultural Worker

H-2A is for temporary agricultural workers. The employer must get a certification from the U.S. Department of Labor that no qualified U.S. workers are available and the employee must be paid the prevailing wage.

H-2B Other Temporary Workers

This status allows you to work for an employer in a temporary position. Short-term and start-up projects often have positions considered temporary. H-2B status requires proof of the unavailability of lawful U.S. workers. You may get an H-2B visa for a period up to one year at a time with a three-year time limit. Obtaining H-2B status is often very difficult, and it's even more difficult to extend your stay beyond one year. As of Jaury 18 , 2014 nationals from only some countries are eligible to participate in the H-2B program.

Gregory's story illustrates H-2B status.

Gregory's Story

Gregory from Quito, Ecuador, is a skilled artisan with ten years' experience making marble tabletops with complicated engravings. A U.S. company would like him to come to the United States for one year to help develop their new line of marble tabletops. The project will involve making tabletops and training American workers. The employer anticipates that within the year, the table production unit of the U.S. company will be on its feet and will no longer need Gregory's services. Gregory's U.S. employer, with the help of a lawyer, advertises the job offer at the prevailing wage in a local paper. No qualified worker applied for the job. The Department of Labor grants the employer a labor certification valid for one year. The employer then files an H-2B petition with the USCIS and they approve it. The USCIS forwards the approved petition to the U.S. consulate in Quito, where Gregory obtains an H-2B visa valid for one year.

H-3: Trainee

H-3 status is available for you to receive income for work in a training program if the training is not available in your home country. H-3 status usually has a two-year limit. To get an H-3 visa, you need not have a college degree. Your employer may pay you a salary, and the amount may be less than the prevailing wage. You must provide details about the training program, and your employer must prove that you will not be displacing a U.S. worker. Your employer must also show that any productive work that you perform will be secondary to the training you receive.

Vanessa's story illustrates the H-3 trainee visa.

Vanessa's Story

Vanessa, from Venezuela, does not have a college degree, but she wishes to participate in a two-year training program for account executives in a major international stock brokerage company. The company is based in the United States.

The company will pay her $40,000 a year during the training period. Vanessa needs an H-3 visa to participate in the program. In order to get her H-3 status, Vanessa's employer/trainer must establish that she will participate in an organized training program. The employer/trainer must provide a detailed explanation to the USCIS stating the reading materials that are required, the subjects that will be considered and the process for evaluation. It is not enough to say that Vanessa will learn on the job during those two years.

Vanessa's employer will also have to prove that the training she will receive is unavailable in Venezuela and that the primary purpose of Vanessa's employment is training, not creating immediate profits for the company. Since she is learning American stock and commodities training, this should be no problem. In fact, the purpose of the program is to train people for employment in the foreign offices of the U.S. company.

H-4: Spouse or Dependent of H-1A, H-1B, H-1B1H-2, or H-3 Workers

The spouse and dependents of individuals in H status can be in the United States in H-4 status. Except for the spouse of an H-1B worker, a person in H-4 status cannot legally work in the United States. But there is nothing to stop an H-4 applicant from getting his or her own H-1, H-2, or H-3 visa. A person in H-4 status can attend school without changing to F-1 status.

I   I: International Journalist

To qualify for I visa status a foreign newspaper, magazine, television station or network, or other mass media organization must be employing you. You may remain in the United States for as long as your employment continues, but you can only work for your foreign employer. If you wish to change your foreign employer you must file the USCIS Form I-539 Application to Extend/Change Nonmmigrant Status.

J   J-1: Exchange Visitor

J-2: Spouse and Dependent Children of J-1

J-1 exchange visitor status is used primarily to bring students, scholars, and researchers to the United States. It is also available to some businesspeople, high school exchange students, college graduates, nannies, and international camp counselors. You get a J-1 visa by participation in a program administered through the Department of State Bureau of Educational and Cultural Affairs (formerly known as USIA).

J-1 exchange visitors commonly receive financial support from the U.S. government, from their own government, or from the college or university they attend in the United States. Some, but not all, J-1 exchange visitors are subject to a two-year home residence requirement. Compliance with this requirement means returning to your home country for two years after the J-1 visa expires. If you are subject to the requirement, you cannot change status to temporary worker or permanent resident until you have satisfied the requirement or you have received a waiver of the requirement. If you are subject to this requirement, you must comply with the condition or obtain a waiver of the requirement in order to change status to H-1B temporary professional worker, H-2 temporary worker, H-3 trainee, L-1 intracompany transferee, F-1 student, or permanent resident. Waivers are often difficult to obtain.

Not every J-1 exchange visitor is subject to the two-year requirement. You are subject to the two-year foreign residence requirement only if:

- Your participation in the program was funded in whole or part, directly or indirectly, by a U.S. government agency or an agency of your home country.

- An agency of the government of your home country says that they need the skills you developed as an exchange visitor.

- You are a foreign medical graduate.

For you to qualify for J-1 status, a J-1 program must accept you. The program sponsor then issues DS-2019 confirming your acceptance. You present the DS-2019 to a U.S. consular officer abroad to obtain the J-1 visa. As a prospective J-1, you can sometimes obtain a B-2 visitor's visa to come to the United States.

 To get a J-1 visa, you must have a residence abroad that you do not intend to abandon.

Your spouse and unmarried minor children may accompany you to the United States and may remain with you while you are in lawful J-1 status. Unlike the F-2 dependent or the F-1 student, J-2 dependent spouses may receive USCIS work authorization. They must show that they are working to meet the financial needs of themselves and/or their children and not to support the J-1 visa holder.

K   K-1: Fiancé or Fiancée Visa

K-2: Minor Unmarried Children of K-1 Visa Holders

K-3: Spouse of a U.S. Citizen

K-4: Minor Unmarried Children of K-3 Visa Holders

K visas are available for a fiancé(e) or spouse of a U.S. citizen and for the unmarried children under age twenty-one of the fiancé(e) or spouse. You can usually get a K visa more quickly than an immigrant visa. For more on K visas, see chapter 15.

L   L-1: Intracompany Transferee

L-2: Spouse and Dependents of L-1

To qualify as an L-1 transferee, you must have been employed abroad as an executive, as a manager, or in a position requiring specialized knowledge. You must have been employed in that capacity for one continuous year out of the three years prior to your being transferred to the United States. The required period of one year of continuous employment is reduced to six months in some cases where the employer has filed a blanket L-1 petition.

The work you will do in the United States must be for the same company or an affiliate or a subsidiary of that company. The USCIS approves L-1 status for initially up to three years, one year if you are coming to work in an office that is new or has been open for less than one year. You can then apply for extensions of up to two-year intervals for a total of seven years as a manager or an executive but only five years in a position that requires specialized knowledge.

The spouse of an L-1 status-holder may apply for USCIS employment authorization.

M   M-1: Technical or Vocational School Student

M-2: Spouse and Dependents of M-1

You may get M-1 status to attend schools offering technical or vocational education. Programs include such subjects as auto mechanics, paralegal studies, secretarial skills, beauty and cosmetics, keyboard operation, and computer programming.

M-1 students are barred from changing to F-1 status while in the United States and can only change to H-1B status if the student did not get the qualifying education through M-1 status. An M-1 student who wants to become an F-1 student has to leave the country and apply for an F-1 visa at a U.S. consulate abroad. M-1 students may sometimes work, but the options are very limited. Your foreign student advisor can advise you about your work options.

N **N-1 The Parent of Certain Unmarried Minors Who Are Special Immigrants**

N-2 The Unmarried Minor Child of an N-1 and the Unmarried Minor Child of Certain Special Immigrants

Certain G-1 nonimmigrants qualify for permanent residence as Special Immigrants. If you are under twenty-one and you get permanent residence as a G-1 special immigrant, you can bring your parents here as N-1 nonimmigrants until you reach the age of twenty-one. If you are a G-1 special immigrant, you may also bring your unmarried children under the age of twenty-one to the United States as N-2 nonimmigrants. Finally, if you bring your parents to the U.S. as N-1 nonimmigrants, they may bring with them their unmarried children under twenty-one. The N visa is available to the parents of G-1special immigrants and to the children and parents of the G-1 special immigrant.

NATO-1 Through NATO-7

NATO visas are only for people coming to the United States under the NATO treaty and their dependents and personal employees.

O **O-1: Individuals of Extraordinary Ability**

O-2: Spouse and Dependents of O-1

The O-visa category is for individuals with extraordinary ability in the sciences, the arts, education, business, or athletics, shown by sustained national or international acclaim. You can get an O-visa even if you are not extraordinary, if you accompany an O individual to the United States to help in an artistic or athletic performance. You must be an integral part of the performance and have critical skills and experience that others cannot perform.

P **P-1 Internationally Recognized Athletes and Group Entertainers**

P-2 Entertainers Coming Through an Exchange Program

P-3 Artists and Entertainers Coming to Give Culturally Unique Group Performances

P-4 Spouse and Dependents of P-1, P-2, and P-3 Visa Holders

The P-1 visa category allows you to enter the United States to perform as an athlete at an internationally recognized level of performance. You can also get a P-1 visa as part of an entertainment group recognized internationally as outstanding in the field. You, as an individual, need not be internationally recognized if your team or group is.

P-2 status is to come to the United States to participate in an international cultural exchange. P-3 status allows you to come here to give a culturally unique performance. For P-2 and P-3 status, you and your group need not be internationally recognized as outstanding in your field.

Admission in P status can be for an initial period of up to five years with an extension for up to five years.

Q **Q-1 Cultural Exchange Visitors**

Q-2 Spouse and Dependent Children of Q-1 Exchange Visitors

The Q-1 visa allows you to come to the United States for up to 15 months to participate in an international cultural exchange program. The USCIS must approve the program. The program's purpose, and your purpose in coming to the United States as a Q exchange visitor, must be to help the U.S. public learn about foreign cultures. You may be paid for work you do in Q status.

Q(ii): Irish Peace Process Cultural and Training Program

In late 1998, Congress added this new visa category for nonimmigrants from Northern Ireland and surrounding counties. The law allowed 4,000 visas to be issued per year for each of three years. This program sunset on September 30, 2008.

R-1: Status for Religious Workers

R-2: Spouse and Dependent Children of R-1 Religious Workers

You can get an R visa if you are coming to the United States to do religious work as a minister, a professional religious worker, or a person in a religious vocation or occupation such as a liturgical worker, cantor, or missionary. To qualify for an R visa, you must have been a member of the religious denomination making the application for at least two years immediately preceding the application for admission. In addition, you must show that you are qualified in the religious occupation or vocation. The initial period granted to an R worker is for up to two and a half years. You can apply for an additional two and a half years.

S-1: Criminal Informants

S-2: Informants on Terrorism

Every year, the USCIS may admit up to 200 people to help in criminal prosecution and fifty more to provide information on terrorist activities. The spouse and children of S nonimmigrants can also come to the United States as S nonimmigrants. Some S nonimmigrants qualify to become permanent residents.

T: Victims of Trafficking

Victims of international smuggling. Holders of T visas often qualify eventually for permanent residence based on T status.

TN: NAFTA Professionals

The TN visa is available to Canadian and Mexican nationals coming to the United States in order to do professional work. (For more on the TN visa, see chapter 14.)

TD: Spouse and Unmarried Children Under Twenty-One of TN Workers

U-1: Victim of Criminal Activity

U-2: Spouse, Child, or Parent of a U-1

Victims of physical or mental abuse and their families may qualify for a U visa. An applicant must file a petition with the USCIS and prove that he or she has suffered substantial physical or mental abuse as a result of having been a victim of any one of a list of twenty-seven criminal activities. The list includes rape, torture, domestic abuse, and enslavement prostitution. U visa holders often qualify eventually for permanent residence based on U status.

V: Spouses and Minor Children of Permanent Residents

The V visa allows certain spouses and children of legal permanent residents to come to the United States while waiting to get permanent residence. To get a V visa, your permanent resident parent or spouse must have petitioned for you on or before December 21, 2000, and you must have been waiting for permanent residence at least three years. V visas are rarely used these days.

Chapter 12 - B-1/B-2 Visitors for Business or Pleasure and the Visa Waiver Program

Every year, millions of people come to the United States to visit or do business. Tourists and others coming for personal reasons need B-2 visas. Business visitors use B-1 visas. Often a visitor's visa will be noted as B-1/B-2, which means you can use it for either business or personal visits.

In this chapter, I explain who is eligible to visit the United States and provide practical hints for getting a visitor's visa. Citizens of some countries can visit the United States without a visa under the Visa Waiver Program, and I also explain this program. Canadians may also visit without first obtaining a visitor's visa.

B-1 Visitor for Business

You qualify for a B-1 visa if you are coming to do business in the United States, but you will not be employed by a U.S. company. Examples of situations where you may qualify for a B-1 visa are:

- You are a representative of a foreign company coming to the United States to take sales orders.

- You are coming to organize trade for a foreign company.

- You are coming to the United States to investigate investment possibilities.

- You are coming to the United States to speak at a conference and you are receiving only expenses rather than a salary.

- You are an athlete coming to the United States to participate in athletic events where your only earnings will be either because of success in those events (such as prize money in a prize fight or golf tournament) or for endorsement activities (such as a tennis player receiving money for a shoe contract).

- You are coming to negotiate a contract for a foreign company.

- You are coming because you are involved in a legal proceeding.

- You are coming to do independent research.

- You are coming to engage in academic activity and you are receiving an honorarium. The activity may not last more than nine days at a single academic institution. The activity must be sponsored by a DHS approved institution of higher education or affiliated nonprofit entity or a nonprofit or governmental research organization. You may not accept honoraria from more than five institutions or organizations within a six-month period.

The more specific you can be, the better. You should have enough personal financial resources or support from your company so that you won't have to work for a U.S. company to support yourself while in the United States. To get a B-1 visa, you must have a residence abroad that you have not abandoned. Consular officers may ask you to provide evidence of your ties to your country. For example, bring with you a letter from your school or employer or proof that you own a business.

Normally, when you enter the United States on a B-1 visa, you will be admitted for 90 days. The USCIS may grant you an extension of your stay if you can establish a need. Or, if you have proof as to why you will need to be in the United States on business for more than 90 days, you can ask the USCIS inspector at your port of entry to admit you for a longer period.

Virginia's and Jorge's stories provide examples of legitimate B-1 activities.

Virginia's Story

Virginia owns a small shoe manufacturing company in Bogota, Colombia. She recently developed a new shoe line and wants to present her company's new designs to wholesalers and retailers in the United States. When she applies for her B-1 visa, she takes a copy of her company's incorporation papers, a letter from her bank showing the resources of the company, and a list of her appointments in the United States. Virginia has no problem getting a B-1 visa.

Jorge's Story

Jorge, from Mexico, has a Ph.D. in biology. He is a world-renowned expert on infectious diseases, and recently developed a new test to determine if a person is HIV positive. He has been invited to be the keynote speaker at a three-day national health conference in Philadelphia, Pennsylvania. The conference planning committee is covering his out-of-pocket expenses by giving him a $2,000 honorarium. Jorge can prove to the consular officer who interviewed him that if someone hired him to work three days in the United States, his fee would be thousands of dollars more than the honorarium. Jorge qualifies for a B-1 visa. If Jorge wanted to work temporarily in the United States for a U.S. company, he could get an H-1B visa (see chapter 14 for more on H-1B status).

B-2 Temporary Visitor for Pleasure

A B-2 visa allows you to come to the United States for personal reasons other than work or study.

- You are coming as a tourist.
- You are coming for medical treatment.
- You are coming to attend a funeral.
- You are coming to attend a wedding, graduation, baptism, or bar mitzvah.
- You are coming to visit friends or relatives.

To get a B-2 visa, you must have a residence abroad that you have not abandoned. This is often difficult to prove if you are a resident of a developing country. U.S. consular officers in developing countries often suspect that an individual seeking a B-2 visa would like to stay and work in the United States, or simply to live in the United States permanently. If you believe that a consular officer may be suspicious about your intentions, you should plan to show that you have reasons to want to go home at the end of your visit to the United States. You should document your ties to your country. Examples are a letter from your employer if you are working, a letter from your school if you are studying, proof of family ties, and proof of any property you hold.

A consular officer is likely to be more sympathetic if you can show that you are coming for a specific event such as a wedding or college graduation. You should be prepared to explain in detail what you will be doing in the United States, whom you will be staying with, and how you will pay for your trip. It is better if you have a round-trip ticket.

With a B-2 visa, the USCIS usually admits you to the United States for six months. You may apply for extensions after that. It is unusual for the USCIS to give a B-2 visa holder more than one six-month extension.

Joyce's story gives us an example of how to get a B-2 visa.

Joyce's Story

Joyce, from Jamaica, wants to visit New York. During the visit, she would like to attend her sister's wedding. Joyce also wants to visit several colleges to see if studying in New York is best for her. She explains all of this to the consular officer, who then denies her application. The officer is sure that Joyce will not come back to Jamaica if she gives her a B-2 visitor's visa. Joyce returns to the U.S. consulate the next week with an old passport showing that she has been to the United States several times and each time returned within the time allowed by the USCIS. She also brings a letter from her high school showing that she only has to complete one more semester to get her diploma. Finally, she presents an invitation to her sister's wedding which is three months away, where they list her as a bridesmaid. This time Joyce convinces the consular officer that she will return after her visit, and the officer grants her a B-2 visa.

Visa Waiver Program

Under the Visa Waiver Program (VWP), the citizens of some countries don't need B-1 or B-2 visas to visit the United States for business or pleasure. These countries are Andorra, Australia, Austria, Belgium, Brunei, Czech Republic, Estonia, Chile, Denmark, Finland, France, Germany, Greece, Hungary, Latvia, Iceland, Ireland, Italy, Japan, Liechtenstein, Lithuania, Slovakia, South Korea, Luxembourg, Monaco, the Netherlands, New Zealand, Norway, Portugal, San Marino, Republic of Malta, Singapore, Slovenia, Spain, Sweden, Switzerland, Taiwan and the United Kingdom.

Occasionally countries are added or deleted from the list. If you come from a Visa Waiver country, you can enter the United States without a B-1 or B-2 visa and remain here for no longer than 90 days. The Department of State puts countries on the list for the VWP after it's been established that their citizens are rarely refused visitors' visas at U.S. consulates. Canadians may also enter without a visa for up to a six month visit.

If you enter the United States under the VWP, you cannot extend your stay past 90 days except in very unusual circumstances, and you cannot change to another nonimmigrant status while in the United States. And VWP entrants who overstay or otherwise violate their status cannot reenter under the VWP. To reenter as a visitor, the USCIS you'll need a B-1 or B-2 visa.

Electronic System for Travel Authorization (ESTA)

VWP visitors must apply for authorization and pay an administrative fee before traveling to the United States. You no longer can simply show up at a U.S. port of entry, show your passport and enter. Under enhanced security requirements, you need to register online and pay the fee by credit card.

It's best if you can register at least seventy-two hours before boarding. An even better idea is to register as soon you start thinking about traveling to the United States. Then, if ESTA rejects your registration, you can apply at a U.S. consulate abroad for a visitor's visa. For more information about ESTA and to register go to **https://esta.cbp.dhs.gov/esta/**.

Chapter 13 - F-1 Student Status

To get an F-1 student visa, you first must be accepted by a college, or university accredited by U.S. Immigration and Customs enforcement to admit foreign students. You can also apply for a F-1 visa to attend a grammar school, junior high, or high school. You must show that you have enough money or financial support to study in the United States without working, and you must prove that you do not intend to immigrate to the United States.

The Student and Exchange Visitor Information System (SEVIS)

In response to the events of 9/11, the Department of Homeland Security, implemented regulations to better monitor international students in the United States. Those regulations included an internet-based tracking system, the Student and Exchange Visitor Information System (SEVIS). SEVIS regulations require schools to regularly report on changes in a student's academic standing, address and immigration student status. SEVIS is managed by U.S. Immigration and Customs Enforcement, but the USCIS and U.S. consulates abroad have access to your SEVIS information. Among other things, your school's Designated School Official, commonly called an international student advisor, must now report to DHS the following information:

- Start date of the student's next term or session.
- Student's failure to enroll.
- Student dropping below a full course of study without prior authorization by the DSO.
- Any failure to maintain status or complete the program.
- Change of the student's or dependent's legal name or U.S. address.
- Any disciplinary action taken by the school against the student as a result of the student being convicted of a crime.
- Student's graduation prior to the program end date listed on the Form I-20.
- Within 21 days of a change in the name, U.S. address or curriculum of a school, a DSO must update SEVIS with the current information within a 30 days.
- The DSO must report the failure of the student or exchange visitor to enroll or commence study.
- Date of the student's enrollment in an approved institution or exchange program.
- Degree program and field of study.
- Date of the termination of enrollment and the reason for termination.

You can see that the SEVIS monitoring requirements and the other new regulations necessitate a higher degree of understanding and compliance by international students.

Acceptance by a School, College, or University

As a prospective student, you must meet the standards set by the institution for the admission of international students. Some schools are easy to get into. For others, particularly prestigious universities, it's much harder. You should call or write to any school that you are interested in attending, read their catalog, and follow their application procedures carefully.

Many schools require a foreign student to take the Test of English as a Foreign Language **(TOEFL)** as part of the application process. The school usually waives the test if the student is from a country where most residents speak English (or if the language of instruction at the student's high school was English). For example, a school won't require the test of students from Australia and Great Britain, but they may require it of students from India or Kenya. Schools that offer classes in the student's own language or that offer classes in English as a Second Language **(ESL)** do not usually require the **TOEFL**.

Form I-20

Once a school accepts you for admission and evaluates your ability to pay for your education, the school's Designated School Official issues you Form I-20, Certificate of Eligibility for Nonimmigrant F-1 Student Status. Before issuing Form I-20 to you, the school must make sure that you have sufficient financial resources to study full-time without working illegally.

Evidence of Financial Support

As noted elsewhere in this chapter, an F-1 student can only work in the United States under limited circumstances. So to get an F-1 visa, you must show that you can support yourself, paying for both your tuition and living expenses. You'll present evidence that you can pay for your education first to your school. The money can be from your own funds or those of close family members. Since living and studying in the United States can be expensive, an important part of applying for F-1 status is providing evidence of financial support.

Your Form I-20 will note the estimated cost of one year's study at the school. If you apply for F-1 status, you must show that you have the money to pay the cost of your first year of study in the United States. You must also have dependable financial resources for the rest of the educational program. You can show proof of financial capability in several ways.

One way of proving the ability to pay for your education and living expenses is through an Affidavit of Support. Someone in your immediate family, like a parent, brother, or sister, usually completes the Affidavit of Support. It should be dated less than six months from the date of submission.

Besides the Affidavit of Support, you will need letters from a bank, tax records, or other evidence confirming the financial resources of whoever signs your Affidavit of Support. You may present an Affidavit of Support from someone other than a member of your immediate family, but it's often not very helpful.

If you have the personal resources to pay for your own education, you don't need an Affidavit of Support. However, you'll need to show that you can maintain yourself throughout your course of study. You must present evidence of bank accounts, a trust, or similar income.

If a distant relative or friend will be supporting you, it's best for that person to put the money directly into your personal bank account because an Affidavit of Support may not be enough to convince a consular officer. Any factors that will reduce your expenses, such as free room and board, should also be presented in order to establish your ability to support yourself without working.

Martin's and Yoshi's stories provide examples of how to prove you can support yourself as a college student.

Martin's Story

Martin, from Ireland, wants to study in the United States. A very prestigious public university in Texas with reasonable tuition fees has accepted him. Despite the relatively low cost for tuition, his family will have great difficulty showing that they can support him without Martin having to work. The college figures room and board to be $7,000 per student, and tuition for nonresidents of the state is $8,000, for a total of $15,000 a year.

Although Martin's father has a good job as an engineer, $15,000 per year is just a little bit more than the family in Ireland can afford. Martin is fortunate, however. Luckily, his older sister lives in the same city as the university and has offered to let Martin stay with her throughout his college years. Martin will have his own room and free meals. Additionally, Martin's sister will give him $50 per week for transportation and entertainment expenses. The only expenses that Martin's father in Ireland must pay are his tuition fees, clothing, and books. By submitting an affidavit (a sworn statement) from Martin's sister, as well as an affidavit from his father (supported by his father's income tax records and a letter from his father's bank), Martin can establish enough financial stability to get the university to issue a Form I-20. When Martin submits the documentation a U.S. consular officer will grant him an F-1 student visa.

Yoshi's Story

Yoshi, from Tokyo, has just received his bachelor's degree in political science at the University of Tokyo. A private university in San Francisco, California, has accepted him to study in their doctoral program. The university has established that living expenses for a student are $9,000 per year and that tuition is $15,000 per year, a total of $24,000. Neither Yoshi nor his family has the money necessary to pay for Yoshi's education. However, Yoshi is able to acquire an F-1 visa by obtaining a letter from the college stating that they are providing him with a full tuition grant. To get the grant, he must teach one class per semester (see "On-Campus Employment" on the next page). He will also receive a scholarship to cover his living expenses. Thus, although Yoshi doesn't have much money, he will not be required to work except on campus teaching for the university.

Spouses and Children of F-1 Students

As an F-1 student, your spouse and dependent children can get a derivative status known as F-2. Your family can apply when you apply for F-1 status or at a later time. If your family members want visas, they will need their own Form I-20. And, they must show the additional amount of expense needed to support themselves. They'll need to supply the USCIS with strong proof of substantial resources, because your family members are not entitled to work in the United States in F-2 status.

In many developing countries, obtaining F-2 visas is very difficult for the wife and children of an F-1 student. The U.S. consul often believes that if the family of the student accompanies the student to the United States, the student will have no reason to return home.

An F-2 spouse or child may only attend college to take occasional courses for recreational or avocational purposes. F-2 children may attend school from Kindergarten to 12th grade. If an F-2 wants to go to college or university full-time, he or she must change to F-1 status.

Working While Studying for the F-1 Student

Many foreign students wish to work to gain experience, interact with U.S. businesses, and supplement family support. Sometimes you need extra funds due to changed financial need, like having a baby. Although you had to show that you could support yourself without working to obtain an F-1 visa, the law provides several possibilities for employment while in F-1 status.

On-Campus Employment

As an F-1 student, you may work up to 20 hours a week while school is in session and full-time during vacations and recess periods. You must intend to register for the next term.

On-campus employment means employment on the premises of the school or at an affiliated off-site location. It means employment on campus of a type normally performed by students. Examples are work in the school library, cafeteria, or student store, or employment that is part of a student's scholarship, fellowship, or assistantship. With off-campus locations for on-campus employment, the place of employment must be associated or educationally affiliated with the school's established curriculum. Or it must be related to contractually funded research projects at the postgraduate level.

On-campus employers usually know that as an F-1 student, you hold a valid Form I-20 that allows you to work up to twenty hours a week. Sometimes you will need a letter from your foreign student advisor in order to prove that the advisor has authorized you to work on campus. The authorization letter from the foreign student advisor will help you to get a social security card. Students who accept on-campus employment are exempt from having to obtain an Employment Authorization Document (EAD) from the USCIS.

Off-Campus Co-Op Programs and Internships

Co-op (cooperative) training programs and internships are called curricular practical training by USCIS. You can get curricular practical training only by participating in a work-study program that is a part of a degree requirement or regular course of study. You cannot qualify for curricular practical training until you have been enrolled in the school for at least nine months. The rules provide an exception to the nine-month rule if you are enrolled in graduate studies that require immediate participation in curricular practical training.

Your foreign student advisor must give you permission to engage in curricular practical training and she/he must also enter the details of your employment into the SEVIS system.
Pre-Completion Practical Training

You may work off campus in a field related to your studies if you work no more than twenty hours a week while school is in session. You may work full-time during vacations and recess periods so long as you intend to register for the next term. If you work full time (more than twenty hours) for twelve months or more you will not be eligible for Optional Practical Training (OPT). Time spent in pre-completion practical training will be deducted from the full-time employment available for post-completion practical training (see "Post-Completion Practical Training," below).

For example, if you work twenty hours per week for six months, you would have three months deducted from the twelve months allowed you for post-completion practical training. Permission for pre-completion practical training requires only that your foreign student advisor certify that the employment is directly related to your major area of study and consistent with your educational level.

Employment Authorization Based on Severe Economic Hardship

Where unforeseen circumstances lead to a change in your economic situation, you may obtain permission to work off campus in any job of your choosing. You may work part-time while school is in session and full-time during vacation periods. Examples of a change in circumstances include the loss of your financial aid or on-campus employment through no fault of your own, an unexpected increase in your cost of living or tuition, large medical expenses, a decrease in the value of currency from your country, or an economic loss affecting your sponsor. Employment based on economic necessity is not deducted from time allowed for post-completion practical training. To qualify, you must have completed one academic year in F-1 status and be in good academic standing. Sometimes the Department of Homeland Security will authorize hardship employment authorization for an entire class of students, as it did after the earthquake in Haiti in 2010 or in 2012 for Syrian students.

Yoshi's Story Continues...

After Yoshi's first year of graduate studies, an economic crisis at the university caused him to lose his scholarship. They also cut back his on-campus teaching.

To prove his new financial need, Yoshi got a letter from the university's financial aid officer explaining the loss of the scholarship. He also got a letter from the dean of faculty regarding the loss of part of his teaching income. He submitted these letters to the USCIS with an affidavit about his financial situation. The USCIS granted him employment authorization to work off campus, part-time. Yoshi got a job as an international commodities trader and became rich overnight!

Post-Completion Practical Training

Under current rules, F-1 students qualify for at least one year OPT for each degree earned. The law calls this "optional" because students have the option of using their practical training rights while still in school. Individuals with a bachelor's degree or higher in a STEM subject, qualify for up to twenty-nine months OPT employment. To qualify for the extra seventeen months OPT, the student's employer must participate in the USCIS's E-Verify employment verification program.

The OPT extension for STEM graduates provides time for employers to petition professional workers for H-1B status.

Those qualifying for only twelve months of post-completion practical training must complete that training within a fourteen-month period following the completion of studies. You get twelve months practical training for each higher degree you obtain. That includes separate twelve-month periods for Associate, Bachelor, Masters, and other graduate degrees.

Martin's Story Continues...

Martin successfully completed his studies for a bachelor's degree in political science. He then obtained permission to engage in post-completion practical training and applied to the USCIS for an Employment Authorization Document (EAD). Martin had no offer of employment when he received the EAD, but authorization was valid for fourteen months. It took two-and-a-half months for Martin to find a job teaching American history at a community college. While his studies were in political science, teaching American history is close enough to his area of study to qualify as practical training. Martin can teach for twelve months in F-1 status as a practical trainee. If he wants to continue to work beyond this year, he has to continue his studies at the graduate level to get another twelve month period of optional practical training or he must change to another status, such as H-1B temporary worker or permanent resident.

Changing to F-1 Status/Getting an F-1 Visa

Once your school's Designated School Official issues you USCIS form I-20, your next step is to apply for F-1 status. If you entered the United States with a nonimmigrant visa and you are still in legal status, you may apply for a change from your current status to F-1 status. You do this by filing USCIS form I-539, Application to Extend / Change Nonimmigrant Status. You MAY NOT attend college in B-1/B-2 visitor status or F-2 dependent status while waiting for the USCIS to consider your change to F-1 status. This rule applies only to B-1/B-2 visitors and F-2 dependents. Other lawfully-admitted nonimmigrants may attend school while waiting to hear on a change of status application. B-1/B-2 visitors and F-2 dependents must wait until the USCIS approves a your change of status before attending school. H-1B, G and other nonimmigrants will not be penalized for beginning classes before getting approved to change to F-1 status.

Sometimes it is difficult for a B-1/B-2 visitor to change to F-1 student status. If you apply within sixty days from the time you arrive in the United States, the USCIS may think that you hid your plans to study in the United States, or might be trying to avoid the possible difficulties of applying for a student visa at the U.S. consulate in your home country. Wherever you apply, it is wise to include with the application for a change of status to F-1 student status, an explanation, in the form of an affidavit, as to why the change is sought and why no F-1 visa application was made in your home country. The affidavit should also explain why you are seeking to study in the U.S. If your desire to study developed after you entered the United States, explain how that happened. If you have concrete plans about how your education will benefit you when return to your home country, mention that as well.

You should NOT have a problem changing from B-1/B-2 status to student status if, at the time you got your B-1/B-2 visa or at the time you entered the United States, a government official noted "intending student" or similar language on your passport.

You must submit your change of status application before your visitors' status expires, unless you have a particularly good reason why you couldn't do that. For more on changing status, see Chapter 17.

Travel Abroad

With security tight at all U.S. ports of entry, you need to take particular care when traveling abroad. Before you leave, check with your Designated School Official to make sure you have (or will be able to get) all the documents you will need to be readmitted to the United States.

1. Valid SEVIS Form I-20 with a signature from your international student advisor. The document must have been issued no more than six months earlier than the time you will return to the United States.

2. Passport valid for at least six months beyond their anticipated return date.

3. Unexpired F-1 visa stamp in your passport. Note that Canadians do not need a visa to enter the United States. In some circumstances, discussed below, you may travel to Canada, Mexico, and islands adjacent to the United States for up to 30 days even if your visa has expired.

4. Evidence of financial support. (See the previous "Evidence of Financial Support" section.)

5. Proof that you are enrolled at your college. That might be a transcript or letter from your international student advisor.

If Your F-1 Visa Stamp Has Expired

If your visa stamp has expired, with limited exceptions for travel to Canada, Mexico or and islands adjacent to the United States, you will need to get a new visa before returning. While U.S. consuls usually grant new visas to students who have maintained status, there is no guarantee. If a U.S. consular officer refuses to issue you a new visa, you may get stuck abroad.

 If your visa has expired do not travel abroad without first speaking to your international student advisor.

If the USCIS has granted you the right to be in the United States for Duration of Status usually indicated by D/S or, until the date on your form I-94 has not expired, you may travel to Canada, Mexico, and islands adjacent to the United States for up to thirty days. However, if you apply for a new visa while abroad and a U.S. consul denies your visa application, you MAY NOT reenter the United States.

Chapter 14 - Temporary Professional

In this chapter, I discuss H-1B, TN, H-1B1, and E-3 status. H-1B, H-1B1 TN and E-3 status are available to temporary workers in professional positions. H-1B1 status is for nationals of Chile and Singapore only. TN status is available only to Canadians and Mexicans under the NAFTA treaty. E-3 status is for Australians. Unlike most permanent employment visas, you can get H-1B1,TN and E-3 status even if many U.S. workers can do the job.

H-1B

You can get H-1B status if you have a four-year college degree or the equivalent in education and experience. H-1B status is available also to certain fashion models. In this chapter, we address those qualifying based on the degree requirement. To meet that requirement, you may have obtained your education and experience either in the United States or abroad. If the job has a license requirement, you must have that license, unless the only bar to getting a license is getting a social security card.

If you have been in the United States illegally, you still might get H-1B status, although you may have to leave the country and get a visa before you can work here.

 Before traveling outside the United States you should be careful about the three and ten years bars which I discussed earlier in this book.

You may even get H-1B status if you have started a permanent residence case, a rule that makes the H-1B different from many nonimmigrant classifications. You can't petition for yourself for H-1B status; your employer must petition for you. In rare situations, a corporation can petition for an individual who is a partial owner of that corporation. The employer must offer you a position where your degree is necessary to do the job. An H-1B employer can be an individual, a partnership, or a corporation.

To get H-1B status, your employer must pay you the prevailing wage for the position or the wage paid to workers in similar positions in the company (called the actual wage), whichever is greater. Employers must also offer H-1B workers the same benefits they offer other workers. These benefits include health, life, disability, and other insurance plans, retirement and savings plans, bonuses, and stock options.

The USCIS will approve an H-1B petition in intervals of up to three years at a time, up to a maximum of six years. Then, in limited circumstances (discussed later), the USCIS may extend your H-1B status beyond six years in one-year, or sometimes three-year intervals.

You Don't Have to Be Special, Just Qualified

U.S. immigration law calls H-1B jobs specialty occupations. But you don't have to be "special" to get H-1B status—you just have to have a four- year degree or the equivalent and a job offer that requires a degree in your specific field. And, unlike most immigrant (permanent) employment-based visa applications, your employer need not prove that no U.S. workers are ready, willing, and able to do your job. Even if hundreds of U.S. workers qualify for the position, your employer can choose you for the job and petition for you for H-1B status.

James's story illustrates how a person with the minimum qualifications can get H-1B status despite there being qualified and lawful U.S. worker applicants for the position.

James's Story

James, from England, managed to get a degree in business management from the University of California at Los Angeles, but just barely. He spent most of his time in college going to parties and as a result, his grades suffered. He did graduate, but he was near the bottom of his class.

James had difficulty getting a job offer after graduation. Finally, through a friend of his uncle, he found a position as a junior hotel executive. The job required a college degree in business administration or hotel management but did not require experience. Although the employer had not been advertising, he routinely got thirty to forty letters per week from qualified applicants looking for a position. Nevertheless, because the employer was a friend of James's uncle, he offered James the position and petitioned for him for H-1B status. James applied to change from F-1 to H-1B status and was successful, despite the large number of qualified workers applying for the position. The USCIS approved his change of status for a period of three years.

The Degree Requirement

A key element in getting H-1B status is proving that the job the employer offers you customarily requires a relevant four-year college degree as a condition of employment. Even if you have a degree, you cannot get an H-1B visa if your degree isn't typically required for the job.

Some professional positions almost always require a bachelor's degree or higher. Examples are schoolteacher, college or university professor, engineer, and architect. Some positions are not so obvious. The position of manager of a small shoe store would not normally require a specific bachelor's degree. You would have great difficulty getting H-1B status to be a shoe store manager. The position of accountant, on the other hand, would usually require a degree in accounting and would support an application for H-1B status.

Take the example of a small manufacturing company that employs a secretary, a sales representative, a buyer, a manager, and an engineer.

The secretary would probably not be considered to be in a specialty occupation. The position rarely requires a four-year degree in a particular field. The sales representative and buyer might be considered professionals, but only if the buying and selling require expertise normally acquired through a college education. An example would be a job selling or buying engineering products or chemicals.

The position of manager may or may not be a specialty occupation. If the manager must understand finance or law, and the volume of business justifies the manager spending most of his or her time using this knowledge, this may be an H-1B position. The manager's job will be considered a specialty occupation if the job requires special knowledge normally acquired through a college education. If the manager's job generally requires less than a college degree, the position will not be considered a specialty occupation. The position of engineer is usually considered a specialty occupation, since to be an engineer, you usually need a four-year college degree in engineering.

The stories of Tommy, Mary, and Carson illustrate the importance of showing the relationship between an H-1B applicant's education and the job duties.

Tommy's Story

Tommy, from Thailand, had studied engineering in his country and wanted to come to the United States to work as an engineer. He had his school records evaluated by a professional academic evaluation service in the United States. The service reported that, indeed, his education was the equivalent of a U.S. bachelor of science degree in engineering. Though he had no work experience, a recruiter from Silicon Valley Engineering Associates, a U.S. company, offered him a job as an engineer. Tommy's is an easy H-1B case. A degree in engineering is a customary degree for a position as an engineer.

Mary's Story

Mary, from Ethiopia, received a bachelor's degree in political science, with a concentration in international relations, from a university in her country. While in New York on holiday, she began looking for a job that would qualify her for H-1B status based on her new degree. She looked for teaching jobs in a variety of subjects, including social science in a high school and history and political science in colleges. She even tried to get a job teaching in a private elementary school. Finally, she obtained a job as an editor for a publication that wrote and distributed high school textbooks about the United Nations and international relations

While Mary had no experience in this area, her bachelor's degree in political science and the fact that she took several courses in international relations qualified her for the position. Her employer explained in a letter to the USCIS that Mary was doing more than just correcting grammar and spelling. She was editing the text for factual accuracy. Her job also required research on world history and government. The USCIS decided that her degree qualified her for the position of editor.

Carson's Story

Carson received his degree in anthropology, studying at City College in New York City in F-1 international student status. His best friend, John, a U.S. citizen, introduced Carson to John's father, John Sr., a frozen food manufacturer and distributor. John Sr. was planning to begin a major campaign to develop, market and distribute frozen foods worldwide. His thought was to develop special products and marketing efforts for each country in the market. Though Carson had never studied business, let alone marketing, he was trained in researching and analyzing national and regional cultures. John Sr. felt these skills would be useful to his marketing efforts, and he sponsored Carson for H-1B status. Though at first the USCIS questioned whether Carson's education qualified him for the job, they eventually approved the petition. The USCIS had inquired about Carson's qualifications, so John Sr. submitted letters from an anthropology professor and a business school professor confirming the important role played by anthropologists in modern product development and marketing strategies.

Despite this evidence, USCIS was unconvinced and denied the employer's H-1B petition.

The Prevailing and Actual Wage Requirement

To get H-1B status, your employer must offer you at least the typical wage paid to other workers doing your job in the geographic area where you will be working. We call this the "prevailing" wage. If the wage paid other workers at the company doing the same work, the "actual" wage, is higher, then the employer must offer that wage. Also, the employer must offer you the same benefits offered to other workers. USCIS regulations provide several ways for your employer to decide the prevailing wage. If the position is covered by a union contract, the contract wage is the prevailing wage. The prevailing wage in cases where the work is done under federal contract is set by federal law. In other cases, the employer typically relies on the U.S. Department of Labor's online wage survey, **http://www.flcdatacenter.com/**, though sometimes DOL will accept a professional survey referred to as "**independent authoritative source**" or "**other legitimate source**."

The Attorney Fee as Part of the Prevailing Wage

A United States Department of Labor rule requires that an employer pay the legal fees and costs to obtain H-1B status for the worker. If the employer does not pay the fees and costs and the wage paid to the worker is less than the required wage for the position, the U.S. Department of Labor could impose penalties including fines, back wages and limitations on employing H-1B workers in the future.

You Must Have an Offer of Employment

The USCIS will not approve an H-1B petition unless a U.S. employer or agent petitions for you. Your employer may be an individual, a partnership, or a corporation. A corporation, solely or majority owned by one individual, will find it difficult to petition for that same individual because USCIS policy requires that the petitioner have "control" over the employee. The USCIS sometimes scrutinizes petitions by new corporations with limited capital to ensure that there is a real business that will have the ability to provide professional-level work to the H-1B worker in his or her field of specialty.

The Labor Condition Application for H-1B Workers

H-1B employers must get a Labor Condition Application (LCA) certified by the U.S. Department of Labor before filing an H-1B petition with the USCIS. In the LCA, the employer attests that the job is being offered at a wage higher than the prevailing or actual wage for the position, that the employer is offering the job at the prevailing working conditions for all other workers in the same job category at the facility, and that the employer has posted a notice of filing the H-1B attestation in two conspicuous locations at the place of employment or has notified the employees' bargaining representative. The notice must be posted for ten days, but the employer may file the Labor Condition Application immediately after posting the notice. The employer must also keep records proving that the statements made in the LCA are true. For more on the LCA, see part II of this chapter.

How Long Can You Work Here in H-1B Status?

The USCIS can approve an initial H-1B petition for up to three years. At that point, you become eligible for one three-year extension. The USCIS will extend your status beyond six years only if you have had a labor certification or I-140 employment-based petition filed before the end of your fifth year of H-1B status and it has been pending for three hundred and sixty-five days or, if your I-140 petition has been approved but you can't get your immigrant visa of a backlog in the immigrant visa waiting lists. Under the one year waiting rule, you can get multiple one-year extensions. The three-year extensions are for individuals facing a quota backlog who are applying in the first, second or third employment-based visa preferences.

Changing Employers, Adding Employers, and the Portability Rule

H-1B status is employer-specific. That means that to work for an employer, the USCIS must have approved an H-1B petition allowing you to work for that particular employer. If you want to change employers, the new employer must first petition for you. If you want to work for two employers at the same time, each must have an H-1B petition approved for you.

Jaime's story illustrates the rule that applies if you have two H-1B employers.

Jaime's Story

Jaime is a professor at California State University in Northridge. He holds a master's degree in mathematics, which he received from a Mexican university. He is studying for his Ph.D. in mathematics at the University of California at Los Angeles. Jaime is a part-time, or adjunct, professor. He teaches two classes each semester at California State University. Jaime wants to teach a third class at Los Angeles Community College. Because H-1B status is employer-specific, that college must first have an H-1B petition approved for Jaime. Los Angeles Community College must get an LCA certified and file the new H-1 petition.

Once Los Angeles Community College files an H-1B petition for Jaime, he may begin teaching classes there. He need not wait for the USCIS to approve that petition, nor must he get a new visa.

Under the H-1B portability rule, if you are already in lawful H-1B status, you can start work for a new or second employer without the USCIS having approved the second employer's petition. To benefit from this rule, the second employer must have filed a nonfrivolous petition before your H-1B stay with the first employer expires. A nonfrivolous petition is one that has some basis in law or fact.

If you have a visa issued based on the first H-1B petition, you may continue to travel on that visa until your stay on that visa expires. If you have two or more approved H petitions you may use a single H visa which is valid until the expiration date of the last expiring petition. Information from all petitons should be noted on the visa.

Jill's story illustrates the H-1B portability rule.

Jill's Story

Jill, a citizen of Italy, came to the United States to work for a U.S. bank as a financial analyst. She holds a degree in economics from the University of Turin, Italy. Her employer petitioned for her to work for three years in H-1B status. The USCIS approved the petition, and Jill got an H-1B visa at the United States consulate in Rome. After two years, she was offered a position at a different bank, also as a financial analyst, but at a higher rate of pay. The new bank petitioned for her to work for them in H-1B status for three years.

The new bank must get an LCA certified before filing the petition, but once the petition is filed, Jill may change jobs. She need not wait until the USCIS approves the petition. Nor does she need to get a new visa. If she stays in the United States, she can work as long as she remains in H-1B status, even if her visa expires. Her current visa is valid for one more year and she can use it to travel in and out of the United States. If she travels outside the United States after the USCIS has approved her H-1B status for the new employer, she can get a new visa, though she need not do that until her current visa expires.

Changes in Employment Conditions

If your job responsibilities change substantially, your employer may need to file an amended H-1B petition for you. Additionally, if your worksite location changes to in an area beyond commuting distance from the area used to determine the prevailing wage, your employer will need to file an amended H-1B petition for you.

Extensions of Stay

You apply for extension of stay by having your employer file a new H-1B petition. If your LCA has expired, the employer will have to support the petition with a new LCA. Also include a letter from your employer confirming your continuing employment in the H-1B position. If you file the extension request before your H-1B status expires, you may continue working for your employer while waiting for the USCIS extension approval. Caution: If you travel abroad after your H-1B visa (the visa stamp in your passport) expires, you'll need a new visa to reenter, and you can't get that visa until the USCIS approves your extension.

Libby's story illustrates the extension rule.

Libby's Story

Libby is an engineer at Applied Engineering Incorporated. She is working for the company in H-1B professional temporary worker status. The USCIS approved her initial H-1B status for three years. Six months prior to the expiration of the three years, the company filed an extension for Libby. The company had to first get a new LCA but was then able to file the petition requesting the extension. Six months is normally enough time for the U.S. Department of Labor to approve a new LCA and for the USCIS to approve a new petition, but in Libby's case the USCIS lost the employer's petition so the employer had to refile it.

Because Libby's employer was able to prove that the petition had been filed before Libby's status expired, she may continue working for the company until the USCIS decides the petition and extension request. If the USCIS eventually approves the petition and extension request, Libby may remain in the United States to work in H-1B status until the end of the three-year period that her employer requested.

Once USCIS approved her H-1B petition and extension of status. Libby traveled to her home country and while there, applied for applied for a visa at a U.S. consulate. A U.S. consular officer granted her a visa with an expiration date that coincides with the end of the initial H-1B period authorized by the USCIS.

Expedited Adjudication

H-1B petition approval usually takes thirty to ninety days, though times will vary greatly from region to region and year to year. If you want the USCIS to decide your case more quickly, you may pay a $1,225 expedite fee. You make the expedite request using USCIS Form I-907, Request for Premium Processing Service. If you pay the fee, the agency promises it will respond to the petition in fifteen calendar days. Each USCIS region has a special mailing address, phone number, and e-mail address for these expedited cases.

The Number of H-1B Visas Available Each Year

The law sets an annual limit on the number of foreigners that can receive H-1B status in a fiscal year. The cap is 65,000 per year with an additional 20,000 H-1B visas available to employees with a U.S. Master's degree or higher. USCIS begins accepting petitions every April for H-1Bs employees who will begin work the following October 1st. Typically, USCIS accepts new H-1B petitions for the first five business days in April, then holds a lottery to pick the petitions it will consider for the 85,000 visas.

Extension applicants are excluded from the count. Also excluded are workers who have H-1B status who change jobs or apply and employees of institutions of higher education and related or affiliated nonprofit entities and nonprofit or governmental research organizations.If you are excluded from the count, you may get H-1B status even after the cap is reached.

Special Rules for H-1B Dependent Employers and Prior Violators of H-1B Rules

The law requires special promises, or attestations, from employers who employ a high percentage of H-1B workers. The law calls these employers "H-1B dependent employers." The same rules apply to employers found to have willfully violated H-1B rules.

> The law defines a dependent employer as any one of the following:
>
> - An employer with twenty-five or fewer full-time employees who has more than seven H-1B workers.
> - An employer with twenty-six to fifty full-time employees who has more than twelve H-1B workers.
> - An employer with more than fifty full-time employees with fifteen percent or more H-1B workers.

Dependent employers must attest that they have not displaced any U.S. worker with an H-1B worker. They must also attest that they won't displace any United States worker employed by them within the period 90 days before and 90 days after the filing of an H-1B visa petition. Similar requirements apply when a dependent employer places an H-1B worker to provide services in another firm.

Dependent employers must also attest that they have taken good-faith steps to recruit in the United States. They must offer the position at the prevailing wage to any U.S. worker who applies and is equally or better qualified than the H-1B applicant. The employer need not recruit if the H-1B worker is a person of extraordinary ability, is an outstanding professor or researcher, or is a multinational manager or executive.

The law does not require the new attestation if a dependent employer is petitioning for an H-1B worker who holds a master's degree or higher (or the equivalent) or who receives wages at a rate of at least $60,000 per year.

No Benching Rule

If you are a full-time employee, your employer must pay you your full salary as noted on your H-1B petition, even if you don't work those hours. The only exceptions are if your employer terminates you, you are voluntarily absent, or you are unable to perform your duties. For part-time employees, the employer must pay wages for the minimum number of hours on the petition. This is called the no benching provision. It is designed to ensure that H-1B workers aren't brought in as full-time workers only to be used and paid when needed as casual workers. Educational institutions may establish salary practices paying for work of less than twelve months if you, as an H-1B employee, agree.

Employer Obligation to Pay Travel Home

If your employer fires you before your H-1B stay expires, the law requires that your employer pay your return transportation to your home country. If your employer refuses to pay, the USCIS won't force payment, but you can may your employer for transportation costs. The USCIS may punish the employer by restricting employment of other H-1B workers.

Your Spouse and Children

If you obtain H-1B status, your spouse and unmarried children, under age twenty-one, may get H-4 status. If they are legally in the United States, they may change to H-4 status by filing USCIS Form I-539, Application to Extend/ Change Nonimmigrant Status. If they are abroad, they may apply for an H-4 visa at a U.S. consulate. H-4 spouses may sometimes work in the United States after receiving USCIS employment authorization. They qualify if the H-1B spouse is the beneficiary of an approved I-140 employment-based green card petition, or the USCIS has granted the H-1B spouse H-1B status beyond six years. They apply using USCIS form I-765, Application for Employment Authorization

TN Status for Canadian and Mexican Nationals

A list of TN professionals can be found in Appendix E. If your work comes under a category listed, sometimes you can get TN status even if you don't have the equivalent of a U.S. four-year college degree. For instance, Canadian baccalaureate degrees, including those which require only three years of study, and Mexican post-secondary certificates, may qualify you for TN status. Management consultants often rely on experience that is less than the equivalent of a bachelor's degree to get TN status.

Getting TN Status

TN and applicants do not need an approved petition to get TN status. If you are in the United States in lawful nonimmigrant status, you may apply to change your status to TN while in the United States. You cannot get TN status if you have started a permanent residence case. If you are abroad and Canadian, to get TN status you present yourself at certain U.S. ports of entry with a letter from a U.S. employer confirming the details of the position offered and proof of your qualifications. If you are abroad and Mexican, you take your job letter and proof of your qualifications to a U.S. consulate abroad where you apply for a TN visa.

H-1B1 Status for Chilean and Singaporean Nationals

Chileans and Singaporeans eligible for H-1B status also qualify for H-1B1 status. In addition, Chileans and Singaporean nationals who are working as Disaster Relief Claims Adjusters and Management Consultants can qualify for H-1B1 status with a combination of specialized training plus three years' experience in lieu of the standard four-year degree requirement for H-1Bs. Only Chilean nationals can qualify as Agricultural Managers and Physical Therapists with a combination of a post-secondary certificate in the specialty and three years' experience.

Getting H-1B1 Status

Like TN's, H-1B1 applicants do not need an approved petition to get H-1B1 status. If you are in the United States in lawful nonimmigrant status, you may apply to change your status to H-1B1 while in the United States. If you are abroad, you present an offer of employment with a certified LCA to a U.S. consular officer at a U.S. consulate or embassy.

E-3

E-3 status is for Australians. To qualify, you must have a four-year college degree or the equivalent in education and experience. That's similar to the rules for most H-1B workers. You need not have a USCIS-approved petition, but you must have an approved LCA. You can get E-3 status in two-year intervals. Unlike H-1B status, you can get unlimited extensions of E-3 status.

Chapter 15 - K Visas for a Fiancé(e) or Spouse of a U.S. Citizen

If you are a U.S. citizen, you may bring your fiancé(e) to the United States on a K visa. A U.S. citizen may also use the K visa to bring a spouse to the United States. The K visa is not available for the fiancé(e) or spouse of a permanent resident.

 K visa holders may bring their unmarried children under the age of twenty-one with them to the United States.

K Fiancé(e) Visa

If you are a U.S. citizen intending to marry a foreigner, you may bring your fiancé to the United States for up to ninety days on a fiancé(e) visa. In most cases, you'll need to prove that you met with your fiancé(e) in the two years prior to the approval of the fiancé(e) petition. The USCIS will exempt you from this "meeting" requirement if traveling abroad will result in your suffering extreme hardship, for instance, you can't travel because of a health problem. The USCIS also can exempt you from the meeting requirement if meeting before the wedding would violate the traditions and customs of your culture, religion, or those of your fiancé(e). An example is where religion prohibits the prospective bride and groom from meeting prior to the wedding day. The fiancé(e) visa is only available abroad. A person in the United States cannot change to K status without leaving the United States.

In order to bring your fiancé(e) to the United States, you file USCIS Form I-129F, Petition for Alien Fiancé. Once the USCIS approves the petition, the agency will send it to the National Visa Center who in turn will forward the petition to the U.S. consul abroad that you designate in the petition. While K visas are nonimmigrant visas, the visa interview with the U.S. consular officer is similar to an immigrant visa interview. The consular officer will carefully evaluate the authenticity of the relationship. Your fiancé(e) will be required to submit a medical exam and proof that he or she won't become a "public charge," that is, that your fiancé(e) can live in the United States without needing public assistance. In proving that your fiancé(e) will not become a public charge, you may use the nonbinding USCIS Form I-134, Affidavit of Support. (For more on the public charge issue, see chapter 5.)

If all goes well, the consular officer will grant your fiancé(e) a visa, and he or she can come to the United States for 90 days. After arrival, he or she may apply for employment authorization using USCIS Form I-765, Application for Employment Authorization. And the K visa holder, while the visa is valid, can travel freely in and out of the United States.

If you marry your fiancé(e), he or she can apply for adjustment of status to permanent residence. (For more on adjustment of status, see chapter 6.) You do not need to file an USCIS Form I-130, Petition for Alien Relative. Instead, include proof of the K visa holder's entry into the United States. USCIS will approve an adjustment of status application even if the marriage takes place after the K visa holder has been in the United States more than ninety days.

The law limits the rights of K visa holders. They may not change to another nonimmigrant status. A K visa holder wanting to enter the United States under a different visa status must apply for a visa at a U.S. consul abroad.

Kelly's story illustrates the rule regarding change of status.

Kelly's Story

Kelly came to the United States on a K visa to marry Sean. They had fallen in love when he was studying at Oxford University in London. Sean returned to his place of birth, New York City, and petitioned for Kelly to join him in K status. Shortly after Kelly arrived, she realized that Sean was not the guy for her. Still, she liked New York, and before her 90-day stay expired, she got a job offer as an architect. She qualifies for H-1B status for temporary professional workers, but despite still being in lawful status, Kelly cannot change from K to another status. In order for her to be able to work in the United States in H-1B status, she must return home to apply at the U.S. consul for an H-1B visa.

Another limitation on K status is that a K fiancé(e) can only adjust status to permanent residence if he or she marries the K petitioner. If the K fiancé(e) qualifies for permanent residence in another category, he or she must leave the United States and apply for an immigrant visa at a U.S. consulate abroad. (For more on adjustment of status and consular processing, see chapter 6.)

Simon's story demonstrates the rule that applies when a K visa holder doesn't marry his or her fiancé(e).

Simon's Story

Simon, a native of Italy, met Sally, a U.S. citizen, when she was visiting Rome. It was love at first sight. They decided to marry, but Sally wanted her fiancé to spend time in the U.S. and meet her family and friends. So, they planned to make New York City their home.

Sally filed an I-129F fiancé(e) petition for Simon. The USCIS approved the petition and eventually it was sent to the U.S. consulate in Rome, where the consul granted Simon's K visa application. Simon then traveled to the United States and the USCIS officer at the airport granted him a ninety-day stay, the maximum for a K visa holder.

Once Sally and Simon spent some time together, they realized that marriage was not right for them, and they broke up. Simon decided to stay in the United States. After several months, he fell in love with another U.S. citizen, Cassandra. Cassandra petitioned for Simon and the USCIS approved the petition. Simon can become a permanent resident based on Cassandra's petition, but he'll have to travel to Italy to be interviewed at a U.S. consulate for his immigrant visa. He cannot adjust status (the process of interviewing in the United States — for more on adjustment of status and consular processing, see chapter 6.) Depending on how long he overstayed past the days granted him by the INS, he may face the Unlawful Presence bar to permanent residence. (For more on the bar, see chapter 5.)

K Spouse Visa

The Legal Immigration and Family Equity Act of 2000 (LIFE) made the K visa available to the spouse of a U.S. citizen. The unmarried children under age twenty-one of that spouse may also come to the United States in K status. To get a K visa, your spouse must be abroad. Even if your spouse is in the United States legally, he or she cannot change to K status from another nonimmigrant status.

If the marriage took place abroad, the visa must be applied for in the country where the marriage occurred.

If your spouse is already the beneficiary of an approved USCIS Form I-130, he or she is not eligible for a K fiance(e) visa. The spouse must wait to apply directly for permanent residence through "adjustment of status" in the United States or for an immigrant visa at a U.S. consulate abroad.

To get your spouse (and your spouse's children) K status, you must first file USCIS Form I-130 for your spouse. Your spouse's unmarried children under twenty-one may accompany your spouse to the United States in K status. Still, I advise that you file for the children, assuming you are their "parent" under immigration laws. That's because as the spouse of a U.S. citizen, your spouse's children do not get the derivative beneficiary benefits discussed in chapter 1.

If you want the child to get permanent residence, you'll eventually want to file an I-130 petition for the child.

Warning: If your spouse is in the United States unlawfully for more than 180 days, and then leaves to apply for a K visa, he or she may be subject to the three- or ten-year bars to reentering the United States. That rule applies to K visa applicants as well as immigrant visa applicants (For more on the "unlawful presence" bar, see chapter 5.) K status works best for people already abroad.

Raphael's and Norma's stories illustrate why a person in the United States may not want to try to get K status.

Raphael's Story

Raphael's wife, Wilma, is a U.S. citizen. Raphael had come to the United States as a visitor from the Dominican Republic and overstayed his visa. Two years after he entered the United States, he married Wilma. She filed an I-130 petition for him, and he simultaneously applied for adjustment of status. He qualifies for a K visa, but it may be more trouble than it is worth. As an applicant for adjustment of status, he can work in the United States and travel abroad with USCIS permission (advance parole).

Norma's Story

Norma came to the United States in F-1 student status. She finished college and was doing her practical training when she married Howard, a United States citizen. (For more on student practical training, see chapter 13.) Norma may file for adjustment of status, work permission, and travel permission with the I-130 petition filed by Howard. She can work and travel while waiting to get her immigrant visa. Getting K status isn't necessary.

As of this writing, the USCIS has yet to issue a special form for K spouse petitions. So, to get a K visa for your spouse, you file petition USCIS Form I-129F.

As is true for K fiancé(e) visas, the consul will require your spouse (and your spouse's children) to submit a medical exam and proof that he or she can live in the United States without needing public assistance. To prove that your spouse won't become a "public charge," you may follow the nonbinding affidavit support rules using USCIS Form I-134. (For more on the medical examination and the public charge rules, see chapter 6.)

Once your spouse and your spouse's children get their K visas, they may apply for admission to the United States at a land, sea, or air port of entry. The USCIS officer will admit your spouse for two years. The USCIS will admit your spouse's children for two years as well, or until the day before the children's twenty-first birthdays, whichever is shorter. Your spouse and your spouse's children may then apply for USCIS employment authorization using USCIS Form I-765, Application for Employment Authorization. And they may travel freely in and out of the United States during the period of their stay.

Chapter 16 - Getting In and Staying In Nonimmigrant Status

With certain exceptions, noted below, to enter the United States as a nonimmigrant, you'll need a nonimmigrant visa. A nonimmigrant visa is a stamp in your passport put there by a U.S. consular officer at a U.S. consulate (in Taiwan you apply at the American Institute). You show it to a Customs and Border Patrol officer at a land, air, or seaport at entry. If the officer admits you, he or she will stamp your passport or other travel document with proof of entry. Once you enter the United States as a nonimmigrant, we say that you are here in nonimmigrant status.

Not every nonimmigrant needs a visa to enter the United States. Under the Visa Waiver Program (VWP), the citizens of certain countries may enter the United States for business or pleasure visits without first getting a visa. (I discussed the VWP in chapter 12.) Most Canadian nonimmigrants don't need a visa to enter the United States. The exception is Canadian treaty traders and treaty investors who do need an E visa. Canadian nonimmigrants seeking entry without a visa must meet all entry qualifications, including, in some cases, an approved petition.

 Until recently, all nonimmigrants completed a card, known as CBP Form I-94, Arrival/Departure Record, and the border officer noted entry information on that form. For nonimmigrants entering without a visa, the form is I-94W. Now, at air and seaports, no I-94 is required. CBP still issues form I-94 at land borders. If you enter by air or sea, you can get proof of lawful entry at **cbp.gov/I94**.

Where to Apply for Your Nonimmigrant Visa

Most often, you must apply for a nonimmigrant visa at a U.S. consulate in the country of your current or last residence. With limited exceptions, the consulate will require a personal appearance.

Some consulates, particularly in developing countries, have high refusal rates. That's why some visa applicants try to get a visa at a consulate in a country different from where they are residing. We call this third-country processing.

 Under current law, you can third-country process only if you are in lawful status, if you never overstayed or were adjudicated to be out of status, if you made a timely application for a change or extension of status and that application is pending, or you can show that "extraordinary circumstances" exist in your case. If you are unlawfully in the United States, in most cases if you want a new visa, you'll have to apply at a consulate in your country of nationality. That can be risky. You should not try that without getting expert legal advice.

How does the U.S. Department of State define "extraordinary circumstances?" If no consulate is operating in your country of nationality, that would almost certainly constitute an "extraordinary circumstance." Physicians who are in the United States as J-1 exchange visitors working in medically underserved areas, and those who are out of status for technical reasons, may also continue to qualify for third-country nonimmigrant visa processing. Extraordinary circumstances may also be shown if your employer filed a change of status application for you but the USCIS didn't approve the change until your status had already expired. You must have been in legal status when your employer petitioned for you and your stay expired only because the USCIS could not approve the change of status in time. Extraordinary circumstances exist also if you applied for an extension of stay before your current stay expired and the USCIS has not yet ruled on your extension request. Finally, A and G visa applicants can still take advantage of third-country processing.

Even if you are in the United States in lawful status, some consular officers discourage "consular shopping"—attempts to find the consulate where you think you are most likely to have your visa application approved. A third-country consular officer is most likely to favorably consider a visa application if you have a legitimate personal or business reason for being in the consular district. Some consulates, however, will accept almost any visa application if the applicant left the United States in lawful status. Consulates frequently change policy regarding whether they accept third-country applicants. Check the website of the consulate where you plan to apply to learn its third-country processing policy.

Making a Successful Nonimmigrant Visa Application

A visa applicant's right to challenge a consular officer's denial of a nonimmigrant visa application is limited. So it is important that you are courteous and clear in your presentation to the U.S. consular officer and that you are as prepared as you can possibly be. You should keep copies of any documents that you submit to the consul, just in case a problem develops.

If you apply for a nonimmigrant visa, you must anticipate two main issues: nonimmigrant intent and grounds of inadmissibility (a bar to an otherwise eligible applicant; formerly called a "ground of exclusion"). I discuss nonimmigrant intent in detail below. In appendix A, I list the grounds of inadmissibility. If you're inadmissible for one of the reasons listed, you may still be able to obtain a nonimmigrant visa, but you may have to apply for a waiver of inadmissibility. If you think that you may be inadmissible, speak to an immigration law expert before applying for a visa.

Proving Nonimmigrant Intent

Having nonimmigrant intent means that you plan to leave the United States when your stay expires. It also means that you're not going to use the nonimmigrant visa as a means to get to the United States so that you can live there permanently. You are most likely to have problems with the nonimmigrant intent issue if you are applying for a B, C, D, or M visa.

No problem frustrates nonimmigrant visa applicants more than having a consular officer deny their application because of a claim of immigrant intent. If you are from a developed country, you will usually not have a problem with proving nonimmigrant intent unless you have previously violated immigration laws or have had a permanent immigrant visa petition filed for you. If you are from a developing country, a consular officer may automatically assume that you have the intention of staying permanently in the United States.

In cases where nonimmigrant intent is an issue, showing the U.S. consular officer that you have strong ties to your country of residence is important. You want to show family, community, or social ties, membership in organizations and religious groups, a family business, ownership of property, and bank accounts.

Mirella's and Juan's stories provide examples of nonimmigrant visa applicants confronting the issue of immigrant intent.

Mirella's Story

Mirella is from Italy and is applying for a student visa to study at Los Angeles City College, a two-year college in California. The college has accepted her, and the school's foreign student advisor sent her Form I-20. Form I-20 proves that she meets the basic qualifications for an F-1 visa.

However, Mirella's mother is a permanent resident of the United States and has petitioned the USCIS to also let Mirella become a permanent resident. When Mirella applies for her visa at the U.S. consulate in Milan, she notes correctly on her nonimmigrant visa application that her mother has petitioned for her. Though Mirella probably won't get her immigrant visa for four or five years, the consular officer who interviews her questions her about whether she truly has nonimmigrant intent.

Will she return to Italy when she completes her studies at Los Angeles City College? Does she plan to continue her studies at a four-year college? If she flunks out of college, will she return to Italy? Is she really just planning to use the F-1 visa as a way to get into the United States while she waits to get an immigrant visa?

Consular officers rarely deny Italians nonimmigrant visas, but it does happen. Whether Mirella gets a student visa depends upon whether she can persuade the consular officer that she will not violate her student status. She will have to convince the officer that if she completes her studies before she qualifies for an immigrant visa, she will return to Italy and wait for her time to immigrate.

Juan's Story

Juan is a citizen of the Dominican Republic who lives in the lovely beachside town of Puerto Plata. He is twenty-five years old and single. He wants to attend the graduation of his sister from New York University. She is the first member of his family to graduate from a U.S. college. When he first goes to the U.S. consulate to apply for a B-2 visitor's visa, the consular officer who interviews him denies his request. The officer doesn't believe that Juan, a young man with no wife or children in the Dominican Republic, will return in two weeks as Juan has said he would.

Juan would have had a better chance of getting a visa if he had brought a letter from his employer, a major bank, showing his salary and explaining that he is up for a promotion to vice president. If Juan had also brought the title to a small home that he owns in the capital of the Dominican Republic, Santo Domingo, and a copy of the graduation notice from New York University listing his sister as a commencement speaker and proof of the specific event (his sister's graduation), the consular officer might have approved Juan's application for a B-2 visitor's visa.

For How Long and for How Many Entries May You Use Your Visa?

If a consular officer grants you a nonimmigrant visa, he or she will put a visa stamp in your passport. The stamp will contain a visa number, the location of the consulate where they issued the visa, an expiration date, and the number of times you can use the visa to enter the United States. The visa may be indefinite and valid for multiple entries, which means that you can enter and leave the United States as often as you like for as long as you live. Or the visa may be limited in time and be valid for only a limited number of entries.

For instance, if yours is a single-entry, one-year visa, you may enter the United States anytime during that year, but once you use the visa, it will no longer be valid for entry into the United States. If you leave the United States after the one entry on a single-entry visa, you will need to apply for a new visa before you return.

With a single-entry visa, you may reenter without a new visa only if you are in status and you are returning from a visit of no more than thirty days to Canada or Mexico. F and J visa holders in status but with expired visas can reenter from trips of no more than thirty days from Mexico, Canada, or the Caribbean.

If you have a multiple-entry visa, you can use it to enter the United States until the visa expires. When you apply for entry into the United States, a border officer will review your documents, noting the type of visa you used to enter. Once you made a lawful entry, your visa may expire, but you may still be in the United States in legal status.

 Isabel's and Sharon's stories illustrate the difference between the validity of your visa and the lawfulness of your status.

Isabel's Story

A consular officer at the United States embassy in Quito, Ecuador, granted Isabel a single-entry H-1B visa. The visa was valid for one month from the time the officer issued it. A company in Houston, Texas, had petitioned the USCIS to allow Sharon to work for them for three years as a senior electrical engineer. The USCIS had approved the petition for a three-year period and sent the notice of approval to Quito.

Two weeks after the consular officer stamped the visa in her passport, on January 15, 2015, Isabel arrived at the airport in New York, where she planned to stay for a week with relatives and sightsee. At the airport, a CBP officer noted in her passport "H-1B, valid until January 15, 2018." Though her visa expired two weeks after she entered the United States, she can live legally in the United States and work for the Houston company until January 15, 2018. If the USCIS grants her an extension of stay, she can remain even longer.

Sharon's Story

Sharon, from Costa Rica, came to the United States on an F-1 student visa to study at the University of Wisconsin. The visa was good for one year. The CPB officer at the airport stamped noted "D/S" (Duration of Status) in her passport. The D/S designation means that Sharon could remain in the United States while she was pursuing a full course of study. After her third year at the university, Sharon decided on a short trip to the beautiful city of Vancouver, Canada. Although her visa had expired, she was in lawful status and did not need to get a new visa. Next summer, when she goes to Costa Rica to visit her parents, she will need to get a new F-1 to reenter the United States.

If a Consular Officer Denies Your Nonimmigrant Visa Application

If a consular officer denies your application for a nonimmigrant visa, the officer will usually tell you the reasons for the denial and you will receive written notice of those reasons. Sometimes you can ask the visa officer to reconsider the denial. For instance, if the officer denied the application because you failed to show sufficient ties to your country, you may be able to return with additional proof, such as a job letter, that you are likely to return to your country. If, however, the consular officer insists on denying the application, it is very difficult to get that decision overturned.

If a consular officer denies your application or request for reconsideration, your only recourse is to seek review from the U.S. Department of State, asking them to reverse the decision of the officer. You do not have the right for a formal appeal. Where the officer's decision is based on a claim that you are intending to live permanently in the United States, what the law calls an "intending immigrant," it is very unlikely that the Department of State will reverse the consular officer's decision. Where an issue of law is involved, such as an interpretation of government regulations or statutes, the Department of State will sometimes reverse the consular officer's decision. To seek review of a visa denial, write to **legalnet@state.gov**.

The Procedure at the Port of Entry

When you present yourself at an air, land, or sea port, seeking entry as a nonimmigrant, a CBP officer will look at your passport, ask you about your purpose in coming to the United States, and decide whether you should be admitted. Usually the inspection is routine. Sometimes the officer will question you carefully or check your luggage. The inspector will then do one of three things: **(1)** admit you **(2)** parole you in pending further proceedings (physically let you in but without legally admitting you), or **(3)** tell you that you are not admissible and ask you to return to where you came from.

If you are applying for entry using a valid visa, you have the right to a hearing before an immigration judge as to your right to enter the United States. If you are applying for entry under the Visa Waiver Program, you waive that right to a hearing.

Changing Nonimmigrant Status

Once you arrive in the United States using a nonimmigrant visa, you may want to change your nonimmigrant status. You might come to the United States as an H-1B professional worker and want to change to F-1 student. Or, if you are here in F-1 student status, upon graduation from college, you may want to become an H-1B temporary professional worker.

A change of status application is usually made by using USCIS Form I-539, Application to Extend/Change Nonimmigrant Status. In some cases, for instance when changing to H-1B professional temporary worker status, the change of status request is included as part of the petition filed by you or your employer. The USCIS is much more likely to change your status if you are in status, that is, if your authorized period of stay hasn't expired. If you are out of status, you must have an exceptionally good reason why your status has lapsed.

Extension of Stay

If you want to stay in the United States beyond the period granted to you by the CBP officer when you entered the country, you'll need to file for an extension of stay on Form I-539. Make sure you file your extension request before your stay expires, or you will need an extraordinarily good excuse as to why you filed late.

Section 4
Asylees and Refugees

How come you got to stay in the United States?" Maria asked her friend Barbara over coffee. "You don't have any family here," she added.

"The USCIS gave me political asylum," Barbara answered. "Convincing the USCIS that I couldn't go back to my country was very hard. But I had a copy of the papers they gave me when they released me from prison, and I gave them statements from my friends from the resistance movement. That convinced them," said Barbara. "Then, one year after they gave me asylum, I applied for permanent residence and the USCIS gave me my green card."

Perhaps the most controversial aspect of U.S. immigration law involves the treatment of those seeking asylum and refuge in the United States. Too often, foreign policy interests and racial discrimination have biased U.S. asylum and refugee policy. It is an area of law constantly debated and litigated, and therefore it is always in flux.

Let's look at the terms "asylee" and "refugee." Asylees and refugees are people who have a well-founded fear that they will be persecuted in their home country because of their race, religion, nationality, political opinions, or membership in a particular social group.

Refugees apply for refugee status at an USCIS office outside the United States. If they are successful, the USCIS gives them travel documents that they can use to enter the United States.

Asylees are people who are already in the United States or at a U.S. port of entry when they apply to live in the United States.

I begin in chapter 17 by explaining how you prove a well-founded fear of persecution; I also discuss the process for filing for asylum. In chapter 18, I explain refugee processing procedures.

These days, getting asylum or refugee status is hard. Don't try to do it on your own. If you are in the United States, talk to an immigration law expert before sending your asylum application to the USCIS. If you are abroad, talk to a representative of a voluntary (not-for-profit) agency or a United Nations High Commission on Refugees (UNHCR) representative before contacting the United States government.

Chapter 17 - Proving Fear of Persecution and Getting Asylum

The regulations and current USCIS practice are designed to provide for a quick resolution to asylum claims by that agency. However, if USCIS does not approve your application and you end up in deportation proceedings, the process slows. Unless you are detained, it could be many years before the matter is decided.

Some criticize the USCIS for being more interested in deporting asylum applicants than in finding genuine refugees. Yet every day, people are granted asylum. Current procedures, while discouraging people with weak or nonexistent cases from applying for asylum just to get work authorization, benefit those with strong applications.

As I explain later, either an immigration judge or the USCIS may grant you asylum. In either case, you must prove that you have a well-founded fear that you will be persecuted if you return home. Sometimes you hear the term "political" asylum used to describe any kind of asylee status. However, you can be an asylee because of many types of persecution, not just political. The persecution can be based on your religion, race, nationality, membership in a particular social group, or political opinion.

 If you are granted asylum, you can work in the United States. One year after your case is approved, you can apply for permanent residence.

The One-Year Rule

Usually, you must file for asylum within one year after you arrive in the United States. The exceptions are if you can prove changed circumstances in your country or "extraordinary circumstances" prevented you from filing within the one-year limit.

Examples of changed circumstances include a change in government in your country or a recent attack on a relative or colleague. An example of a circumstance that may have prevented you from filing would be mental or physical disability.

The one-year rule does not apply to applications for Withholding of Removal or applications under the Torture Convention discussed below.

Proving a Well-Founded Fear of Persecution

Having a well-founded fear of persecution does not necessarily mean that you will be tortured, killed, or even arrested if you return home. Persecution can also mean confiscation of your property, denial of the opportunity to work, and being forced to comply with laws that go against your religious beliefs. You can show a well-founded fear of persecution by proving that you have been persecuted in the past and that conditions have not changed. Or you can give evidence of what is likely to happen to you if you return home. What constitutes "persecution" is a complicated legal question best left to an immigration law expert.

Often, you will have to prove your fear of persecution through your own statements, both written and oral, and the affidavits of friends and relatives. You may also use the statements of experts who have information about conditions in your country and what has already happened and/or what is likely to happen if you returned there, as well as newspaper articles and arrest records.

The persecution does not necessarily have to be at the hands of the government. If you are suffering persecution from a nongovernmental authority—for instance, the majority religious group is persecuting you because you are a member of a minority religious group—and you can prove that the government is unwilling or incapable of preventing the persecution, you may have a claim for asylum. The 1996 immigration law says that you may prove a fear of persecution if you can show that you are a victim of coercive population control, such as forced sterilization or forced abortion. Only 1,000 people per year can get asylum (or become refugees) under this special provision.

You cannot base a case for asylum solely on economic hardship separate from being singled out for persecution—for example, you would starve because poverty or famine is a common condition in your country. Nor is it enough to show that war or civil strife or a repressive government makes it dangerous to everyone in your country. The persecution must be based on one of the five listed criteria: race, religion, nationality, political opinion, or membership in a particular social group.

Ana's story illustrates that proving suffering due to war or national disaster cannot be the basis of an asylum claim.

Ana's Story

Ana was born and raised in Syria. Neither she nor any close members of her family were politically active. They supported neither the government nor the rebels that were trying to overthrow the government. Ana was aware of the political conflict in her country, but she and her family did what they could to stay away from the fighting. Unfortunately, a battle between government and rebel forces broke out near her village. Her parents and her brother and sister were accidentally killed.

Left alone with no means to support herself, she decided to come to the United States to try to get a job so that she wouldn't starve. She made her way to Canada, eventually, with the help of friends in New York, and she paid a smuggler who took her across the border into the United States.

Ana cannot get asylum based on what happened to her family in Syria. Though her life was in danger because of the fighting, she was never persecuted herself for her political opinion, race, nationality, religion, or membership in a particular social group.

Discretionary Denials of Asylum

Even if you can prove a well-founded fear of persecution, an asylum officer or immigration judge may deny you asylum if the officer or judge, considering all the facts in your case, doesn't think you deserve asylum because of negative factors. We call this being denied as a matter of discretion. When an officer or a judge exercises discretion, they weigh negative factors in your case against positive factors. The officer or judge can deny you asylum as a matter of discretion because you could have applied to become a refugee before coming to the United States, because you entered the United States with phony papers, or because you have a troubling criminal record (even if it is not serious enough to automatically bar you from asylum). They may also deny you asylum as a matter of discretion if you were persecuted in the past, but returning home now is safe. Immigration judges routinely deny asylum for one of these reasons.

If you are denied asylum as a matter of discretion, an immigration judge may grant you withholding of deportation, now called "withholding of removal", and you may have the right to remain in the United States but not to become a permanent resident.

Bars to Asylum

Beyond discretionary bars to asylum, there are mandatory bars as well. An asylum officer or immigration judge must deny you asylum if you have firmly resettled in a third country. A third country means a country other than the United States and the country where you fear persecution. The officer or judge must also deny you asylum if you have been convicted of committing a particularly serious crime, including any aggravated felonies, or you have persecuted others. (See appendix B, "List of Aggravated Felonies.")

If you are ineligible for asylum because you have firmly resettled in a third country, a judge may grant you withholding of removal, and you can remain in the United States. If you are ineligible for asylum because you have committed certain serious crimes or persecuted others, the USCIS may try to deport you back to your home country, even if you might be persecuted there. However, under the Convention Against Torture discussed below, you cannot be removed to a country where you will be tortured, regardless of whether you have persecuted others or committed a serious crime.

Firm Resettlement

The rationale behind the firm resettlement law is that a person seeking refugee status does not have the right to choose to live in any country he or she wishes. In order for firm resettlement to be a bar to asylum, you must have had, or been offered, all the rights and benefits of a permanent resident or citizen of that third country: the right to work, the right to attend school, the right to remain indefinitely in the country, and the right to leave and return to that country.

Jacobo's story illustrates the concept of firm resettlement.

Jacobo's Story

Jacobo was a leader in a student movement in support of the Zapatistas, a militant armed group in Mexico that was challenging the authority of the government. Though he never admitted that he was a member of the Zapatista Army, many believed that he had participated in armed actions. Jacobo learned through a friend in the government that the Mexican authorities would soon come to arrest him. He decided to leave Mexico for Spain. He told the Spanish authorities that he planned only to visit their country, but he ended up staying for more than a year, continuing his efforts to support the Zapatista movement.

He came to the United States when a Mexican American student group invited him to speak at the University of Texas in Austin. After just a few weeks in Texas, Jacobo realized that he could do more work for his cause in the United States than in Spain and he decided to apply for asylum.

The fact that Jacobo spent a year in Spain will not automatically disqualify him for asylum. While in Spain, he did not have legal status or permission to work. Although he was safe from persecution in Spain, he neither was firmly resettled nor was offered firm resettlement.

Criminal Activity

If you are convicted of an aggravated felony or felonies and you are sentenced to an aggregate term of imprisonment of at least five years, you become ineligible for withholding of deportation/removal. Thus you will be denied both asylum and withholding of removal, and the government may send you home, unless you will face torture and you are thus protected by the Convention Against Torture.

The Torture Convention Defense

Under the United Nations Convention Against Torture and Other Crimes, Inhumane or Degrading Treatment or Punishment, (often referred to as the Convention Against Torture, CAT), you may not be returned to a country where you will be tortured.

The Board of Immigration Appeals, BIA, has defined torture as including the following:

1. An act causing severe physical or mental pain or suffering that must be "an extreme form of cruel and inhuman treatment" and not lesser forms;

2. The act must be "specifically intended" to inflict severe physical or mental pain or suffering and an act that results in unanticipated or unintended severity of pain or suffering does not constitute torture;

3. The act must have an "illicit purpose" such as "obtaining information or a confession, punishment for a victim's or another's act, intimidating or coercing a victim or another or any discriminatory purpose;"

4. The act must be an intentional government act directed against a person in the offender's custody or control and "negligent acts or acts by private individuals not acting on behalf of the government" are not covered; and...

5. The act "does not include pain or suffering arising only from, inherent in or incidental to lawful sanctions" such as a judicially imposed death penalty.

Unlike for a grant of asylum or withholding of deportation, to benefit under the CAT, you need not prove that you will be persecuted for any particular reason. The fact that you will face torture is enough to prevent the government from removing you.

Only an immigration judge can grant you the right to remain in the United States because you will be tortured if returned home. Relief under the Torture Convention does not make you eligible for permanent residence, nor for relief from government custody. However, unless you are a threat to the community, the government will likely release you if a judge grants you CAT relief.

Defensive Versus Affirmative Asylum Applications

We say you file an affirmative asylum application when you apply for asylum before the government tries to deport you. You should only file affirmatively when you are sure, after talking to an expert, that you have a very strong case. If your application is successful and the USCIS grants you asylum, you'll get work authorization and you'll qualify for permanent residence after one year. If you are here out of status and the USCIS denies your application, they will try to deport you. If you are here in status (for instance, as a legal foreign student) and the USCIS denies your application, you may have a hard time getting a nonimmigrant visa in the future.

If the USCIS denies your asylum claim, you can renew your application before an immigration judge, but, in the end, you may be forced out of the United States.

We say you are filing defensively when you file for asylum only after the government has ordered you to appear for a deportation/removal proceeding and you apply for asylum as a defense. With a defensive application, you have little to lose. You may not win asylum, but unless your application is frivolous—that is, without any merit at all—you aren't penalized for trying. If the USCIS finds that your application is frivolous, you could be barred from later becoming a permanent resident.

Affirmative Applications

You file an affirmative asylum application with the USCIS. No filing fee is required. With the help of your representative, you will include a detailed statement about your claim and the affidavits (sworn statements) of people who can support that claim. If you were arrested for your beliefs, you should include an arrest record, if you have it. You should include anything that you think will help the Judge decide in your favor. Newspaper articles about you, your country, or your beliefs, books, medical records—it's up to you. You must submit a translation for all documents not in the English language. You may supplement your application later, but it is best if you make a strong presentation when you first file your application.

The USCIS will then schedule you for an interview with an USCIS asylum officer at your local USCIS office. An attorney or representative of a recognized not-for-profit organization can represent you at your asylum interview. You may bring witnesses, but the interview is usually short, so it is often better to present written notarized statements than to bring witnesses.

If USCIS approves your application, you can apply for employment authorization (also known as a "work card"). Your spouse and unmarried children under age twenty-one can get asylum as well. If your spouse and children are outside the United States, you can petition to bring them to the U.S. using USCIS Form I-730, Refugee/Asylee Relative Petition. Under the recently passed Child Status Protection Act, a child of an asylee can get "derivative asylum" if the child is not yet twenty-one on the day the USCIS receives the parent's asylum application. That's true even if the child turns twenty-one before the USCIS approves the asylum application of the parent.

If the USCIS does not approve your application and you are out of status, you will receive notice to appear for a deportation (removal) hearing.

At your removal hearing, you may ask the immigration judge to grant you asylum. The judge will have your original application, but you can supplement the record with additional affidavits and documentary evidence. You may also have witnesses testify for you. The immigration judge will take into consideration your credibility (whether you should be believed), whether your statements are trustworthy and believable, and the credibility of your witnesses. USCIS rules specifically state that an applicant's asylum testimony alone may be sufficient to grant an asylum claim.

If the immigration judge grants you asylum, you'll get the same rights and benefits as a person granted asylum by the USCIS. If the immigration judge rules against you, you can appeal that decision to the Board of Immigration Appeals (BIA). The government can appeal also. If the BIA dismisses (denies) your appeal, you can ask a federal court to review the BIA's decision. The government can't remove you from the United States until the BIA decides your case.

The stories of Darian and Sophie illustrate the concepts of affirmative asylum applications.

Darian's Story

Darian's family was very active in their country's politics. They were part of a growing opposition movement seeking greater democracy in their country. Darian was only 20 years old and didn't play an important role in the politics of his country, but he was outspoken against government abuses. After his first year in college, he decided to spend his summer with relatives in the United States. He came into the United States on a visitor's visa with plans to return to finish his senior year in college.

While in the United States, Darian learned that government officials had arrested his father, mother, brother and sister. Newspaper articles in papers back home discussed how the government would try the family for treason. The articles also said that government agents were looking for Darian. Obviously, he could not return home. Darian wasn't wealthy enough to live in the United States without working, and he didn't qualify for a work visa. After discussing his case with a representative of a not-for-profit agency that helps immigrants, he decided to apply for asylum.

Darian got an affidavit from a university professor who was an expert in his country's politics. He also obtained affidavits from relatives in the United States who were knowledgeable about his family's opposition to the government. When Darian sent in his application, he included copies of the newspaper articles about him and his family. He submitted his application with the supporting documents to the USCIS Regional Service Center. An USCIS asylum officer interviewed Darian and granted him asylum. One year later, he will be eligible to apply to become a permanent resident of the United States.

Darian's application was an affirmative application because the government had not been trying to remove him from the United States at the time that he filed the application.

Sophie's Story

Sophie was from Latin America. She managed to come to the United States by crossing the Mexican-U.S. border late one night. Under U.S. immigration laws, she had no right to be in the United States. She found a job working very hard at very low wages. She knew that unless she got USCIS work permission, she would have a very hard time finding employment in the United States. Sophie had heard that the USCIS granted asylum to many people from her country. Though she had never been active in any political activities, she was desperate to get work permission. She went to an "immigration consultant" who charged her $500 and advised her to apply for asylum. The consultant who advised Sophie was neither a lawyer nor a representative of a not-for-profit organization.

With the consultant's help, Sophie applied to the USCIS for asylum. The consultant filled out the form without even asking Sophie the basis for her asylum claim, and Sophie signed it. The USCIS scheduled her for an interview with an asylum officer. At the interview, Sophie had a very hard time answering the officer's questions. She claimed that she had been very active politically in her country, but she had a hard time explaining her point of view. Under questioning from the asylum officer, she kept changing her story. She did not submit any evidence other than her own statement about why she had a well-founded fear of persecution.

The asylum officer gave Sophie a date to come back for the decision in her case. When Sophie returned to the asylum office, she learned that they had denied her asylum application. An USCIS officer gave her a notice to appear for removal proceedings.

Sophie had made an affirmative application for asylum. The USCIS had no knowledge that Sophie was in the United States until she filed the application. Now, because she had made a weak asylum application, she found herself in removal proceedings. Unless Sophie can figure out a legal way to remain in the United States, she will be forced to return to her country.

Defensive Applications

You file defensive applications with the immigration court after the government has already ordered you to appear for a removal hearing. At your hearing, you'll have the right to testify and present witnesses and evidence. If the immigration judge denies your application, he or she may order you to leave the country.

LaNedra's story illustrates the concepts of defensive asylum applications.

LaNedra's Story

LaNedra was a schoolteacher in a poor country. She was very popular with her students and their parents. She had a reputation as an individual who cared about other people. Often, when people in her village had problems with local authorities, they would go to LaNedra and she would speak to the authorities for them. LaNedra never thought of herself as being political, but the local government considered her a nuisance, especially after she organized a group of parents to protest poor conditions in the schools. Once, after she led a demonstration, the police chief arrested her for disorderly conduct. The police chief told her that if she didn't keep quiet, she might end up in prison.

LaNedra was making very little money. She was having great difficulty supporting herself and her two small children. Her husband had died after the birth of their second child, and she was the sole source of income for her family. Because she spoke out against local government abuses, LaNedra had trouble getting a better job. A relative in the United States encouraged LaNedra to come to California where, he said, he could find her work. LaNedra got a visitor's visa and came to the United States.

Life in the United States was very difficult for LaNedra because she didn't have work authorization. She managed to find a job working "off the books" at a garment factory for $100 per week. One day the government raided the factory and arrested LaNedra. She ended up in removal proceedings.

LaNedra had little documentation of what had happened to her back home. Her case will depend primarily on her own testimony. Her claim is genuine but not very strong. But since asylum is her only chance to stay in the United States, she has no reason not to ask the judge for asylum. LaNedra is making a defensive asylum application.

Withholding of Deportation/Removal

Even if a judge denies you asylum as a matter of discretion, you may win the right to remain temporarily in the United States under the withholding of removal law (until April 1, 1997, this was called "withholding of deportation"). Only an immigration judge can grant you withholding of removal.

The test for this relief is harder than for asylum. In order to obtain withholding of removal relief, you must show a clear probability that you will be persecuted if you are sent home. This is a higher standard than the "well-founded fear of persecution" standard used in asylum cases.
With withholding of removal, you don't qualify for permanent residence in one year as you do with asylum. However, you will get USCIS work permission. If you get withholding of removal after the judge denies your asylum application, you still can get permanent residence some other way, such as through marrying a U.S. citizen or through an offer of employment.

You will not be able to get withholding of removal if you have been convicted of a particularly serious crime (such as an aggravated felony), you have persecuted others, you have committed a serious nonpolitical crime outside the United States, you are a danger to the security of the United States, or you are a terrorist.

Applications at Entry (or Within Two Years of Entry) into the United States

If you arrive at a U.S. port of entry without proper entry documents or you are caught trying to sneak into the United States, the government will subject to special expedited asylum processing. You can be detained until the government decides that you have proven that you have a well-founded fear of persecution and that you are eligible for either asylum or withholding of removal.

Under these procedures, the first step is an interview by an asylum officer. If you convince the officer that you have a credible claim of persecution, you will be detained for further consideration of your application. If you can't convince the asylum officer that you have a credible claim of persecution, you have the right to a hearing before an immigration judge. The hearing must be held within seven days. If the judge denies your asylum claim, you'll be sent back to the country you were in just before you arrived in the United States.

Chapter 18 - Refugees and Refugee Processing

Like an asylum applicant, if you want to come to the United States as a refugee, you must prove that you have a well-founded fear of being persecuted in your home country. (For an explanation of what is meant by "well-founded fear of persecution," see chapter 17.) Refugee applicants, like asylum applicants, must prove that they face persecution based on race, religion, political opinion, nationality, or membership in a social group. And, just as in the case of asylees, you may be denied refugee status if you have firmly resettled in a third country or committed certain serious crimes. Also barred from refugee status, without the right to a waiver, are former or current members of the Nazi Party and, those who have participated in genocide., and those convicted of certain serious crimes.

If the USCIS approves your refugee application, your spouse and your unmarried children under age twenty-one may come with you to the United States or follow you here after your arrival. One year after your admission to the United States as a refugee, you may apply for an immigrant visa (green card).

Typically, a refugee is living outside his or her home country, afraid to return home. In exceptional situations, you may apply to be a refugee without leaving your country at USCIS in-country refugee processing centers.

Applying for Refugee Papers

If you want to apply to come to the United States as a refugee, you may contact a U.S. Embassy, an international relief organization (known as a non-governmental organization - NGO) or the United Nations High Commission on Refugees (UNHCR), which has offices in countries throughout the world. U.S. embassies and consulates also can provide you with refugee processing information. Refugee applications are processed at USCIS offices outside the United States.

The yearly quota for U.S. refugee admissions is set by the President after consultation with Congress. Once you have established a well-founded fear of persecution, the USCIS will consider a number of factors in deciding whether they will admit you to the United States as a refugee. Among the factors are family and other ties to the United States, general humanitarian concerns, and the policy interests of the United States.

To get refugee travel papers, you must also have a sponsor who can guarantee your transportation to the United States. The sponsor can be a person or an organization.

Once the USCIS has decided that you meet the qualifications to be a refugee, you must arrange for resettlement in the United States. The USCIS, the UNHCR, or an NGO abroad will help you make contact with a U.S. resettlement agency. Before you are given refugee papers, a U.S. agency must agree to assist you upon your arrival in the United States.

When you arrive in the United States, voluntary agencies offer financial and other forms of support. Refugees can get USCIS work authorization upon their arrival, and they are eligible for most public benefits, such as Medicaid and food stamps.

To travel outside the United States, a refugee can get a "refugee travel document," renewable at one-year intervals.

If your spouse and/or children didn't accompany you to the United States, you can petition or sponsor them to come to the United States. The children must be unmarried and under age twenty-one. **Petition for family members using USCIS Form I-730, Refugee/Asylee Relative Petition.**

Violeta's story helps us to understand refugee processing.

Violeta's Story

Violeta was an active member of the antigovernment movement in Poland in 1987. She often took risks, participating in illegal actions against the government. In one such action during the election, she was arrested and interrogated by police. The police took her passport away and let her go. She was stopped again immediately after she left the police station for not having an ID and was kept in jail for forty-eight hours. When she finally got out, she decided to leave the country. Some of her best friends from the movement had already left for the refugee camp in Latina, Italy and she decided to join them.

In Italy she went straight from the airport to the refugee camp in Latina and declared herself a political refugee. Violeta's friends had since left for the United States. The Tolstoy Foundation, one of many U.S.-based voluntary agencies in Europe that assist refugees, helped her file an asylum application with the Italian government. The Italians denied her application, but she got an appointment for an interview with the USCIS at the U.S. consulate in Rome.

At her interview, she confirmed the facts given in the application, explaining her fear of persecution if she returned to Poland. She gave the USCIS in Rome the names of her friends whom she had conspired with in Poland, the same friends that had been admitted to the United States as refugees. She reconstructed the details of her arrest and political activity. The USCIS agreed to give her refugee status in the United States.

After spending time in the camp in Latina, Italy, she was flown to the United States and reunited with the friends who had sponsored her. After one year, she applied for permanent residence.

Section 5
Special Rules for Special People

Not everyone can receive legal status in the United States. The notion that you can "get in line" and obtain a green card is false. Even if you are of good character and can support yourself through savings or work, you can't necessarily get the right to live in the U.S. permanently unless you qualify under one of the categories noted in this book. Some older people manage to live in the United States most of the year by entering on B-2 visitor's visas then leaving for week or two, without problem, but that's technically a violation of visitor's status. Since the United States has no "retiree" visa, so these retirees are violating our immigration laws. Nor do we have a point system, like some countries, where you can combine your education and family ties to qualify to live here permanently.

The law provides a number of unusual ways to get permission to stay here legally. Some provide temporary status, others lead to permanent residence or U.S. citizenship. I have mentioned some of these "Special Rules for Special People" elsewhere in the book. However, with real immigration reform, with a path to citizenship for undocumented immigrants years away, I felt it valuable to expand on some of these special paths to legal status. If you think you qualify, you should consult an immigration law expert.

In Chapter 19, I review some little-known paths to legal status. In Chapter 20, I review President Obama's programs for granting temporary legal protection for undocumented immigrants.

Chapter 19 - Lesser-Known Paths to Legal Status

Military Accessions Vital to the National Interest program

Members of the U.S. military since September 11, 2001 qualify automatically for U.S. citizenship. Normally, to join the military you must be a permanent resident or U.S. citizen. Under the MAVNI program, individuals lawfully in the U.S. with certain language skills or medical training may enlist. Generally, if you are a graduate of a ten week Basic Combat Training or you accept a commission as Army Officers, you can immediately apply for U.S. citizenship.

Those eligible for MAVNI include asylees, refugees, individuals in the U.S. with Temporary Protected Status (TPS) or Deferred Action for Childhood Arrivals, and those in one of the following nonimmigrant categories: E, F, H, I, J, K, L, M, O, P, Q, R, S, T, TC, TD, TN, U or V. To enlist you must have been lawfully in the United States for at least two years and must not have been abroad for a continuous period of ninety days or more prior to enlistment.

> **For those without medical training, you must have expertise in one of the following languages:**
>
> Albanian, Amharic, Arabic, Azerbaijani, Bengali, Burmese, Cambodian-Khmer, Cebuano, Chinese, Czech, French (limited to individuals possessing citizenship from an African country), Haitian-Creole Hausa, Hindi, Hungarian, Igbo, Indonesian, Korean, Kurdish, Lao, Malay, Malayalam, Moro, Nepalese, Persian [Dari & Farsi], Polish, Portuguese, Punjabi, Pushtu (aka Pashto), Russian, Serbo-Croatian, Sindhi, Singhalese, Somali, Swahili, Tagalog, Tajik, Tamil, Thai, Turkish, Turkmen, Ukrainian, Urdu, Uzbek, and Yoruba.

U Status

U status is available for victims of certain crimes who cooperate in the investigation or prosecution of the criminal activity. **U** status can lead to permanent residence. To qualify, the victim must have suffered substantial mental or physical abuse because of the crime. You may qualify for **U** status if you were the victim of one of the following crimes: Abduction, abusive sexual contact, blackmail, domestic violence, extortion, false imprisonment, felonious assault, female genital mutilation, felonious assault, being held hostage, incest, involuntary servitude, kidnapping, manslaughter, murder, obstruction of justice, peonage, perjury, prostitution, rape, sexual assault, sexual exploitation, slave trade, torture, trafficking, witness tampering, and unlawful criminal restraint. Having been a victim of related crimes, or of intent or conspiracy to commit these crimes may also be qualifying crimes.

Sometimes "indirect" victims of a crime qualify for **U** status. Indirect victims include family members of the direct victim, where that victim died due to murder or manslaughter or is incompetent or incapacitated. In these cases the "family" is the spouse and children under twenty-one. If the direct victim was under twenty-one, his or her siblings under eighteen qualify as well. In addition to family members, indirect victims sometimes include witnesses to a crime.

If you are a crime victim, a representative of a federal, state, or local law enforcement agency, prosecutor, judge or other authority responsible for investigating or prosecuting the crime, must certify your cooperation by signing a "a certificate of helpfulness." That requires that you, a parent or guardian or a counselor or social worker have useful information about the crime.

Getting law enforcement certification can be the most difficult part of a **U** visa case. In large urban cities with substantial immigrant populations, law enforcement officials are familiar with **U** status certification. In smaller jurisdictions, you may need someone to advocate for you.

Beyond your having been a crime victim and getting law enforcement certification, you must be otherwise admissible to the United States. I discuss grounds of inadmissibility in Chapter 5. For **U** visas, USCIS can waive those grounds, and often do.

USCIS will grant **U** status, with the right to employment authorization, in four-year intervals. After three years in **U** status, you can apply for a green card. With your green card application, you must submit proof that you did not unreasonably refuse to provide assistance in the criminal investigation or prosecution. If you are under twenty-one, your spouse, children, parents (only you are unmarried) and siblings under eighteen at the time of you file for **U** status may qualify as well. If you are twenty-one or over, your spouse and unmarried children under twenty-one qualify.

Special Immigrant Juvenile Status (SIJS)

If you are under twenty-one and unmarried and not living with your parents, or your parents have abused or neglected you, you may qualify for **SIJS**. Qualified children may apply to a family or juvenile court for that protection. A United States state court must decide that you are a dependent of the court, or legally place you with either a state or private agency or a private person including your relative. Once you have this determination from the state court, you can immediately apply for a green card. The court must find that it is not in your best interest to be returned to your home country. You must submit your **SIJS** green card application before you turn twenty-one, but you may be twenty-one or over when USCIS makes a decision on your application. Anyone unmarried, under twenty-one who is not living with their parents should speak to an immigration law expert about the possibility of applying for **SIJS**.

One note: If you get a SIJS green card and later become a U.S. citizen, you cannot petition for your biological parents.

Monica's story illustrates how **SIJS** can lead to a green card.

Monica's Story

Monica came to the United States at age sixteen from El Salvador, to live with her U.S. citizen aunt in Detroit. Her parents arranged for her to be smuggled across the Mexican border. She began high school, where a counselor learned that she was undocumented and that her parents were back in El Salvador. The counselor arranged for her to get help from a not-for-profit legal service provider. A lawyer helped find a family court judge to assign her aunt as her guardian. The family court judge found that her parents could not provide for her in El Salvador and that it was is in Monica's best interest to remain in the United States. With the judge's order, Monica applied for SIJS and USCIS granted her permanent residence.

Temporary Protected Status (TPS)

When civil unrest or natural disaster makes it risky for a foreign national to return to their home country, USCIS, on direction from the Department of Homeland Security (DHS), will sometimes grant individuals from that country Temporary Protected Status **(TPS)**. The individuals get protection from deportation and may qualify for employment authorization. They can get permission to travel abroad, called "advance parole' as well. You can find a list of countries whose nationals qualify for TPS at **uscis.gov**. In recent years, DHS has granted TPS to the following nationalities: El Salvador, Guinea, Haiti, Honduras, Nicaragua, Liberia, Sierra Leone, Somalia, Sudan and Syria.

TPS, by design is a temporary program and can be terminated, but program termination is rare. Though the TPS programs typically have an application cutoff date by which you must have been in the United States, once USCIS grants you TPS, you can expect that it will be extended.

An example is TPS granted the tens of thousands of Haitians in the United States when a devastating earthquake hit Haiti on January 12, 2010. The program initially benefitted Haitians in the U.S. when the earthquake hit, but that cutoff was extended one year to January 12, 2011. Haitians may now claim for TPS until January 22, 2016.

Though TPS does not provide a direct path to a green card, if you travel with advance parole, and you are the immediate relative of a U.S. citizen—the spouse of a U.S. citizen, the unmarried child under twenty-one of a U.S. citizen and parent of a U.S. citizen where the citizen child is at least age twenty-one—you may interview in the United States for permanent residence. Plus, if you travel abroad with advance parole for a green card interview, you won't be penalized for having been in the United States unlawfully.

Jean and Jose's stories illustrate how a person with TPS can help you get a green card.

Jean's Story

Jean came to the United States in 2005 to visit his sister, a U.S. citizen. He decided to stay and attend college in the U.S., but he never changed his status to international student, so he fell out-of-status. Meanwhile, his sister petitioned for him for permanent residence. He knew however, that he could not qualify for a green card in the United States. As explained in Chapter 6, because Jean had been in the U.S. illegally, he would have to travel to Haiti for his immigrant visa interview. Additionally, as explained in Chapter 5, once he left the United States, he would be barred from returning for 10 years.

When the earthquake hit Haiti and President Obama announced the Haitian TPS program, Jean applied and USCIS approved his application. He also applied for advance parole and USCIS granted that application as well. Once Jean got to the front of the line under the visa quota system as the brother of a U.S. citizen, he renewed his advance parole and traveled to his interview in Haiti. Because he traveled with advance parole, the "unlawful presence" bar discussed in Chapter 5 did not apply. The U.S. consul in Haiti granted him an immigrant visa, which he used to travel to the United States. His green card came in the mail a few weeks later.

Jose's Story

Jose and his family came to the United States in 2000, fleeing the civil strife in El Salvador. Neither he nor his family were politically active, but they lived in a part of the country where the fighting was fierce. They traveled to Mexico, and with the help of a smuggler, they snuck into the United States. Jose was sixteen at the time.

In 2001, individuals from El Salvador became eligible for TPS. Jose and his family applied and USCIS approved their applications. In 2012, after USCIS had granted him advance parole, Jose returned to El Salvador to visit his ailing grandmother. When he returned, he married his fianceé Frieda, a U.S. citizen. Since a U.S. border officer inspected and admitted Jose at the time of his last entry, he can interview in the United States, a process called "adjustment of status" discussed in Chapter 6. That's a lot safer than having to travel to El Salvador for his green card interview.

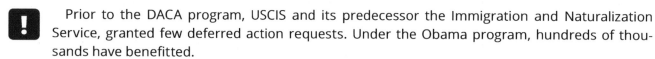

Chapter 20 - President Obama's Executive Action Programs

On June 15, 2012, President Obama announced a program to provide protection from deportation and employment authorization to certain undocumented youth. Known as **Deferred Action for Childhood Arrivals (DACA)**, the program grants "deferred action" in two year intervals. Deferred action refers to a USCIS program that allows deserving individuals to stay in the United States, despite their being deportable.

! Prior to the DACA program, USCIS and its predecessor the Immigration and Naturalization Service, granted few deferred action requests. Under the Obama program, hundreds of thousands have benefitted.

Obama designed the program to provide relief for undocumented immigrants who came to the United States before age sixteen, who had been in the United States for five years, and who had not yet reached age thirty-one on the day of the President's announcement.

On November 20, 2014, President Obama announced an expansion of DACA and a new program called **Deferred Action for the Parents of American Citizens and Permanent Residents (DAPA)**. The expanded DACA program would benefit individuals who had entered before age sixteen, who had lived here since January 1, 2010, with no upper age limit. DAPA would benefit undocumented immigrants who had lived here since January 1, 2010 who had a U.S. citizen or permanent resident child.

! The original DACA program, the one announced in 2012, continues. USCIS is granting extensions beyond the original two years deferred action. However, as of this writing, the Federal Courts have prevented the Obama administration from proceeding on expanded-DACA and DAPA. With the program stalled, USCIS has yet to issue rules regarding the two new programs nor is an application form available.

In this chapter, I provide detailed information on DACA, and a brief outline of expanded-DACA and DAPA. It is likely that USCIS rules for the new programs will be similar to the existing DACA program, but it is impossible to know for sure.

Some undocumented youth are afraid to apply for DACA, fearing that a new administration will deport those who have registered for the program. The opposite is more likely. If you successfully are granted DACA, you will have the freedom to come out from hiding sour immigration status to your employers, friends and neighbors. You will build a zone of protection around yourself.

If a President gets elected based on an anti-immigrant platform, people with DACA will likely have more protection than those who do not have any form of legal right to be here. As I often say when speaking and advocating for these new laws, if my sister or mother qualified, I would tell them to apply.

DACA Benefits

If USCIS grants you DACA, you will get protection from deportation unless you commit certain crimes. You will get other benefits as well.

Permission to Travel Abroad

If USCIS grants you DACA, you may apply for permission to return to the United States after travel abroad. USCIS calls the permission "advance parole." Your prior immigration law violations won't keep you from reentering the United States. That's true even if an immigration judge had ordered you deported. **If an immigration judge ordered you deported but you never left, consult an immigration law expert before leaving the United States.** You want to avoid "self deportation." With expert help, you may be able to reopen your deportation proceedings and so travel abroad won't be a problem.

Your pre-DACA Criminal convictions also should not be a problem, provided you revealed them when you applied for DACA and your were not barred from DACA because of those convictions.

To qualify for advanced parole, you must have a business, educational or humanitarian reason to travel. Examples of business reasons are to sell property or deal with an estate. Examples of educational reasons are study abroad programs and attending educational conferences. Examples of humanitarian reasons are to visit a sick relative, attend a funeral, and if you are lucky, in some cases you can get advance parole to attend an immigrant visa interview.

Advance Parole and the Path to Permanent Residence

In two important ways, getting DACA may help you become a permanent resident. The DACA program does not provide a direct path to a green card, but the availability of advance parole may smooth the way.

First, if you entered the United States without being inspected by a U.S. border officer, reentering with advance parole means that your last entry was lawful. That is, an immigration officer inspected and admitted you. As discussed in detail in chapter 6, if you were inspected and admitted and you are an immediate relative of a U.S. citizen, you can interview in the U.S.—the process called "adjustment of status." That's true despite your time in the United States without legal status. The immediate relative category includes the spouse, unmarried child children under twenty-one and parents of U.S. citizen children at least age twenty-one.

Suppose you are not an immediate relative of a U.S. citizen but qualify for a green card in some other category; perhaps as a needed worker; perhaps as a brother or sister of a U.S. citizen.

Check the list of categories in Chapter 1, but no matter which category, you may be able to get a green card despite your having been in the U.S. unlawfully. You would need to travel home for your green card interview, but if you travel with advance parole, you would not face the "unlawful presence" bar to permanent residence discussed in Chapter 5. USCIS has granted some advance parole requests for individuals to travel to immigrant visa interviews, but it is unclear if that policy will continue. I hope it does.

Terry and Esmeralda's stories illustrate how advance parole can lead to permanent residence.

Terry's Story

Terry, from El Salvador, entered the United States by crossing the Mexican border at night. He came to the country with his father when Terry was just fifteen years old in 1990. They both managed to evade the U.S. border patrol. USCIS granted Terry DACA in late 2012. When his grandmother in El Salvador took ill in 2014, he applied to the USCIS for advance parole, presenting a doctor's letter explaining his grandmother's grave condition.

Terry's Story (Continued)

With his advance parole document in hand, Terry returned to El Salvador where he spent two weeks visiting with his grandmother and his mother whom he had not seen in more than six years. He returned to the United States, presenting his DACA employment card, advance parole document and Salvadoran passport to a U.S. border office at Los Angeles International Airport and returned to his home in Los Angeles.

In 2015 Terry married his girlfriend Gladys, a U.S. citizen. As explained in Chapter 6, since he was admitted and inspected at entry, his marriage to a U.S. citizen means he can interview here for permanent residence—the process called adjustment of status. USCIS will ignore his prior unlawful presence.

Esmeralda's Story

Esmeralda came to the United States from Mexico on a visitor's visa in 1995, at age fourteen, to visit her U.S. citizen sister. She enjoyed her time in the United States and she decided to stay. Her sister filed a family-based immigration petition for her, and USCIS approved the petition. Many years later, in 2011, when she got to front of line for a green card, her lawyer told her she would need to return to Mexico for a green card interview at the U.S. consulate in Juarez, Mexico. She could not interview in the United States because she had been in the country illegally and was not an "immediate relative" of a U.S. citizen. However, because she had been here unlawfully so long, she would be barred for returning for ten years. Learn more about the unlawful presence bar to a green card in Chapter 5.

In 2012, USCIS granted her DACA. She reactivated her immigrant visa case at the U.S. consulate in Juarez. She managed to convince USCIS to grant her advanced parole so she could go to her interview in Juarez without triggering the unlawful presence bar. She traveled to her interview in May 2015, all went well, and she returned with an immigrant visa. Had something gone wrong at her interview, she would have been readmitted to the United States to continue life here with DACA.

Travel Within the United States and U.S. Territories

Many undocumented immigrants travel throughout the United States without problems. If you have a government I.D., U.S. travel is rarely a problem. Still, some undocumented immigrants are concerned that an incident on a plane, for instance an arrest of another passenger, will result in the authorities learning that they are here unlawfully. Once you get DACA, that will no longer be a concern.

Driver's License

In most states, with DACA you can get a driver's license. Some with DACA prefer a driver's license to their DACA employment authorization card as a form of identification since it doesn't identify them as an undocumented immigrant.

Social Security Card

Since with DACA you get an employment authorization card, you can get also a social security card. When you work with a social security card, you start earning credits toward retirement benefits. To get Social Security retirement benefits while in the United States you would need to become a permanent resident. Depending on where you retire however, you might be able to get your benefit if you retire abroad, even if you don't get a green card first.

Financial Aid

At the time of this writing scholarship programs are targeting college students with DACA for special financial aid programs. Some states and cities are considering providing grants and loans for DACA college students.

DACA Requirements

To get DACA, you must meet the following eligibility requirements:

- You entered the United States before your sixteenth birthday;

- You were physically present in the United States on June 15, 2012 and at the time you register for DACA;

- You have continuously resided in the United States since June 15, 2007 up to the present time;

- You entered the United States without inspection or if you entered the United States legally, your status was expired as of June 15, 2012;

- You do not have lawful status on the day you file the application;

- You are in school, have a high school degree or General Education Degree (GED or TASC) certificate, or have been honorably discharged from the U.S. Armed Forces or Coast Guard;

- You have not been convicted of a felony, a "significant misdemeanor," or three or more other misdemeanors, and you do not otherwise pose a threat to national security or public safety or any crime for which a judge sentenced you to more than ninety days or more in jail; and...

- You are at least fifteen years old (unless you are in immigration proceedings in which case you be able to apply before age fifteen).

Let's take a look at some of these requirements in more detail.

Proving Entry Prior to Age Sixteen

You will need a birth certificate to prove your age, and a document to prove your presence in the U.S. before turning sixteen. An affidavit (a sworn statement) even from a reliable source such as a government official, is not sufficient. Examples of acceptable proof of entry prior to age sixteen include your passport with an entry stamp or your Arrival/Departure Document (Form I-94/I-95/I-94W), U.S. school records, Immigration and Naturalization Service or Department of Homeland Security documents showing your presence or date of entry, U.S. travel records, hospital or medical records, employment pay stubs, official records from a religious entity confirming participation in a religious ceremony, copies of money order receipts for money sent in or out of the country, birth certificates of children born in the United States, dated bank transactions, automobile license receipts or registration, rental agreement contracts, tax receipts, and insurance policies.

Proving Presence in the United States on June 15, 2007

As with proving presence in the United States before age sixteen, you will need a document created in the normal course of activity to prove you were here on June 15, 2007. The documents mentioned for proving you were here before turning sixteen are examples. However, you need not provide a document with the June 15, 2007 date. For instance, if you have a document proving you were here on May 1, 2007 and another showing presence on June 30, 2007, that should be sufficient. We call this proving your case through "circumstantial" evidence.

Continuous Presence from June 15, 2007 to the Time of Filing

No one can prove presence in the United States every day for five years or longer. Try to provide at least one document per month if you can. School or work records, if you have them, are the easiest way to prove continuous residence. Do the best you can. Short trips abroad do not interrupt "continuous presence."

Unlawfully in the United States on June 15, 2012

If you entered illegally, by sneaking into the United States or you entered with false documents and never attained legal status, you meet this requirement. If you entered legally, and overstayed the time allowed to be in the United States, you meet this requirement as well. If you entered legally, but your stay has no end date, your situation may be more complicated.

Nonimmigrants such as temporary workers and students qualify as unlawfully here for DACA only if they became unlawfully here through the passage of time. Or, if an immigration judge found them deportable. Simply violating status, for instance by working without USCIS permission, in not sufficient. USCIS considers F-1 international students to be unlawfully here for DACA if the student's foreign student advisor noted the student's termination in the government's SEVIS records.

The Education Requirement

USCIS has been generous in interpreting the education requirement. Of course if you have a high school diploma or Graduate Education Development (GED) degree (a high school degree you receive by taking a test as opposed to graduating from a school), you'll be fine. The "honorably discharged" from the military is not really an option since undocumented immigrants can't join the military.

If you are not in school, you can enroll in an English language program, GED or TASC study program or vocational education program and you will qualify immediately for DACA.

Criminal Record Issues

If you have ever been arrested or charged with a crime, follow **"Wernick's Rule:" If you have a criminal record, see an immigration law expert before applying for an immigration benefit.** Immigration rules regarding the impact of criminal activity are incredibly complex. If you have a criminal record, applying for an immigration benefit could result in your being deported.

That said, only a very few DACA applicants will find themselves barred from getting DACA because of a criminal record. These days, when an undocumented immigrant commits a serious crime or is incarcerated, usually immigration deports them.

USCIS will deny you DACA if you were convicted of any felony. Generally that means a crime where the possible sentence is more than one year's jail time. USCIS will deny you DACA also if you were convicted of three or more misdemeanors, defined by USCIS as a crime for which a judge could order your incarceration for between five days or more but less than one year. Finally, conviction for even one "significant misdemeanor" is a bar to DACA. A significant misdemeanor is an offense of domestic violence; sexual abuse or exploitation; burglary; unlawful possession or use of a firearm; drug distribution or trafficking; or, driving under the influence.

Finally, USCIS will deny you DACA if a judge sentenced you to time in custody of more than ninety days. A suspended sentence will not count against you for the purpose of this rule.

Applying for DACA

In order to submit a request for DACA, you must mail the following forms simultaneously, along with supporting documents: Form I-821D, Consideration of Deferred Action for Childhood Arrivals, Form I-765, Application for Employment Authorization, and Form I-765WS, Worksheet. You submit also a money order or check for $465. The $465 covers the cost of the employment authorization document and biometrics (fingerprinting). Fee waivers are available but only in very limited situations. If you want to try to get USCIS to waive your DACA filing fee, you must submit a fee waiver request before applying for DACA. If USCIS grants the request, you then submit the fee waiver approval with your DACA application.

> **To get USCIS to waive the DACA filing fee, you must prove one of the following:**
>
> - You are under eighteen years of age, homeless, in foster care, or otherwise lacking parental or other familial support and your income is less than 150% of the U.S. poverty level,
>
> - You cannot care for yourself because you suffer from a serious chronic disability and your income is less than 150% of the U.S. poverty level, or,
>
> - You, accumulated $10,000 or more in debt in the past 12 months as the result of unreinbursed medical expenses for yourself or an immediate family member and your income is less than 150% of the U.S. poverty level.

After USCIS receives your DACA application, it will mail you receipts for Form 821-D, Consideration of Deferred Action for Childhood Arrivals and Form I-765, Application for Employment Authorization. You can then track your case at **uscis.gov** by clicking the "Check Your Case Status" link and entering your receipt number in the "case status" box. Next, USCIS will send you a biometrics' appointment notice. If USCIS grants your request for DACA, it will send you an I-821D Approval Notice, followed by an I-765 Approval Notice and finally your Employment Authorization Document—your work permit.

If USCIS denies your DACA and employment authorization document, your only option is to reapply. You cannot appeal a DACA denial but you can request a review of your denial due to administrative errors on the part of USCIS.

Expanded DACA

When President Obama announced an expanded program on November 20, 2014, immigrant advocates had planned to begin helping potential applicants by February 18, 2015. Unfortunately a lawsuit brought by 26 Republican governors resulted in an injunction (an order stopping) that prevents the federal government from proceeding with the expanded DACA program. With the program stalled, the USCIS has not issued expanded DACA instructions nor an expanded DACA form.

When the courts allow the program to proceed, we expect the expanded DACA rules to be similar to the current DACA rules with these exceptions:

Under expanded DACA, you have lived continuously in the United States since January 1, 2010. The day you must have entered will move up from June 15, 2007. Also, expanded DACA will not have an upper age limit. So, individuals who were over thirty-one on November 20, 2014, qualify.

 ## DAPA

Court intervention has also stalled President Obama's DAPA program. When the program proceeds, it will benefit the parents of U.S. citizens and permanent residents who have been living in the United States since January 1, 2010. To benefit your U.S. citizen or permanent resident child must have been born or a parent/child relationship created by November 20, 2014. You must have been present in the United States on November 20, 2014 through the time you apply for DAPA. Under DAPA, you need not meet an education requirement, but the criminal bars will apply.

Acknowledgements

Some outstanding legal experts helped make sure that Wernick's Guide to U.S. Immigration and Citizenship is up-to-date and accurate. Writing for the public, as I do in my weekly column in the *New York Daily News* and in my syndicated column for King Features Syndicate, I've got to get it right the first time. That's why special thanks goes to the people who reviewed my drafts and others who helped me understand and present the law. Of course, all final decisions regarding the content of the book were my own.

A few people deserve special mention. Elinor Drucker-Rahmani, a colleague at CUNY Citizenship Now!, reviewed the entire manuscript offering many suggestions. Tamara Bloom and Thomas Shea, also with Citizenship Now!, graciously allowed me to use their work in Chapters 10 and 11, providing the best how-to guide to completing the N-400 naturalization application available. Tom also reviewed Chapter 6, "Applying for an Immigrant Visa", making several significant contributions. Julie Dinnerstein, a New York attorney and a leading expert on family-based immigration reviewed Chapter 2, greatly improving that chapter. Andrew Fair, also an attorney in New York with an advanced understanding of employment-based immigrant visas reviewed Chapter 3, providing important insights. Phyllis Jewell, a business immigration law expert in San Francisco, was extremely generous in her contribution to chapter 14, "Temporary Professional Workers."

Maria Violetta Szulc conceived the stories that introduce the book and each section. A recent immigrant, Maria also helped make sure the book was understandable to non-lawyers—not an easy task.

Thanks also to Peter Rubie, my literary agent of many years, for having confidence that I had something to offer the public and helping me find publishers who agreed with that assessment.

Special thanks to Highline Editions in New York: Publisher, Robert Astle; CEO, David Lane, Stratus/Highline Editions in UK; General Manager, Jillian Ports; Designer, Kate Murphy; Cover Designer; Ervin Serrano; Editorial Assistant, Brooke Kressel–Magin; Marketing and Social Media, Brielle Cummings.

Previous Editions

U.S. Immigration & Citizenship: Your Complete Guide- 4th Edition

Clerisy Press, Emmis Books

November 1, 2004

ISBN-10: 157860169X

ISBN-13: 978-1578601691

U.S. Immigration & Citizenship

Prima Lifestyles

January 15, 2002

ISBN-10: 0761536280

ISBN-13: 978-0761536284

U.S. Immigration & Citizenship

Prima Lifestyles

March 3, 1999

ISBN-10: 0761517154

ISBN-13: 978-0761517153

U.S. Immigration & Citizenship

Prima Publishing

March 1997

ISBN-10: 0761504508

ISBN-13: 978-0761504504

Inmigracion y Ciudadania en Estados Unidos

Clerisy Press, Emmis Books

May 1, 2005

ISBN-10: 1578601762

ISBN-13: 978-1578601769

Inmigracion y Ciudadania en Estados Unidos. (Nueva edicion 3CDs)

Coral Communications Group, LLC

October 1, 2009

ISBN-10: 1877951803

ISBN-13: 978-1877951800

Appendix A - Grounds of Inadmissibility

Below I list the most important reasons why you might be barred from entering the United States or getting an immigrant or nonimmigrant visa. For some of these grounds of inadmissibility, the USCIS might waive your inadmissibility. If any of these bars apply to you, speak to an immigration law expert before applying for an immigrant or nonimmigrant visa. (For more on inadmissibility in the context of an application for an immigrant visa, see chapter 5.)

- You have a communicable disease of public health significance including tuberculosis, chancroid, gonorrhea, granuloma inguinale, infectious leprosy, lymphogranuloma, venereum, or infectious syphilis.

- You have a physical or mental disorder and a history of behavior associated with the disorder that may pose or has posed a threat to the property, safety, or welfare of yourself or others. This might include alcoholism or addiction to a noncontrolled but mind-altering substance.

- You are a drug abuser or drug addict. Usually this refers to habit-forming narcotic drugs.

- You have been convicted of, or you admit to having committed, a crime involving moral turpitude that is not a purely political offense. This includes attempts of conspiracy to commit crimes involving moral turpitude.

- You have been convicted of committing, or you admit to having committed, a violation of any law or regulation relating to controlled substances as defined in federal law. In addition to cocaine and heroin, this includes LSD, amphetamines, barbiturates, Seconal, and angel dust. This exclusion includes attempts and conspiracy to commit this crime.

- You have been convicted of two or more offenses where the total sentence of confinement actually imposed was five years or more.

- A consular or an USCIS officer has reason to believe that you have been an illicit trafficker in a controlled substance or that you have assisted, abetted, conspired with, or colluded with others in the illicit trafficking of controlled substances.

- You are a prostitute, you have committed acts of prostitution, you are coming to the United States to engage in prostitution, or you have procured or attempted to procure or import prostitutes. This ground of exclusion applies to events that occurred within ten years of your application for a visa or entry into the United States.

- An USCIS or a consular officer believes that you are coming to the United States to engage in espionage or sabotage or to try to overthrow the U.S. government by force, violence, or unlawful means, or that you are coming to engage in terrorist activities.

- The U.S. government believes that your entry or activities would have potentially serious adverse foreign policy consequences.

- You are, or have been, a member of or affiliated with a communist or other totalitarian party.

- You participated in Nazi persecutions or genocide.

- You are likely to become a public charge.

- You were previously excluded and/or deported from the United States.

- You got a visa or tried to get a visa or you entered the United States or you tried to enter the United States by fraud or willful misrepresentation of a material fact.

- You are a stowaway. However, this bar only applies if you are caught trying to enter the United States. Once you enter the United States, having been a stowaway will not bar you from becoming a permanent resident.

- You are a smuggler.

- You committed document fraud.

- You are coming to the United States to practice polygamy.

- You are permanently ineligible for citizenship.

- You are accompanying an inadmissible alien whose exclusion is due to infancy, sickness, or physical and mental disability.

- You detain, retain, or withhold custody of a child outside the United States after receipt of a court order granting custody of the child to a U.S. citizen, where the child has a lawful claim to U.S. citizenship.

- You are coming to the United States in a category which requires that you obtain a certification from the Department of Labor showing there are no U.S. workers ready, willing, and able to handle your job, and you do not obtain such certification.

- You are a medical graduate of a unapproved medical school who has not successfully completed qualifying exams and who is not competent in oral and written English and you are coming to the United States to perform services as a member of the medical profession.

- You knowingly made a frivolous application for asylum after the USCIS had advised you of the consequences of filing a frivolous application.

- You haven't been vaccinated against vaccine-preventable diseases, including at least the following diseases: mumps, measles, rubella, polio, tetanus and diphtheria toxoids, pertussis, influenza type B, and hepatitis B.

- You incited terrorist activity under circumstances indicating an intention to cause death or serious bodily harm.

- You failed to appear at your removal hearing without reasonable cause. This will bar you until you have been outside the United States for at least five years.

- You have falsely claimed U.S. citizenship to get a federal or state benefit.

- You came here as a nonimmigrant and you got public benefits for which you were ineligible. This bars you until you have been outside of the United States for five years.

- You came here as an F-1 student to attend elementary or high school and you violated your status. This bars you until you have been outside the United States for five years.

- You were removed (deported or excluded) from the United States. This bars you until you have been outside the United States for five years. If you have been removed twice or convicted of an aggravated felony, you will be barred for 20 years.

- You left the United States after having been in the country unlawfully for more than 180 days. This will bar you for three years, but you may be eligible for a waiver.

- You have been in the United States unlawfully for one year or more. This will bar you for ten years, but you may be eligible for a waiver.

- You voted unlawfully.

Appendix B - List of Aggravated Felonies

People convicted of aggravated felonies, prior to November 29, 1990, are permanently ineligible for naturalization. People convicted of aggravated felonies are also permanently ineligible for asylum. If you have a criminal record, see an immigration law expert before making any application to the INS. Here's a layperson's list of what may constitute an aggravated felony:

- Murder.
- Rape.
- Sexual abuse of a minor.
- Drug-trafficking crimes or any illicit trafficking in any controlled substances.
- Illicit trafficking in destructive devices.
- Any offense related to laundering of monetary instruments if the amount exceeds $10,000.
- Most offenses involving explosives or arson.
- Offenses relating to the receipt, manufacture, or possession of firearms without proper licenses or taxes.
- Most crimes of violence (not including a purely political offense) for which the term of imprisonment imposed (regardless of any suspension of such imprisonment) is at least one year.
- A theft offense (including receipt of stolen property) or burglary offense for which the term of imprisonment imposed (regardless of any suspension of such imprisonment) is at least one year.
- Ransom offenses, including using interstate communications to demand ransom or threaten kidnap; using mails to make threatening communications; making threatening communications from foreign countries; receiving, possessing, or disposing of ransom money or property.
- Child pornography offenses, including employing, using, or coercing minors to engage in pornography; selling or transferring custody of a child with knowledge that the child will be used for pornography; receiving or distributing child pornography.
- RICO (the Racketeer-Influenced and Corrupt Organizations Act) offenses for which a sentence of one year imprisonment or more may be imposed.
- Offenses relating to owning, controlling, managing, or supervising a prostitution business.
- Offenses relating to involuntary servitude.
- Offenses relating to spying and national security.
- Treason and concealing and failing to disclose treason.
- Fraud or deceit crimes in which the loss to the victim exceeds $10,000.
- Income tax evasion where the loss to the government exceeds $10,000.
- Alien smuggling for commercial gain where the term of imprisonment imposed (regardless of any suspension of imprisonment) is at least one year (exception: only one offense where the person smuggled was your spouse, parent, or child).

- Document fraud under which the person's actions constitute trafficking in the documents and the sentence imposed (even if suspended) is at least one year (except where you committed the offense to assist your spouse, parent, or child).

- An offense for failing to appear for sentence where a defendant has been convicted of a crime with a possible sentence of 15 years or more.

- Offenses involving obstruction of justice, perjury, or subornation or helping another person commit perjury or bribery of a witness, for which a sentence of at least one year may be imposed.

- Offenses relating to commercial bribery, forgery, counterfeiting, or trafficking in vehicles, for which a sentence of at least one year may be imposed.

- Offenses committed by an alien ordered previously deported.

- Offenses relating to the failure to appear in court for a criminal offense for which a sentence of two or more years may be imposed.

- Any attempt or conspiracy to commit any of the above acts, committed within the United States.

- Any attempt or conspiracy to commit any of these acts violating a law in a foreign country where the term of imprisonment was completed within the previous 15 years.

Appendix C- List of Countries That Recognize Dual Citizenship with the United States

Afghanistan	Albania	Algeria
Angola	Antigua and Barbuda	Armenia
Australia	Bangladesh	Barbados
Belarus	Belize	Benin
Bosnia and Herzegovina	Brazil	Bulgaria
Burkina Faso	Burundi	Cambodia
Canada	Cape Verde	Central African Republic
Chad	Chile	Colombia
Costa Rica	Cote D'Ivoire	Croatia
Cyprus	Czech Republic	Dominica
Dominican Republic	Ecuador	Egypt
El Salvador	Fiji	Finland
France	Ghana	Greece
Grenada	Guatemala	Haiti
Hong Kong	Hungary	Iceland
Iran	Iraq	Ireland
Israel	Italy	Jamaica
Jordan	Latvia	Lebanon
Libya	Liechtenstein	Macedonia
Maldives	Mali	Mauritius
Mexico	Morocco	New Zealand
Nicaragua	Nigeria	North Korea (PRK)
Panama	Pakistan	Peru
Philippines	Poland	Portugal
Romania	Russia	Senegal
Sierra Leone	Slovenia	South Africa
Sri Lanka	St. Christopher	St. Kitts and Nevis
St. Lucia	St. Vincent Sudan	Swaziland
Sweden	Switzerland	Syria
Taiwan	Togo	Tunisia
Turkey	Tuvalu	Uganda
United Kingdom	Uruguay	Venezuela
Vietnam		

Dual Citizenship Generally Not Allowed After U.S. Naturalization

The countries below limit dual citizenship (being a citizen of two countries at once). For more information about losing your present citizenship when you naturalize as a U.S. citizen, speak with a representative of your government before filing for naturalization. Even if your country allows Dual Citizenship you are required by U.S. law to use a U.S. passport to leave and re-enter the United States.

Andorra	Argentina	Austria
Azerbaijan	Bahamas	Bahrain
Belgium	Bhutan	Bolivia
Botswana	Brunei	Cameroon
China	Congo	Cuba
Denmark	Djibouti	Equatorial Guinea
Estonia	Ethiopia	Gabon
Georgia	Germany	Guinea
Guinea-Bissau	Guyana	Honduras
India	Indonesia	Japan
Kazakhstan	Kenya	Kiribati
Kuwait	Kyrgyz Republic	Laos
Lesotho	Liberia	Lithuania
Luxembourg	Madagascar	Malawi
Malaysia	Malta	Marshall Islands
Mauritania	Micronesia	Moldova
Monaco	Mongolia	Mozambique
Myanmar (Burma)	Namibia	Nauru
Nepal	Netherlands	New Guinea
Norway	Oman	Palau
Papua New Guinea	Paraguay	Principe Island
Qatar	Rwanda	Samoa
Sao Tome and Principe	Saudi Arabia	Seychelles
Singapore	Slovakia	South Korea
Spain	Surinam	Tanzania
Thailand	Tonga	Trinidad and Tobago
Ukraine	United Arab Emirates	Uzbekistan
Vanuatu	Yemen	Zambia
Zimbabwe		

Appendix D
The Oath of Allegiance

I hereby declare, on oath, that I absolutely, and entirely, renounce and abjure all allegiance and fidelity to any foreign prince, potentate, state or sovereignty of whom or which I have heretofore been a subject or citizen; that I will support and defend the Constitution, and laws, of the United States of America against all enemies, foreign and domestic; that I will bear true faith and allegiance to the same; that I will bear arms on behalf of the United States when required by the law; that I will perform noncombatant service in the Armed Forces of the United States when required by the law; that I will perform work of national importance, under civilian direction, when required by the law; and that I take this obligation freely, without any mental reservation, or purpose of evasion; so help me God.

Appendix E - A List of NAFTA Professionals

Each occupation listed requires either a baccalaureate degree from a U.S. or Canadian college or university or a licenciatura degree from a Mexican college or university, unless otherwise specified. In certain occupations, a state license is an acceptable substitute for a baccalaureate or licenciatura degree (note where specified below). The degree need not be earned in a four-year program of study.

Other requirements apply to particular occupations. Disaster relief insurance claims adjusters require a baccalaureate or licenciatura degree or three years of experience in claims adjustment, and completion of training in disaster relief insurance adjustment. Management consultants require a baccalaureate or licenciatura degree or five years of experience in consulting or a related field. Librarians require a master's degree in library science. Where a specific educational requirement is imposed for a given occupation, it is applied strictly; it may not be met by the substitution of equivalent credentials, such as education and training.

Accountant
baccalaureate or licenciatura degree; or C.P.A., C.A., C.G.A., or C.M.A.

Architect
baccalaureate or licenciatura degree; or state/provincial license

Computer Systems Analyst
baccalaureate or licenciatura degree; or postsecondary diploma or certificate, and three years' experience

Disaster Relief Insurance Claims Adjuster
baccalaureate or licenciatura degree, and successful completion of training in disaster relief insurance adjustment; or three years' experience in claims adjustment and successful completion of training in disaster relief insurance adjustment

Economist
baccalaureate or licenciatura degree

Engineer
baccalaureate or licenciatura degree; or state/provincial license

Forester
baccalaureate or licenciatura degree; or state/provincial license

Graphic Designer
baccalaureate or licenciatura degree; or postsecondary diploma or certificate, and three years' experience

Hotel Manager
baccalaureate or licenciatura degree in hotel/restaurant management; or postsecondary diploma or certificate in hotel/restaurant management, and three years' experience

Industrial Designer
baccalaureate or licenciatura degree; or postsecondary diploma or certificate, and three years' experience

Interior Designer
baccalaureate or licenciatura degree; or postsecondary diploma or certificate, and three years' experience

Landscape Architect
baccalaureate or licenciatura degree

Land Surveyor
baccalaureate or licenciatura degree; or state/provincial/federal license

Lawyer (or Notary in province of Quebec)
LL.B., J.D., LL.L., B.C.L., or licenciatura degree (five years); or membership in a state/provincial bar

Librarian
M.L.S. or B.L.S. (for which another baccalaureate or licenciatura degree is a prerequisite)

Management Consultant
baccalaureate or licenciatura degree; or five years' experience in consulting or related field*

Mathematician (including Statistician)
baccalaureate or licenciatura degree

Range Manager/Conservationist
baccalaureate or licenciatura degree

Research Assistant (in postsecondary educational institution)
baccalaureate or licenciatura degree

Scientific Technician/Technologist
must possess theoretical knowledge of any of the following disciplines: agricultural sciences, astronomy, biology, chemistry, engineering, forestry, geology, geophysics, meteorology, or physics; and must have the ability to solve practical problems in the discipline or apply principles of the discipline to basic or applied research

Silviculturist (Forestry Specialist)
baccalaureate or licenciatura degree

Social Worker
baccalaureate or licenciatura degree

Technical Publications Writer
baccalaureate or licenciatura degree; or postsecondary diploma or certificate, and three years' experience

Urban Planner (Geographer)
baccalaureate or licenciatura degree

Vocational Counselor
baccalaureate or licenciatura degree

Medical/Allied Professionals

Dentist
D.D.S., D.M.D., Doctor en Odontologia, or Doctor en Cirugia Dental; or state/provincial license

Dietitian
baccalaureate or licenciatura degree; or state/provincial license

Medical Laboratory Technologist (Canada)/Medical Technologist (Mexico and the United States)
baccalaureate or licenciatura degree; or postsecondary diploma or certificate, and three years' experience

Nutritionist
baccalaureate or licenciatura degree

Occupational Therapist
baccalaureate or licenciatura degree; or state/provincial license

Pharmacist
baccalaureate or licenciatura degree; or state/provincial license

Physician (teaching or research only)
M.D. or Doctor en Medicina; or state/provincial license

Physio/Physical Therapist
baccalaureate or licenciatura degree; or state/provincial license

Psychologist
state/provincial license or licenciatura degree

Recreational Therapist
baccalaureate or licenciatura degree

Registered Nurse
state/provincial license or licenciatura degree

Veterinarian
D.V.M., D.M.V., or Doctor en Veterinaria; or state/provincial license

---

Scientists

Agriculturist (Agronomist)
baccalaureate or licenciatura degree

Animal Breeder
baccalaureate or licenciatura degree

Animal Scientist
baccalaureate or licenciatura degree

Apiculturist
baccalaureate or licenciatura degree

Astronomer
baccalaureate or licenciatura degree

Biochemist
baccalaureate or licenciatura degree

Biologist
baccalaureate or licenciatura degree

Chemist
baccalaureate or licenciatura degree

Dairy Scientist
baccalaureate or licenciatura degree

Entomologist
baccalaureate or licenciatura degree

Epidemiologist
baccalaureate or licenciatura degree

Geneticist
baccalaureate or licenciatura degree

Geochemist
baccalaureate or licenciatura degree

Geologist
baccalaureate or licenciatura degree

Geophysicist (Oceanographer in the United States and Mexico)
baccalaureate or licenciatura degree

Horticulturist
baccalaureate or licenciatura degree

Meteorologist
baccalaureate or licenciatura degree

Oceanographer (see Geophysicist, Physicist)

Pharmacologist
baccalaureate or licenciatura degree

Physicist (Oceanographer in Canada)
baccalaureate or licenciatura degree

Plant Breeder
baccalaureate or licenciatura degree

Poultry Scientist
baccalaureate or licenciatura degree

Soil Scientist
baccalaureate or licenciatura degree

Zoologist
baccalaureate or licenciatura degree

Teachers

College
baccalaureate or licenciatura degree

Seminary
baccalaureate or licenciatura degree

University
baccalaureate or licenciatura degree

* Management consultants provide services that are directed toward improving the managerial, operating, and economic performance of public and private entities by analyzing and resolving strategic and operating problems and thereby improving the entity's goals, objectives, policies, strategies, administration, organization, and operation. Management consultants are usually independent contractors or employees of consulting firms under contracts to U.S. entities.

INDEX

Addendum

Visa Bulletin Change Allows for Early Adjustment Application Filing

In Chapter 6, we wrote that to submit your application for adjustment of status, (the process of applying for permanent residence while in the United States) you must have a priority date that is "current" for your visa category in the month during which you submit that application. Beginning October 2015, the U.S. Department of State modified this rule to allow those eligible for adjustment of status to file before their priority date becomes current.

The D.O.S. is now publishing two separate visa bulletin charts for both family-based applicants and employment-based applicants. One chart, called the "Application Final Action Dates," provides the same information as early visa bulletins. That is, you can get your immigrant visa if your priority date, your place in line for a green card, is prior to the cutoff date noted in the bulletin. A new, second chart, called the "Dates for Filing Applications," provides a date you can apply for adjustment of status. To file your application, you must have a priority date prior to the cutoff date in the second chart. Put another way, to get your green card, your priority date must still be current, but based on the second chart, you apply for adjustment of status before your priority date is "current". Filing early gives you many benefits. You can get employment authorization, advance parole (travel permission) based on a pending adjustment application and as explained in Chapter 4, in some employment-based cases, you leave the mployer who sponsored you and still get your green card.

Let's take a look at the November 2015 visa bulletin to see how the new rule works.

VISA BULLETIN: NOVEMBER 2015
APPLICATION FINAL ACTION DATES FOR FAMILY-SPONSORED PREFERENCE CASES

FAMILY-SPONSORED	ALL CHARGEABILITY AREAS EXCEPT THOSE LISTED	CHINA (Mainland born)	INDIA	MEXICO	PHILIPPINES
F1	22 FEB 08	22 FEB 08	22 FEB 08	01 DEC 94	01 JUN 02
F2A	15 MAY 14	15 MAY 14	15 MAY 14	01 APR 14	15 MAY 14
F2B	08 FEB 09	08 FEB 09	08 FEB 09	22 AUG 95	01 NOV 04
F3	15 JUN 04	15 JUN 04	15 JUN 04	15 JUN 94	08 OCT 93
F4	01 MAR 03	01 MAR 03	01 MAR 03	01 APR 97	15 JUN 92

FAMILY-SPONSORED	ALL CHARGEABILITY AREAS EXCEPT THOSE LISTED	CHINA (Mainland born)	INDIA	MEXICO	PHILIPPINES
F1	01 MAY 09	01 MAY 09	01 MAY 09	01 APR 95	01 SEP 05
F2A	01 MAR 15	01 MAR 15	01 MAR 15	01 MAR 15	01 MAR 15
F2B	01 JUL 10	01 JUL 10	01 JUL 10	01 APR 96	01 MAY 05
F3	01 APR 05	01 APR 05	01 APR 05	01 MAY 95	01 AUG 95
F4	01 FEB 04	01 FEB 04	01 FEB 04	01 JUN 98	01 JUN 93

You can see that the estimated application filing dates are typically earlier than the final action dates. Latisha's case illustrates how the new rule works.

Latisha's Story

Latisha came to the United States from Jamaica as an F-1 international student. She is twenty-two years old and unmarried. Her mother, a U.S. citizen, filed a family petition, USCIS form I-130, for her under the first family-based preference on April 30, 2009. Latisha has maintained her status, taking the required number of courses and never working without permission. Because her mother filed for her prior to the application filing cutoff date of May 1, 2009, as explained in chapter 6, Latisha qualifies to interview in the United States for permanent residence. She could file her adjustment of status application on November 1, 2015, and along with is, an application for employment authorization and for advanced parole (travel permission).

USCIS will issue Latisha employment authorization and an advanced parole document. The agency will consider her application and, if she remains eligible, grant her permanent residence.

Expansion of F-1 OPT STEM Program

In chapter 13, I point out that a student graduating with a bachelor's or master's degree in Science, Technology, Engineering, or Math qualifies for an additional period of Optional Practical Training beyond the 12 months typical for international students. At the time of publication, the government has proposed increasing the number of extra months of OPT to STEM graduates to twenty-four months OPT for a total of thirty-six months. To confirm that the regulation became law, visit my website at **www.allanwernick.com.**

Notes